The Michigan
DIVORCE BOOK
A guide to doing an uncontested divorce without an attorney

without minor children

By Michael Maran • Michigan Attorney

GRAND RIVER PRESS

Grand River Press
P.O. Box 1342
E. Lansing, MI 48826

The Michigan Divorce Book: A Guide to Doing an Uncontested Divorce without an Attorney (without minor children)
by Michael Maran

Published by:
Grand River Press
P.O. Box 1342
E. Lansing, MI 48826

Printing history:
First edition: January 1986
Second edition:
  First printing: June 1989
  Second printing: September 1990
Third edition:
  First printing: May 1993
  Second printing: October 1994
  Third printing: January 1996
Fourth edition:
  First printing: February 1998
  Second printing: November 1999
Fifth edition:
  First printing: March 2001
  Second printing: March 2002
  Third printing: July 2003
Sixth edition:
  First printing: January 2004
  Second printing: January 2005
  Third printing: November 2005
Seventh edition:
  First printing: March 2007
  Second printing: November 2007
Eighth edition:
  First printing: January 2009
  Second printing: December 2009
  Third printing: November 2010
Ninth edition: March 2013

ISBN 978-0-936343-22-8
Printed in the United States of America

- The Michigan Divorce Book: A Guide to Doing an Uncontested
  Divorce without an Attorney (without minor children) $28.95

  Update $1.00

- The Michigan Divorce Book: A Guide to Doing an Uncontested
  Divorce without an Attorney (with minor children) $34.95

  Update $1.50

TITLE	PRICE	QUANTITY	TOTAL

Subtotal	
Add 6% Sales Tax	
Postage	$3.00
TOTAL	

Method of Payment:

☐ Check or money order (payable to Grand River Press)

☐ Charge: ☐ Visa   ☐ MasterCard

Account # ☐☐☐☐☐☐☐☐☐☐☐☐☐☐☐☐☐☐

Expiration Date _____ Signature _____

Name _____

Address _____

City _____ State _____ Zip _____

Please send form to: **Grand River Press, P.O. Box 1342, East Lansing, Michigan 48826**

Dedication:
V. Cramer

Illustrations:
Patric Fourshe

Lettering and layout:
Altese Graphic Design

Editing:
Mark Woodbury

Contents

Chapter 2

Doing Your Divorce

Appendices

Forms

Preface

Do your own divorce? The idea may sound crazy to many people. After all, doesn't everyone need a lawyer to get a divorce?

The fact is, you have the right to do your own divorce, just as you have the right to represent yourself in any legal matter. The right of legal self-representation is so important it's protected by the Bill of Rights in the U.S. Constitution (it falls under the First Amendment's right of petition for redress of grievances). In Michigan, legal self-help is also guaranteed by Sec. 13 of Art. 1 of the Michigan Constitution of 1963, which says: "a suitor in any court of this state has the right to prosecute or defend his suit, either *in his own proper person* or by an attorney." (Emphasis added.)

Despite these guarantees, the right to represent yourself in court doesn't mean very much if you don't know what you're doing once you get there. That's where this book comes in.

Chapter 1 describes divorce, tells you what an uncontested divorce is and helps you decide whether you can handle it yourself. Chapter 2 has instructions and sample forms to guide you through a divorce. And last but not least, blank forms are included in the back of the book which you can tear out and use to file your own divorce case.

Chapter 1

PART I: Introduction to Divorce

PART II: Uncontested Divorce

PART III: Doing an Uncontested Divorce Yourself

PART I: Introduction to Divorce

Asked about the origin of divorce, the French philosopher Voltaire said he didn't know exactly, but assumed that divorce was invented a few weeks after marriage. His reasoning? A couple married, quarreled and were ready for divorce a few weeks later.

Although it was meant as a joke, Voltaire's remark wasn't that far from the truth. Divorce *has* been around almost as long as marriage. The Babylonian Code of Hammurabi, the oldest known code of law, authorized divorce on several grounds, including a wife's barrenness, disloyalty, neglect or disease. According to the Bible, a Hebrew husband could divorce his wife for "uncleanness" by handing her a "bill of divorcement" and sending her away.

It was this law that Jesus was quizzed about by the Pharisees when they asked him: "Is it lawful for a man to divorce his wife?" The Gospel of St. Mark says Jesus condemned the practice, adding: "What therefore God hath joined together, let not man put asunder." Yet St. Matthew's account of this incident is different. It says that Jesus permitted divorce on grounds of wives' "fornication." Other New Testament scripture is also contradictory; some passages are hostile to divorce, while others seem to tolerate it.

With all this confusion, the Bible can be interpreted to either allow or disallow divorce. Catholic countries sided with the Mark Gospel and forbade divorce. But Protestant countries—with the notable exception of England—followed Matthew and allowed divorce on grounds of adultery and sometimes desertion.

When it came to law, America usually took its cue from England, so it should have observed the English ban on divorce. But divorce became firmly established in this country after the first American divorce was granted in

1639 by the Massachusetts Bay Colony to Mrs. James Luxford for her husband's bigamy.

There were several reasons for that. In a way, America itself was the child of divorce: the "divorce," in the guise of the American Revolution, from England. It's even possible to read the Declaration of Independence as the petition for that divorce. This interpretation isn't as far-fetched as it seems.

Thomas Jefferson, the author of the Declaration of Independence, had handled divorce cases as a young lawyer, and the catalog of grievances and wrongs found in the declaration echoed those from his divorce practice.

There were also practical reasons for the American love affair with divorce. During the colonial era, divorce was forbidden in England, France, Italy and several other European countries. Many immigrants to America were fleeing these repressive divorce laws as much as religious or political persecution. Once here, they were in no mood for tough European-style divorce laws.

By the mid-19th century, almost all the states had divorce laws. Typically, these laws permitted divorce on a variety of fault grounds. According to this fault system, divorce was available only when one spouse had committed marital misconduct. This gave the faultless spouse grounds for a divorce.

On the other hand, an at-fault spouse wasn't entitled to get a divorce. A peculiar divorce doctrine called recrimination prevented anyone with "unclean hands" from asking for a divorce. Recrimination effectively barred an at-fault spouse (who often wanted out of the marriage the most) from getting a divorce, unless the faultless spouse was willing to excuse the marital misconduct. By using this divorce veto, the faultless spouse could blackmail the at-fault spouse—by demanding extra property, support or other concessions—as the price for the divorce.

During this era, Michigan divorce law was typical of the fault divorce laws. The 1846 divorce law had seven fault grounds for divorce: 1) adultery 2) physical incompetence 3) imprisonment 4) desertion 5) husband's drunkenness 6) extreme cruelty 7) husband's neglect. It also had a strict recrimination doctrine.

But not every state was as generous with divorce grounds as Michigan. Before 1967, New York had a notoriously tough divorce law, which allowed divorce only on grounds of adultery. South Carolina was even worse. Divorce was legalized in that state after the Civil War and then abolished in 1878. Divorce was finally re-established in South Carolina in 1949, after an absence of 71 years!

When people were frustrated by strict divorce laws in their home states, they often fled to other states with better laws. This so-called migratory divorce was possible because the United States, unlike most countries, doesn't have a uniform national divorce law. Instead, divorce is regulated by each state. With 50 different divorce laws, it's no wonder that migratory divorce has been a problem in America since colonial times.

Many states tried to stop migratory divorce by adopting divorce residence requirements or erecting other barriers. But a handful of states encouraged divorce migration as a boost to local tourism. Nevada even managed to make migratory divorce its largest industry for a while. In 1907, William Schnitzer, a sharp New York lawyer, noticed that Nevada had a lax divorce law, with a short residence period, seven grounds for divorce and no recrimination doctrine. Schnitzer opened an office in Reno and soon divorce migrants flocked there. Other lawyers followed in Schnitzer's footsteps and migratory divorce flourished in Nevada.

As easy as migratory divorce was, it was still very expensive. There was the cost of getting the divorce, not to mention the expense of traveling to another state and living there during the residence period. As a result, migratory divorce was a luxury only the wealthy could afford.

Among those making the trek to Nevada was Nelson Rockefeller, then governor of New York. Millionaire Rockefeller got a Nevada divorce in 1962 while thousands of his fellow New Yorkers were stuck at home without a divorce remedy. Rockefeller's divorce caused a furor, and many think it cost him the Republican presidential nomination in 1964.

By the 1960s, all the controversy over migratory divorce had created the mood for change. California took the first step in 1969 when it adopted a "no-fault" divorce law. Previously, California had had a fault divorce law with several fault grounds (adultery, extreme cruelty, willful neglect, etc.). It replaced these with two no-fault grounds: incurable insanity and irreconcilable differences. What's more, the new California law banished fault from the other divorce issues of alimony, child support and property division.

The California no-fault law revolutionized divorce in America, as other states rushed to enact similar no-fault laws. Within five years, 45 states had adopted no-fault divorce. By 1986, when final holdout South Dakota gave in, every state had some type of no-fault divorce.

Michigan was among the first states to adopt no-fault divorce in the early 1970s. But in Michigan the transition from fault to no-fault divorce wasn't as smooth as it was in other states. At first, Michigan lawmakers were poised to adopt a sweeping California-style no-fault divorce law removing fault from divorce entirely. Michigan lawyers were horrified at this idea because they feared that no-fault divorce meant no-lawyer divorce. The lawyers lobbied furiously against the no-fault proposal. Ultimately, a deal was reached providing for no-fault divorce grounds, but with fault left intact for most of the other divorce issues. This no-fault divorce law took effect on Jan. 1, 1972, and is still the law today.

In the last few years, no-fault divorce has stirred up new controversy. Feminists have complained that no-fault divorce can be unfair to women. Their reasoning: no-fault destroyed the divorce leverage women once had, leading to smaller property division and support settlements for them. Some conservatives argue that no-fault divorce actually encourages divorce, bringing more of the social problems associated with divorce.

In Michigan, no-fault critics have introduced bills in the legislature to repeal parts of the no-fault law, and re-introduce fault into divorce grounds. These proposals got a lot of press, but haven't gone anywhere as legislators have shied away from re-opening the debate on no-fault divorce.

Do-It-Yourself Divorce

During the era of fault divorce, few dared to do their own divorces because they were hard to handle. But a no-fault divorce is really just a clerical task, which even a nonlawyer can manage. As soon as no-fault laws were adopted, nonlawyer entrepreneurs set up do-it-yourself divorce services to help people do their own divorces.

In Michigan, two such operations sprang up in 1972 after the no-fault divorce law went into effect: Harry Gordon Associates in Oak Park and Gordon, Graham and Cramer in Detroit. Harry Gordon Associates sold a divorce kit with forms and instructions. Gordon, Graham and Cramer offered personalized services, including preparation of papers, filing and help with court appearances.

Alarmed at this threat to their business, Michigan lawyers sought to enforce the unauthorized practice of law statute against their new rivals. Like most states, Michigan has an unauthorized practice law barring non-lawyers from practicing law. This law permits you to represent yourself, but you must be a lawyer to represent others.

In 1972, courts invoked this law and ordered Harry Gordon Associates and Gordon, Graham and Cramer out of business. Facing jail if they disobeyed, most of the firms' operators reluctantly closed. But Virginia Cramer, one of the partners in Gordon, Graham and Cramer, refused to be intimidated. She re-emerged with a new divorce service similar to her old one. Just like before, lawyers tried to stop her claiming that she was engaged in the unauthorized practice of law.

After battling in court for several years, the parties ended up before the Michigan Supreme Court in the case known as *State Bar of Michigan v. Cramer*. The issue in the case was whether Cramer had violated the unauthorized practice law by providing personalized legal services. The court decided that she had when she gave clients *specific* legal information (telling them what to do in their particular situations). On the other hand, the court said that nonlawyers like Cramer could offer *general* legal information in the form of books or legal kits.

Thanks to the apparent ban on nonlawyer divorce services, few such firms exist in Michigan. Without this option, most divorce do-it-yourselfers have had to rely on self-help divorce books or kits. Since the 1970s, several legal aid organizations and women's groups have offered do-it-yourself divorce kits. This book has its genesis in one such kit published in 1981. It was enlarged into book form in 1986, and has been revised several times since then.

PART II:
Uncontested Divorce

Before you start your divorce, it's important to talk with your spouse and see if you agree on the divorce issues. This will determine whether your divorce will be contested or uncontested.

A disagreement over the divorce issues usually means a contested divorce. You are entitled to represent yourself in a contested divorce. But your spouse would probably get a lawyer, providing an edge over you during the divorce. That's why you shouldn't represent yourself in a contested case.

On the other hand, if you and your spouse agree on all the divorce issues, you have an uncontested divorce. You ought to be able to handle this kind of divorce yourself without a lawyer. But see Part III for several situations in which even an uncontested divorce may be too complicated for you to do yourself.

What sort of agreement do you need for an uncontested divorce? A formal written agreement—called a separation or settlement agreement—won't be necessary. Michigan doesn't require these in uncontested cases, as some states do. Instead, an informal agreement or understanding should be enough.

Sometimes you may not need an agreement at all. Needless to say, it's impossible to discuss divorce with a spouse who has disappeared. In that case, the spouse's absence should permit you to go ahead and get an uncontested divorce just as if s/he were agreeing to it.

Divorce Issues

During your talk, you and your spouse may quickly agree that your marriage must end. But a divorce is more than simply ending a marriage. In a divorce with minor children, there are a lot of divorce issues dealing with the children. Even in divorces without minor children, there are three important divorce issues:

- end of marriage
- property division
- alimony

These are the issues you and your spouse must agree on to have an uncontested divorce. To help you reach agreement, the rest of this chapter examines these issues in detail.

End of Marriage

Above all else, a divorce means ending your marriage. To accomplish that, you need specific grounds (reasons). As explained in Part I, Michigan once had fault grounds, such as adultery, desertion, extreme cruelty, etc., for divorce. But in 1972, Michigan adopted these no-fault grounds for divorce:

There has been a breakdown of the marriage relationship to the extent that the objects of matrimony have been destroyed and there remains no reasonable likelihood that the marriage can be preserved.

If you look at these grounds closely, you see that three things must exist to get a divorce: 1) a marital breakdown ("breakdown of the marriage relationship") 2) that is serious ("to the extent that the objects of matrimony have been destroyed") 3) and permanent ("there remains no reasonable likelihood that the marriage can be preserved").

At first, when the no-fault law was new, courts had trouble applying the no-fault grounds. Judges continued to probe into the reasons for marital breakdowns, as they had under the old fault law. Some judges even denied divorces when they felt that a marriage hadn't really broken down or could be saved.

By the late 1970s, courts were applying the no-fault law more liberally. These days, courts don't investigate the marital breakdown very much, and divorces are granted for almost any reason. As a result, the end-of-marriage issue is seldom contested in divorces any more.

Glossary

Uncontested divorce–divorce where spouses agree on all the divorce issues.

No-fault divorce–all Michigan divorces, whether contested or uncontested, are no-fault divorces since they must use no-fault grounds.

Property Division

Years ago, divorce property division was little more than divvying up pots, pans and clothing. But today a lot more may be at stake. Wendy McCaw, wife of cellphone magnate Craig McCaw, may have received the largest ($460 million) divorce property division. Other big winners include wives of Hollywood celebrities like Mel Gibson's first wife Robyn ($425 million) and Maria Shriver, Arnold Schwarzenegger's ex ($250-375 million).

What all these divorces have in common is that they happened in western states with community property laws. In these states, marriage is considered an equal financial partnership, so most property acquired during a marriage belongs to the spouses equally, regardless of which spouse earned or owned it. And when a marriage ends—by death or divorce—each spouse gets one-half of the marital property.

Only nine states, mostly in the South and West, have community property. The rest, including Michigan, have a different system of property ownership and division. At one time, Michigan divided property during divorce strictly according to ownership: Each spouse got whatever they owned. This system was simple and neat, but it discriminated against wives because husbands usually owned most property.

Accused of unfairness, Michigan adopted an equitable distribution system of property division in divorce cases. Like community property law, equitable distribution recognizes that marriage is a financial partnership, giving each spouse a share of the property regardless of ownership.

Despite that similarity, community property and equitable distribution divide property very differently. Spouses always get equal shares of community property. In equitable distribution, the shares can be equal or unequal. All the law asks is that the division be "just and reasonable" or "equitable" under the circumstances.

The flexibility of equitable distribution shows up in court decisions. For example, in Michigan divorces wives have gotten as much as 90% or as little as 10% of the property. Under equitable distribution, such lopsided divisions are permissible if justified by the facts of the case. Nevertheless, these are exceptional cases. In the vast majority of divorces, a 50-50 split, or something close to it, is the equitable division.

Court-Ordered Property Division

When spouses wrangle over property, the court must divide it for them during a trial. According to equitable distribution, the division must be "just and reasonable" or "equitable." But since these general principles don't give enough guidance, courts have developed nine specific factors for property division:

- duration of the marriage
- contribution of the parties to the marital estate
- age of the parties
- health of the parties
- life status of the parties
- necessities and circumstances of the parties
- earning abilities of the parties
- past relations and conduct of the parties
- general principles of equity

In many states, property divisions are based solely on economic factors. If fault is taken into account, it's only to the extent that fault has had an impact on the property. For example, California ignores fault in property divisions except when one spouse has squandered the community property. In that case of "economic fault," the other spouse gets a greater share of the property.

Most of Michigan's property division factors are also economic. But fault creeps into divorce when the property division is contested through the "past relations and conduct of the parties" factor. And in Michigan, this fault isn't confined to misuse of property. It can include almost any type of marital misconduct, no matter how embarrassing or lurid.

Since equitable distribution is designed to be flexible, courts can weigh the property division factors much as they wish. They can focus on the important factors in the case, while disregarding others that don't apply. Courts may also consider other things through the catch-all "general principles of equity" factor.

Courts can avoid all that if the parties have a prenuptial agreement, since the agreement will normally control the division of property. Prenuptial agreements (also called antenuptial agreements or marital contracts) are contracts between spouses-to-be spelling out how property shall be divided when the marriage ends by death or divorce.

Michigan courts weren't always willing to use prenuptial agreements during divorce. For years, they refused to enforce these agreements believing that they encouraged divorce. But in 1991, the Michigan Court of Appeals reversed that rule and decided that prenuptial agreements are enforceable when: 1) the agreement was fairly entered into before the marriage 2) the agreement itself was fair at the time it was signed 3) facts and circumstances haven't changed enough since the agreement was signed that would make it unfair to enforce the agreement.

Uncontested Property Division

Before you and your spouse agree on a property division, you must know the extent and value of your property. "Can I Get a Fair Property Division?" on page 31 has important information about that. It tells which property is divisible in a divorce, and how to value it.

After you agree on a property division, the court should approve it because you have more control over property division than other divorce issues. If you happen to have a prenuptial agreement dealing with divorce, you should be able to use it to divide your property, unless the agreement is "unfair" (see above for the fairness requirements for prenuptial agreements). Whatever you decide about property division, see "Property Division Provisions" on page 163 in Appendix F for information about providing for and carrying out the division.

Alimony

From the start, American courts awarded support in the form of alimony to wives. In 1641, just two years after the first American divorce, Massachusetts Bay Colony passed a law giving wives a right to alimony.

During this era, courts regarded alimony as wife-support, and husbands never got it. But in the 1960s, states revised their alimony laws to make it payable to either men or women. Michigan amended its alimony law in 1970 to permit alimony for men.

Since then, there have been some well-publicized cases of women paying alimony to men. Actresses Jane Seymour and Roseanne Barr reportedly paid their former husbands alimony. And even among the less famous, men are receiving alimony more often as women achieve financial parity with men. But typically, men are the alimony payers and women are the recipients.

Despite all the attention it gets, alimony has never been very common. At the beginning of this century, alimony was awarded in a scant 9.3% of divorces. Although exact figures are hard to come by, that percentage seems to have increased during the next 50 years. One study of California divorces in 1968 found that wives received alimony in 20% of divorces. But by 1975, only 14% of divorce cases included alimony.

As the number of alimony orders declined, the duration of alimony also shrank. Years ago, alimony was usually an open-ended award which continued indefinitely until the wife remarried or died. Nowadays, alimony is likely to be for a limited time—maybe a year or two—to help the recipient get back on his/her feet after divorce. This kind of short-term alimony is sometimes referred to as rehabilitative or transitional alimony.

In Michigan, alimony can be paid during a divorce or afterward. Alimony during a divorce is available as preliminary relief, but only through a temporary order issued after a motion and hearing. See "Do I Need 'Preliminary Relief'?" on page 37 for more about preliminary alimony.

Whether or not preliminary alimony has been ordered, alimony can be granted in the Judgment of Divorce at the end of the divorce. In most cases, alimony takes the form of cash payments payable periodically.

These payments won't last forever because divorce judgments invariably make alimony subject to conditions ending it. These conditions are negotiable, but most judgments contain several of the following:

Death. Alimony is almost always terminated when the recipient dies (as explained below, there are sound tax reasons for making such a provision). Alimony doesn't automatically end when the payer dies, and it can survive and become a debt of his/her estate. Nevertheless, judgments often terminate alimony when payers die.

Remarriage. Alimony often ends when the recipient remarries, but seldom ends if the payer remarries.

Cohabitation. To prevent recipients from choosing cohabitation over remarriage as a way to keep alimony, the alimony may end if the recipient cohabitates with a member of the opposite sex.

Date. Alimony may end on a specific date.

Modification. In Michigan, true alimony has customarily been open to modification when there has been a change in the parties' circumstances. A modification could result in an increase, decrease or even termination of the alimony.

Michigan law does allow divorce parties to designate alimony as non-modifiable. However, this has to be done carefully in a negotiated divorce settlement; you can't do it in an uncontested divorce without input from the defendant. Thus, all alimony described in this book remains modifiable.

Types of Alimony

Alimony is a slippery word because Michigan law and federal law define alimony differently. Adding to complications, Michigan court rules use the phrase "spousal support" instead of alimony. Because of this, the forms in this book also use spousal support to mean alimony, although the text will use the familiar term alimony.

Michigan divorce law regards as alimony any divorce-related payments of money or other property from one (ex)spouse to the other for purposes of support. As explained before, alimony usually takes the form of cash payments paid periodically (weekly, monthly, etc.). There is another kind of so-called alimony, alimony-in-gross, which is often paid in several lump-sum payments. Despite its name, alimony-in-gross is really division of a liquid asset: money. Thus, alimony-in-gross is really property division and not true alimony.

The federal tax code has its own rules for defining alimony. The tax law generally disregards what parties call their payments. Instead, it considers support payments as alimony if they are:

- paid in cash (including checks or money orders)
- made to a spouse or to someone on his/her behalf

- made in a divorce document (such as a divorce order or judgment)
- made when the spouses are living apart (subject to several exceptions, including payment of temporary alimony)
- end on the death of the recipient-spouse
- not provided as child support
- not designated as something other than alimony

These tax rules are important because payments that qualify as alimony get special tax treatment. The payments are deductible by the payer and counted as income for the recipient.

Payment of Alimony

Like child support, alimony is normally paid by immediate income withholding to the state disbursement unit (SDU). But it's possible set up other payment methods, and have alimony paid to the SDU without immediate income withholding or even directly to the payee. See "Choosing an Alimony Payment Method" on page 175 for more about these and other payment options.

Court-Ordered Alimony

When spouses contest the issue of alimony, the court must decide the issue in a trial. To determine whether alimony is payable, the court considers the following factors:

- length of the marriage
- ability of the parties to work
- source of and amount of property awarded to the parties
- age of the parties
- ability of the parties to pay alimony
- present situation of the parties
- needs of the parties
- health of the parties
- prior standard of living of the parties and whether either is responsible for the support of others
- past relations and conduct of the parties
- general principles of equity

Like property division, the procedure for deciding alimony is flexible, so a court may apply these factors as it chooses. It can weigh the factors unequally, disregard ones that don't apply or add others that seem important through the catch-all "general principles of equity" factor.

Most of the alimony factors are economic. That makes sense because what alimony is really about is the need of one spouse for support and the ability of the other to pay it. But fault can creep in through the "past relations and conduct of the parties" factor. As with property division, fault in contested alimony cases may include almost any evidence of marital misconduct.

After a court decides that alimony is due, it must then determine the amount. In Michigan, there are no uniform alimony guidelines as there are for child support. So most judges set alimony on a case-by-case basis using the following factors:

- length of the marriage
- contributions of the parties to the joint estate
- age and health of the parties
- parties' stations in life
- necessities of the parties
- earning ability of the parties

In 1983, Washtenaw County rejected the case-by-case approach and adopted an alimony formula. It judges the strength of an alimony claim (length of the marriage, age, income and job skills are the most important factors), adjusts the claim for other factors and then provides for a mathematical computation of alimony. Recently, other counties have begun using Washtenaw's formula or adaptations of it. This suggests a need for a uniform state-wide formula, which may be developed in the future.

Uncontested Alimony

Since alimony isn't ordered in most divorces, divorce judgments usually waive (surrender) alimony. Sometimes it's possible to reserve alimony, allowing you to ask for it after the divorce. Or you and your spouse can agree to have alimony granted by including an alimony order in your divorce judgment.

"Alimony Provisions" on page 172 in Appendix F has more information about all those methods of dealing with alimony. It also includes two basic alimony orders for short- and long-term periodic alimony, which you can adapt to your situation.

Other Divorce Issues

Ending the marriage, property division and alimony aren't the only divorce issues. But any other divorce issues are relatively minor and seldom contested.

Name change for women is one such minor issue. After a divorce, women often want to drop their married names and resume maiden or former names. For them, Michigan law offers two name change methods: 1) common law name change by usage 2) court-ordered name change from: (a) the court when the divorce is granted (b) a separate name change case later.

The usage method is the easiest because all you do is choose a new name and begin using it regularly. No court order is necessary. The name change is legal as long as you're not adopting a new name for a fraudulent or improper purpose.

The trouble with the usage method is that it's no longer very effective. These days, with the general anxiety about security and special concern about identity theft, authorities want official proof of name changes; informal name changes aren't acceptable any more. As a result, most women choose formal court-ordered name changes.

It's easy for a woman to change her name during divorce. When the divorce is final, the court can allow the wife, whether she is plaintiff or defendant, to adopt a different surname (last name). She may resume a maiden or former name, or choose any other surname. The only restriction is that the name change mustn't be sought with "any fraudulent or evil intent" (to avoid past debts, hide from law enforcement officials, etc.). The divorce papers in this book have provisions for women to ask for and receive name changes.

Some women who ultimately want to change their names aren't ready for name changes during divorce. For personal or other reasons, they may want to keep their married names for a while, and then change later.

Women seeking name changes post-divorce must file separate name change cases. Before filing, they must satisfy a one-year county residency requirement. They must be fingerprinted by the police and submit to a criminal background check. After publishing a legal notice in the newspaper, they must attend a court hearing to get the name change.

Needless to say, this procedure takes much more effort than a divorce name change. That's why most women, if they have a choice, choose a name change during divorce.

Name change at divorce is seldom an issue for men, because men don't customarily change their names at marriage. However, today some men add their wives' surnames to their own, by hyphenation, at marriage, and may then want to drop the addition at divorce.

Michigan divorce law isn't very helpful for men in this predicament. The law has no provision for male name changes during divorce. To change their names at divorce, men must do it by custom and usage under the common law method, of file a separate name change case, outside of divorce, to get a formal a court-ordered name change.

PART III: Doing an Uncontested Divorce Yourself

Most uncontested divorces go smoothly. But divorce remains a difficult legal procedure, and can sometimes get complicated. There may be a problem with jurisdiction, trouble serving the divorce papers, difficulty dividing the property or the danger of spouse abuse. All these problems and more can make your divorce—although it's uncontested—too difficult for you to do yourself.

Am I Married?

It may seem silly, but the first thing you should do before a divorce is make sure you are really married. If you discover that you aren't married, you won't need a divorce to split up.

The legality of a marriage is judged by the law of where it began, not where it ends. If you were married in Michigan, you look at Michigan marriage law. Those married out of state must consider the marriage law of that place.

Michigan authorizes two types of marriage: 1) ceremonial marriage, performed by most clergymen and some government officials 2) secret marriage, a rather obscure form of marriage before a probate judge for the benefit of: (a) people with a good reason to keep their marriage secret (b) children under the age of 16 in certain circumstances. Other states have different types of ceremonial marriage, which are valid in Michigan.

Most states have abolished common law marriage, in which couples informally agree to live together as husband and wife. However, many states had it in the past. Michigan recognized common law marriage until Jan. 1,

1957. Today, only the District of Columbia and the following states permit common law marriage:

- Alabama
- Colorado
- Iowa
- Kansas
- Montana

- Rhode Island
- South Carolina
- Texas
- Utah

If your common law marriage began in one of these states, it's legal in Michigan. Or if it began in Michigan before Jan. 1, 1957, or in other states while they recognized the institution, it's also valid here.

If you doubt whether you are really married, check with the official of the office where you believe your marriage license is filed. In Michigan, that official is the county clerk who issued the license to you; in other states it might be someone else.

Another way to trace marriage records is through a state vital records office. Every state has an office that compiles records of marriages, divorces, births and deaths. By writing to the vital records office of the state in which you think you were married, you can get a copy of your marriage license, if one exists.

After you confirm that you are married, you should also make sure that your marriage hasn't already ended by divorce or annulment. Unlike common law marriage, there is no such thing as informal "common law" divorce. So despite what some people think, tearing up your marriage license, giving back wedding rings, etc. will not make you divorced. Therefore, any divorce that your spouse may have gotten must have been court-ordered.

If you think that you may have been involved in a prior divorce, investigate and see whether a divorce judgment (also known as a decree or order in some states) was ever issued in the case. The court where the divorce was filed will have record of the judgment. If you don't have much information about the divorce, use the procedure described above to contact the vital records office of the state where the divorce was filed. It should have a record of the divorce judgment, if in fact one was issued.

Naturally, your spouse's death also ends your marriage. You might not know about this if you've separated from your spouse and remained out of touch. If you suspect that your spouse has died, you can confirm that by checking to see if a death certificate was filed. In Michigan, death certificates are filed with the county clerk of the place of death. If you don't know the county, use the state vital records office. A quicker way to check on the death of anyone is through the Social Security Administration's (SSA) death index.

More Information

To obtain Michigan marriage, divorce and death records, contact Michigan's vital records office:

Department of Community Health
Vital Records Office
201 Townsend St.
Capitol View Bldg. 3rd Floor
Lansing, MI 48913
(517) 335-8666

Or order Michigan vital records on-line at www.michigan.gov/mdch, then to Birth, Death, Marriage and Divorce Records.

To find vital records offices in other states, go to www.vitalrec.com. This Web site can also help you find vital records in foreign countries. Or get the *International Vital Records Handbook*, 5th ed., Thomas Kemp, Baltimore: Genealogical Publishing Co., 2009.

The SSA's death index lists deceased people whose survivors have received social security death benefits. Not everyone applies for or receives these benefits, so the index isn't 100% complete, but it's a good place to start. The index is available at www.familysearch.com for free.

It's also possible to have your spouse legally declared dead after a long disappearance. Like most states, Michigan has an Enoch Arden law (so called after the shipwrecked sailor of the Tennyson poem who returned from ten years at sea to find his wife remarried), which allows a person to be declared dead after seven years of complete absence.

Do I Really Want to End My Marriage?

When you get a divorce, the marriage between you and your spouse is ended finally and irrevocably. This allows each of you to remarry, if you wish. As someone divorce-bound, you're probably well aware of these and other benefits of divorce.

But as you prepare to divorce, don't forget the many advantages of remaining married. Recently, when Vermont lawmakers were debating their controversial same-sex civil union law, legal experts there counted around 300 benefits of marriage offered by state law. Michigan law certainly provides as many or more. All in all, marriage offers many valuable rights, such as: 1) support 2) property rights 3) estate and will rights 4) private benefits 5) public benefits 6) miscellaneous rights.

To be sure, some of these rights can be continued or compensated after a divorce. You can sometimes get postdivorce support in the form of alimony, and your property rights, including rights in retirement plans, can be recovered in the property division of the divorce.

But many marital rights are lost forever by a divorce. After a divorce, you lose all rights to your spouse's estate, including: 1) the right to inherit a share of his/her estate if s/he dies without a will 2) the right to take a minimum share of the estate, if the will slights you 3) dower (an estate that widows have in their husbands' real property) 4) miscellaneous allowances from your deceased spouse's estate. Divorce also automatically revokes all distributions of property and some appointments in your spouse's will which benefit you.

You may also lose valuable private benefits, often provided by an employer, available through your spouse, such as retirement, fringe, life and health plan benefits. There are substitutes for some of these, such as COBRA-provided health care coverage (see "Health Care Coverage" on page 104 for more more about this type of coverage), but never completely and usually at a higher cost.

DIVORCE IN HASTE; REPENT AT LEISURE.

More Information

On divorce and social security, get "What Every Woman Should Know" (SSA Pub. No. 05-10127) from your local social security office, by calling the SSA at (800) 772-1213 or at www.ssa.gov/pubs/10127.html.

See "Can I Get A Fair Property Division?" on page 31 for resources about retirement benefits.

Good information about these and other topics:

Divorce & Money, 10th ed., Violet Woodhouse and Dale Fetherling, Berkeley: Nolo, 2011

The Dollars and Sense of Divorce, Judith Briles, et al., Chicago: Dearborn Financial Publishing, 1998

More Information

Some non-profit counselors are listed in the yellow pages under "Social Service Organizations." For-profit counselors appear under the "Marriage, Family, Child & Individual Counselors" category.

The **American Association for Marriage and Family Therapy** provides referrals to family counselors at (703) 838-9808, or try their online referral service at www.TherapistLocator.net.

The death of your spouse after your divorce will leave you without public benefits, such as wrongful death claims or survivor's benefits from worker's compensation or no-fault automobile insurance, that you might have enjoyed had you remained married. What's worse, if you happen to divorce before the tenth anniversary of your marriage, you may lose the right to get social security benefits based on your spouse's earnings record.

Divorce also jeopardizes other miscellaneous marital rights that you may have never thought about. For example, aliens (noncitizens) can lose entrance or residence rights when they divorce U.S. citizens. After a divorce, you cannot file a joint income tax return, and may face a bigger tax bill. Marriage also entitles you to discounts on airplane tickets, hotels, etc., which single people don't always enjoy.

After considering all that marriage offers, you may decide that it isn't so bad after all. If you think that your marriage can be saved, you may find marriage counseling helpful. Many religious and human service organizations provide counseling, usually without charge. Private marriage and family counselors offer similar services. These private counselors charge fees for their services, but some health plans pay for the cost.

Is Divorce the Best Way to End My Marriage?

Divorce isn't the only cure for a bad marriage. By declaring a marriage nonexistent, an annulment also ends the marriage. A legal separation—known as separate maintenance in Michigan—ends a marital relationship, although the marriage itself is left intact. Like divorce, an annulment or separate maintenance allows the court to decide the issues of property division and alimony. Before you choose a divorce, consider whether an annulment or separate maintenance might be better for you.

Annulment

Many people don't really understand annulment. For one thing, they often confuse legal annulments with religious annulments. Legal annulments are granted by courts of law, and affect one's legal rights. Some religious denominations, notably the Roman Catholic Church, offer religious annulments. These end marriages in the eyes in the church, restoring various religious privileges. A religious annulment is obtained from the religious organization and has absolutely no effect on legal rights.

Another misunderstanding about annulments is that they are routinely available for spouses who have been married for a short time and simply want to "call the whole thing off." The fact is, the length of a marriage is often insignificant: A marriage of a few days may not be annullable, just as a marriage of many years can be annulled. The real distinction between divorce and annulment is that a divorce ends a valid marriage, while an annulment is a legal declaration that no marriage ever existed because of a serious legal defect in the marriage at the time it was performed.

Like most states, Michigan presumes that marriages are legally valid. As a result, minor legal defects in a marriage, such as irregularities in the marriage ceremony, lack of authority of the person who performed the ceremony, etc., are excusable. But if the legal defect is serious, the marriage is subject to annulment. In Michigan, the serious legal defects providing grounds for an annulment concern whether the spouses: 1) had the legal capacity to marry 2) properly consented to marriage.*

Glossary

Divorce–legal procedure that ends a marriage.

Annulment–says that a marriage is legally defective and never really existed.

Separate maintenance–like a legal separation, allowing the spouses to live apart with marriage still intact.

Legal capacity. One must satisfy several requirements to marry in Michigan. If a spouse failed to meet any of these requirements when the marriage was performed, the spouse lacked the legal capacity for marriage. This defect can provide grounds for annulment:

¶ *Bigamy.* A spouse marries while already married to someone else.

¶ *Incest.* The spouses are related too closely by blood (you cannot marry a parent, child, grandchild, grandparent, brother or sister, aunt or uncle, niece or nephew or first cousin) or marriage (a stepparent, stepchild, stepgrandchild, son- or daughter-in-law, father- or mother-in-law, spouse of a grandchild or grandparent-in-law are all not marriageable).

¶ *Same-sex marriage.* Michigan doesn't permit same-sex marriage, or recognize same-sex marriages from other states.

¶ *Underage.* Eighteen is the age of consent to marry in Michigan. Men and women 16-18 can marry if they obtain the proper parental consent. Under some circumstances, children under 16 can marry with parental consent in a secret marriage in probate court. Anyone who marries while underage and/or without the proper parental consent, lacks the legal capacity to marry.

¶ *Mental incompetency.* Mental incompetency of a spouse at the time of a marriage is an additional legal incapacity. Onset of mental incompetency after marriage doesn't affect the marriage.

¶ *Physical incapacity.* Sterility and some kinds of sexual dysfunction, which exist at the time of the marriage, are also recognized as incapacities.

---

*　As mentioned before, the legality of a marriage is judged by the law of the state where it began. These annulment grounds apply to Michigan marriages only. There may be different annulment grounds for out-of-state marriages.

Consent. According to Michigan law, both spouses must give proper consent to their marriage. If a spouse's consent is absent or defective, for any of the reasons below, the marriage may be annulled:

¶ *Force.* A spouse's consent to the marriage is obtained forcibly. Ordinarily, the force must be the use or threat of physical force, but in some cases extreme psychological duress will qualify as force.

¶ *Intoxication.* A spouse's consent to the marriage might be defective if s/he is under the influence of alcohol or drugs when the marriage is performed.

¶ *Fraud.* Fraud is a misrepresentation that causes someone to do something. If fraud is used to obtain consent to a marriage, the fraud can invalidate the marriage. Michigan law is clear that the fraud must affect an essential part of the marriage. For example, a spouse's misrepresentation about his/her ability to have or want children, or about an intention to engage in cohabitation or sexual relations, may be important enough to annul the marriage. But misrepresentations by a spouse about character, wealth, family background or premarital life don't provide fraud grounds for an annulment.

¶ *Sham marriage.* Even when consent to a marriage is given voluntarily and knowingly, the consent might be defective if it wasn't seriously intended. Marriages based on such false consent are regarded as sham marriages, making them subject to annulment. An example of a sham marriage is a marriage by an alien (noncitizen) who marries a U.S. citizen solely to obtain permanent residence in this country. In that case, the alien's marriage may appear to be proper, but it is really nothing more than a ruse to obtain residence in this country.

If you possess any of these grounds for annulment, you may be able to end your marriage by annulment. Or you can disregard the annulment grounds, file for divorce and end your marriage that way. Which is the better choice?

There is no simple answer to this question because divorces closely resemble annulments. Both procedures end marriages and free spouses to remarry. They both divide property. But alimony, especially long-term alimony, is difficult to get in an annulment.

An annulment may be quicker than a divorce. Annulments don't have waiting periods as divorces do (see "How Long Will My Divorce Take?" on page 28 for information about divorce waiting periods). And there are no state or county residence requirements for annulments as there are in divorce cases (see "Can I Get a Divorce in Michigan?" and "Can I File the Divorce in My County?" on pages 24-26 for more on state and county divorce residence requirements).

On the other hand, the grounds for annulment are harder to prove and easier to defend against than the no-fault divorce grounds. What's worse, most annulment grounds are based on fault. This means that an annulment can be messy, like divorce was under the old fault law.

If you believe that you have grounds for an annulment and cannot decide whether to file for divorce or annulment, talk with a lawyer about which procedure to use. Act quickly because it's possible to lose annulment grounds by waiting too long. If you decide to seek an annulment, have the lawyer represent you because this book doesn't have instructions or forms for annulment.

Separation

Unlike divorce or annulment, separation doesn't end a marriage. It merely ends the marital relationship between the spouses, leaving the marriage itself intact. Despite that fact, there may be sound reasons for choosing separation over divorce or annulment.

Years ago, people often separated to avoid the social stigma of divorce. With divorce more common now, this stigma has faded. Nevertheless, some people may still want to separate and remain married for social or religious reasons.

Some couples choose separation for more practical reasons. As explained before, spouses can lose valuable marital rights when their marriage ends. Since separation doesn't break the legal bond of marriage, it preserves these marital rights. With this in mind, spouses may decide to separate temporarily, and divorce later when losing these rights isn't so important. For example, spouses married eight or nine years might agree to separate for a few years, and then divorce, so they can qualify for social security benefits based on each other's earnings under the ten-year rule mentioned above. Or they may remain married to preserve benefits like health plan coverage.

Informal Separation

You don't need to go to court to separate. As a matter of fact, spouses can separate informally and live apart indefinitely. Separated spouses usually work out arrangements for property division and sometimes alimony. To avoid disputes, some estranged spouses enter into written separation or settlement agreements. These agreements spell out how property division and alimony are handled during the separation. In addition, the agreement can settle these issues for any divorce following the separation.

An informal separation—even one with a written separation agreement—is difficult to maintain. If the spouses disagree about something, they have no place to resolve their dispute. As a result, some separated spouses seek a formal, court-ordered separation, which is popularly known as a legal separation.

Legal Separation: Separate Maintenance

Michigan law provides for a special type of legal separation called separate maintenance. Separate maintenance doesn't end the marriage. But it settles the issues of property division and alimony while the spouses live apart.

The procedure for getting a separate maintenance is like that for a divorce. Even the same no-fault grounds are used. Despite the resemblance, it's much harder to get a separate maintenance because Michigan law allows a defendant in a separate maintenance case to ask for a divorce instead. After the request, the court must grant a divorce if the marriage is broken. Therefore, it's impossible to get a separate maintenance without the approval of the other spouse. All this makes separate maintenance difficult, so see a lawyer if you want one.

Can I Get a Divorce in Michigan?

After deciding that a divorce is what you want, you must then determine whether you can get one in Michigan. Not everyone is entitled to divorce in Michigan. To get a divorce in this state, Michigan courts must have jurisdiction to hear your divorce case. Jurisdiction is based on the residences of you and your spouse.

Residence

Residence is vital to your case as the basis for jurisdiction. But what is it really? Residence has different legal meanings. For the purposes of divorce, residence means your permanent home, or the place you intend to stay.

Long-time residents of Michigan don't have to worry about residence. But if you've moved to the state recently, you can establish residence by: 1) registering to vote here 2) getting a Michigan driver's license and/or registering a vehicle in the state 3) owning or leasing real property here (it's even better if you file for a homestead property tax exemption at your Michigan address) 4) working and filing income tax returns here 5) maintaining financial accounts here 6) joining church, trade, professional or social organizations in Michigan.

Once established in Michigan, residence isn't lost by temporary absences out of state, such as vacations or business trips. Nor is it disturbed by leaving the state under military or government orders. For example, a resident of Michigan who enters the U.S. military or foreign service usually remains a Michigan resident during active duty wherever assigned.

Residence may be important for the purposes of jurisdiction before you file a divorce, but it's much less important afterward. In fact, after you file the divorce you or your spouse can move anywhere—in or outside Michigan—without losing jurisdiction for your divorce.

Glossary

Plaintiff–spouse who files for divorce.

Defendant–spouse against whom divorce is filed.

Jurisdiction–power of a court to decide a divorce case.

Venue—in divorce cases, the correct county for divorce-filing.

Divorce Jurisdiction

Michigan divorce jurisdiction is based on the past and present residences of the spouses. These residences determine whether there is either full or limited jurisdiction for the case. A court can take full jurisdiction when at

Michigan Divorce Jurisdiction

	Defendant is a Michigan resident (and has been for at least 180 days immediately before the divorce is filed)	Defendant once resided with plaintiff in Michigan during their marriage, then moved out of state	Defendant never resided with plaintiff in Michigan during their marriage
Plaintiff is a Michigan resident (and has been for at least 180 days immediately before the divorce is filed)	Full jurisdiction immediately*	Full jurisdiction immediately**	Limited jurisdiction immediately**
Plaintiff once resided with defendant in Michigan during their marriage, then moved out of state	Full jurisdiction immediately	No jurisdiction until plaintiff (or defendant) moves back to Michigan and has resided here at least 180 days immediately before the divorce is filed, then full jurisdiction**	
Plaintiff never resided with defendant in Michigan during their marriage	Full jurisdiction immediately		No jurisdiction until plaintiff (or defendant) moves to Michigan and has resided here at least 180 days immediately before the divorce is filed, then only limited jurisdiction**

* In fact, either plaintiff or defendant can satisfy the 180-day residence requirement by having resided in Michigan at least 180 days immediately before the divorce is filed.

** Full jurisdiction can also be obtained on a nonresident defendant by serving him/her while present in Michigan, such as during a visit to the state.

least the defendant-spouse is residing in Michigan (the plaintiff-spouse may be residing here as well), or when the spouses resided together in Michigan at some time during their marriage. Limited jurisdiction exists when only the plaintiff-spouse resides in Michigan and the defendant never resided here with him/her during their marriage.

Like other states, Michigan also imposes a residence requirement on divorce to discourage migratory divorce. In Michigan, the residence period is 180 days. The chart above depicts Michigan divorce jurisdiction with the residence requirement added.

The concept of jurisdiction is difficult, but it's important because it determines how much of your case the court can decide. As explained in Part II, divorce is divisible into several issues: end-of-marriage, property division and alimony. For reasons that are too complicated to explain here, certain divorce issues may need a particular type of jurisdiction. For example, property division and alimony require full jurisdiction, while ending a marriage can use either limited or full jurisdiction.

When a court has full jurisdiction, it can do a divorce completely. It can end the marriage, divide the property and award alimony. With only limited jurisdiction, a court can end the marriage, but it cannot decide property division or alimony.

Divorces with minor children almost always require full jurisdiction. But divorces without minor children can sometimes get by with limited jurisdiction. If you have little property, and don't seek alimony, limited jurisdiction may be enough. If not, contact a lawyer to see about getting full Michigan jurisdiction or filing for divorce in the defendant's state.

Can I File the Divorce in My County?

Assuming Michigan courts have some type of jurisdiction for your divorce, you must then file in the Michigan county with proper venue. In divorce cases, venue exists in the county where either you or your spouse has resided at least 10 days immediately before the divorce is filed. Incidentally, residence for venue purposes is a place of permanent habitation, just as it is for jurisdiction.

Naturally, when you both reside in the same county, the divorce must be filed there. But when you reside in different Michigan counties, venue is proper in either county. For the sake of convenience, most people choose to file in their own counties.

If the defendant resides out of state, venue will be in the Michigan county where the plaintiff resides. In those rare cases with out-of-state plaintiffs, venue will be in the Michigan county where the defendant resides.

What If My Spouse and I File for Divorce at the Same Time?

This is the dueling divorces problem: You and your spouse file for divorce around the same time, perhaps even before the divorce papers are served on each other. If both cases were filed in Michigan, the one filed first has priority and the later one must be dismissed (to dismiss the second case, see Appendix E about voluntary dismissal of divorce cases).

When the divorces are filed in different states, the situation is a little more complicated. If both states have full jurisdiction, the first case filed usually has priority. But if only one state has full jurisdiction, that state can do the divorce completely and its case should be the one to go forward.

Can My Spouse Be Served with the Divorce Papers?

Regardless of the type of jurisdiction for a divorce, the defendant must get notice of the divorce. Like other lawsuits, notice in divorce cases is provided by serving the initial divorce papers on defendants. Service is explained in detail in Chapter 2.

At this point, you should know that service is easy and cheap if your spouse is available to receive the divorce papers. In that case, you can obtain service by any of three methods: 1) acknowledgment 2) mail 3) delivery. It doesn't matter where your spouse lives, because these service methods can be used anywhere in or outside Michigan.

Service can be difficult if a defendant is elusive (you know where the defendant is, but s/he is eluding or avoiding you). It's even more difficult if the defendant has disappeared (you don't know the whereabouts of the defendant). Luckily, the court rules provide for forms of alternate service to give hard-to-find defendants some type of notice (Appendix B has more about obtaining alternate service on elusive or disappeared defendants).

Thanks to this wide choice of service methods, you can be confident that when there is jurisdiction for your divorce there will be a way to serve the defendant.

What If My Spouse or I Am Imprisoned?

Incarceration of a spouse naturally puts a great strain on a marriage. If the marriage should break, the imprisonment also creates special problems for the divorce, whether the prisoner is plaintiff or defendant.

Divorce by an Imprisoned Plaintiff

Before filing, an imprisoned plaintiff must choose the correct county for filing. Choice of county is called venue and is controlled by the county residence of the divorce parties.

Prisoners are subject to special residence rules for venue. According to Michigan law, prisoners are presumed to remain residents of the county they resided in immediately before imprisonment. However, prisoners can become residents of the county of imprisonment if they can prove that they intend to reside there after release. Keep these residence rules in mind as you choose venue as directed in "Can I File the Divorce in My County?" above.

Prisoners shouldn't have any difficulty serving their non-institutionalized spouses with divorce papers. The three regular methods of service (acknowledgment, mail, delivery), plus alternate service methods, are available to prisoners. Service by mail is probably easiest and cheapest. All these service methods and rules are explained in "Service" on page 69.

Plaintiff-prisoners do face a special problem at the end of divorce, during the final hearing. Ordinarily, divorce plaintiffs must appear personally in court and give some brief testimony for the Judgment of Divorce. To satisfy the court appearance requirement, some counties transport prisoners to court for final hearings in divorce. But transportation is expensive, especially for counties with large prison populations.

As an alternative, many counties allow and encourage prisoners to give their testimony in written or electronic form. The court rules permit this

---

More Information

About divorce problems for prisoners, including giving final hearing testimony from prison, contact:

Prison Legal Services of Michigan
209 E. Washington Ave.
Jackson, MI 49201
(517) 780-6639

More Information

To locate a prison inmate for service and/or obtain the inmate's prisoner identification number, use a prison locator service.

You can locate Michigan prisoners through the **Michigan Department of Corrections'** Offender Tracking Information System (OTIS) at www.mdocweb. state.mi.us/otis2/otis2.html.

For prisoners in other state prisons, see the Johnson and Knox book cited on page 123. It lists prison locator services nationwide.

The federal **Bureau of Prisons** has a federal prison locator at www.bop.gov/iloc2/Locate Inmate.jsp.

because they excuse court appearances in exceptional cases. Prisoners should contact prison legal services for help with giving final hearing testimony without a court appearance.

Filing against a Defendant-Prisoner

There are fewer problems in a divorce against an incarcerated defendant. Before filing, the plaintiff must consider the venue rules while choosing where to file (see "Can I File the Divorce in My County?" on page 26 for more about venue). Typically, plaintiffs file in their home counties, so the residence of a defendant-prisoner isn't an issue. But if you want to file where a defendant-prisoner resides, see the section above about how the residence of prisoners is established.

Probably the best way to serve a defendant in prison is by mail. Service by mail is described in "Service" on page 69, along with the other service methods. When your service-helper mails the service papers to the defendant, make sure the defendant's prisoner identification number appears next to the defendant's name in the address on the envelope. Many prisons require this number for delivery of mail to inmates. If the defendant refuses to take and sign for the mailing, you can always use service by delivery, through the sheriff's office in the county where the prison is located.

What If My Spouse or I Am in the Military?

Military service adds both practical and legal problems to a divorce. As a practical matter, it may be difficult to find and serve papers on a defendant-servicemember stationed at a faraway military base. There are also state and federal military relief laws protecting active-duty servicemembers from hard-to-handle lawsuits. The federal law, the Servicemembers Civil Relief Act (SCRA), can be an especially stiff challenge when the servicemember is a defendant who is uncooperative or unresponsive.

Appendix D has complete information about dealing with military servicemembers whether as divorce plaintiffs or defendants.

How Long Will My Divorce Take?

Uncontested divorces take longer to complete than most uncontested lawsuits because Michigan law imposes two statutory waiting periods on divorces:

- 60 days in cases without minor children
- six months in cases with minor children

The waiting periods serve to delay divorces. The chief reason for the delay is to give the parties a chance to cool off, and possibly reconcile, after the heat of the divorce filing has passed.

In your case, the 60-day statutory waiting period applies. This means that at least 60 days must elapse between the day you file your divorce and the day you finish it in court at the final hearing.

In addition to the statutory waiting period, there may also be unpredictable court-caused delays. Some courts are very busy and may not be able to hear your divorce immediately after the statutory waiting period expires. As a result, your divorce will take at least 60 days, and maybe a while longer if the court is busy.

How Much Will My Divorce Cost?

Doing your own divorce saves you lawyer fees, but not the court fees of the case. These court fees are due in all divorces—with or without lawyers. The court fees for uncontested divorces without minor children include the following items:

Filing fee. The fee for filing a divorce is $150.

Service fee. You can expect to pay $0-50 to have the divorce papers served. The amount of the service fee depends on the method of service you use. Service by acknowledgment is usually available for free. Service by mail is around $10. Service by delivery is usually $23-50. If you use a sheriff for service by delivery, the sheriff charges a base service fee, currently $23, plus mileage (billed at a state government rate) to and from the defendant. Commercial process servers' fees for service by delivery may be slightly higher.

Motion fee. You must pay a $20 fee whenever you file a motion. You must file at least one motion in an uncontested divorce: a motion for a default judgment in the middle of the case. You probably won't have to file another motion unless you have to ask for something extraordinary, like alternate service.

Excluding a service fee, your court fees should be $170 (a $150 filing and $20 motion fee). Add to that a service fee, which depends on the method of service you choose.

Thanks to a landmark U.S. Supreme Court decision, poor people don't have to pay these court fees. In *Boddie v. Connecticut*, the supreme court decided that states must give everyone access to divorce, since they alone have the power to grant divorces. This means that those who can't afford divorce court fees are entitled to exemptions from payment. After the *Boddie* decision in 1971, Michigan adopted fee exemption rules for all types of cases, including divorce. See Appendix A for information about qualifying and applying for a fee exemption.

Divorce Children

	Children included in divorce	Comments/exceptions
Children born during plaintiff's and defendant's current marriage	Yes	But paternity of children born during a marriage can be disproved by evidence that the father is not really the father. If paternity is disproved, the child would usually not be included in the divorce.
Unborn children of the marriage (= wife's pregnancy)	Yes	
Children born during a previous marriage of plaintiff and defendant	Yes	
Children born to plaintiff and defendant outside of their marriage	Yes, if...	Paternity has been established before the divorce or if it can be proved during the divorce.
Children legally adopted by plaintiff and defendant during their marriage	Yes	
Stepchildren of plaintiff or defendant	No	But if a stepchild was adopted by plaintiff or defendant in a stepparent adoption, it will be a legally adopted child of theirs.
Children given up for adoption, or children over whom both plaintiff and defendant have lost parental rights	No	But if only one parent has lost parental rights, include the children in the divorce and explain the circumstances of the parent's loss of parental rights.

Do I Have Children in My Divorce?

To get a divorce without children, you mustn't have any "divorce children" on the day you file for divorce. Since you obtained this edition of *The Michigan Divorce Book*, you obviously believe that you don't have any divorce children. But before you make this assumption, consider the minor and adult children who make up the divorce children, as defined in the chart above.

The minor children are your children who are under 18 on the day you file for divorce. In some cases, divorce children also includes adult children. According to Michigan law, children between the ages of 18 and 19½ are entitled to support if they are: 1) regularly attending high school on a full-time basis with a reasonable expectation of completing sufficient credits to graduate from high school 2) residing on a full-time basis with the recipient of the support or at an institution. These children must be added to your divorce, and child support must be provided for them. Adult divorce children won't be governed by custody, parenting time or residence of children orders since these stop at age 18.

If you have any of these minor or adult divorce children, you must use a different divorce procedure for cases with minor children. You may be able to use *The Michigan Divorce Book (with minor children)* to do the divorce. See the order form at the front of the book for ordering information.

Can I Get a Fair Property Division?

As explained in "Property Division" on page 9, you are entitled to an equitable division of your property in a divorce. But exactly which property is subject to division?

Some states have rigid schemes for dividing property in divorces. They classify property as either marital-community property or nonmarital-separate property. In these states, only marital-community property is divisible during divorce.

In Michigan, by contrast, divorce property division is more flexible. Everything the spouses own is potentially subject to division. Despite what many people believe, this may include property the spouses brought into their marriage. It can also reach inheritances, will gifts or other gifts (including wedding gifts) received before or during the marriage.

Ordinarily, premarital property, inheritances and gifts are left out of divorce property division, and the spouse who owns this property keeps it. But the nonowner-spouse may claim a share of this property when: 1) s/he or the parties' children need the property for support 2) s/he has contributed to "acquisition, improvement or accumulation" of the property.

Saying that all property is potentially divisible in a divorce begs the question of what is property? Does it include everything the spouses possess or only those things with a definite market value?

A generation ago, everyone agreed that divisible property was confined to real property (land and buildings) and personal property, such as cash, bank accounts, stocks, bonds, household goods, tools, motor vehicles, etc., with a definite market value. But during the last 20 years, the definition of property has steadily expanded to include almost anything of value, regardless of whether it has a market value. So besides the familiar old property that has always been divided in divorces, there are several types of "new" property that may also be divisible:

Retirement benefits. For years, courts refused to divide retirement benefits, such as pensions, despite the fact that these benefits are often the most valuable thing spouses own. Ultimately, courts realized the unfairness of that position and now nearly all states permit the division of pensions and other retirement benefits.

Today, Michigan courts divide almost any type of retirement benefit provided by public- or private-sector employers, including pensions, 401(k),

More Information

About the treatment of retirement benefits during divorce, see *Your Pension Rights at Divorce: What Women Need to Know* (3rd ed.) available for viewing online (the print edition has been discontinued) at www.pensionrights.org, then to Get the Facts, to Books.

profit-sharing, employee stock ownership (ESOP) and saving/thrift plans. Also divisible are individual retirement benefits, such as individual retirement arrangement (IRA), simplified employee pension (SEP) and Keogh (HR-10) plans. The only type of retirement benefit immune from division is social security because it already has a built-in means of paying benefits to divorced spouses (see "Do I Really Want to End My Marriage?" on page 19 for more about obtaining social security off your spouse's earnings record).

Employee benefits. Employees are often eligible for valuable fringe benefits, such as health plan coverage, sick and vacation pay, expense accounts, club memberships, meal allowances, lodging, discounts, etc. Some of these benefits, such as banked sick and vacation pay, have been divided in divorce cases in Michigan.

Life insurance. Life insurance is often overlooked during property division, but it's divisible if it has a cash value. Whole life insurance policies usually have a cash value; term insurance policies ordinarily don't.

Businesses. Businesses, such as a sole proprietorship (one-person business) or an interest in a partnership or a small corporation whose stock is not traded publicly, are also divorce property.

Education. Michigan was one of the first states to include education in divorce property divisions. According to Michigan law, education leading to an *advanced* degree (graduate, law, medicine, etc.) is divisible when the degree was the result of a "concerted family effort." What this means is that the nondegree-spouse contributed financial or other support to the spouse earning the advanced degree. If so, the nondegree-spouse's contribution can be valued and awarded to him/her.

Legal claims. Some legal claims that a spouse has against third parties, such as personal injury or workers' compensation claims, are property that can be divided in divorces. For example, in one Michigan case a husband was awarded $700,000 for a libel claim, and the divorce court ruled that his wife was entitled to about half of the money.

Spouses may also have legal claims against each other that can be decided in a divorce. At one time, it was impossible for spouses to sue each other for personal injuries. This immunity has recently been abolished and spouses are adding personal injury claims to divorces more often.

Debts. Although it's hard to think of debts as property, they should be weighed during the property division because debts influence the overall fairness of the division.

Whether your property is old, new or a mixture of both, you must have a good grasp of the extent and value of your property. Otherwise, you and your spouse risk agreeing to an inequitable property division. In all, you should do three things before you agree to a property division: 1) *inventory* your property 2) *value* it 3) find a way to *divide* it.

Inventorying Property

Property division begins with a complete inventory of all the property you and your spouse own. Ordinarily, only property owned when the divorce is filed will be divided. Property transferred before the divorce* or acquired during the divorce is normally left out of the division. So take your inventory just before you file.

As you inventory your property, you may find that you don't know very much about it. In many marriages, one spouse handles the finances, leaving the other spouse in the dark. Luckily, there are several informal ways to get the financial information you need for the inventory.

Start with documents around the house, such as paycheck stubs, bank statements and retirement plan booklets. If you and your spouse have a joint safe deposit box, go through the box. You might find deeds, land contracts, stocks, bonds and life insurance policies hidden there.

Your recent joint personal tax returns, especially any schedules attached to these returns, can reveal valuable information about real property (schedules D and E) bank accounts (schedule B), and businesses (schedules C and F). Likewise, joint business income tax returns have important information about businesses. If you have discarded these returns, you can order copies by submitting Form 4506 to your IRS filing center.

Have you and your spouse applied for a loan recently? If so, you probably prepared a financial statement as part of the loan application. Since federal law makes it a crime to submit false information in the statement, it can be a reliable source of financial information.

If these informal methods fail to give you the financial information you need, there is a formal fact-finding device called discovery. Discovery comes in several forms, including depositions (oral interrogation out of court), interrogatories (written questions) and requests for documents. All these discovery methods are available during divorce to get you the financial information you need. The trouble is, discovery is difficult for nonlawyers to use. If you think you need it, contact a lawyer for help.

Valuing Property

There are many methods of valuing property. Michigan law doesn't say which method must be used, but fair market value seems to be the accepted measure of value.

Fair market value is usually defined as the price property would bring in a sale between a willing buyer and willing seller. When the property is subject to a debt, an adjustment may be necessary. For indebted property, the equity value of the property—its fair market value minus the debt against it—is often used instead of gross fair market value.

---

* But see "Does My Property Need Protection?" on page 36 for how courts can stop a spouse from transferring property to keep it out of the divorce.

More Information

There are several free online real property valuation Web sites. The best of these are:

- Zillow.com
- RealEstateABC.com
- Listingbook.com

Stock quotes are available through most Web home pages and in the financial section of many newspapers.

The U.S. government savings bonds Web site, www.savingsbonds.gov, has a Savings Bond Calculator to figure the redemption value of E/EE and I bonds.

NADA has an online version of its bluebooks at www.nadaguides.com with values for automobiles (cars, trucks, vans, etc.), classic cars, motorcycles, boats, recreational vehicles and manufactured homes. The similar Kelley Blue Book can be accessed at www.kbb.com.

Schroeder's Antiques Price Guide, 29th ed., Paducah, KY: Collector Books, 2011, is the best general price guide for antiques.

2012 Davenport's Art Reference & Price Guide , Alison Becker, Phoenix: LTB Gordonsart, Inc., is a reliable price reference for fine art.

More Information

To find an appraiser, look in the yellow pages under "Appraisers."

Or contact one of the appraisal trade associations for a referral to a certified appraiser near you:

American Society of Appraisers at (800) 272-8258 or www.appraisers.org

International Society of Appraisers at (312) 981-6778 or www.isa-appraisers.org

Appraisers Association of America at (212) 889-5404 or www.appraisersassoc.org

To value real property, you can either: 1) compare your property to the sale prices of other similar property sold recently in your neighborhood 2) double the amount of your property's tax assessment, since assessments are usually around 50% of market value.

You should be able to establish the fair market value of most kinds of personal property informally without going to the trouble and expense of getting formal appraisals.

Cash or near-cash assets (bank accounts, certificates of deposit, money market funds, etc.) are worth their present account balances. The value of stocks, corporate bonds and other securities are listed daily in the *Wall Street Journal*. Use the current redemption value for series E/EE and I U.S. savings bonds. You can value whole life insurance by figuring the cash surrender value on the policy chart, or by asking the insurance company or your insurance agent for this value.

The value of motor vehicles can be obtained from National Automobile Dealer Association (NADA) bluebooks. There are also price guides for stamps, coins, jewelry and antiques. You can estimate the value of household goods and tools by comparing them to similar used items.

If these resources don't provide accurate valuations of your property, you can always get formal appraisals. There are appraisers who are competent to value many types of property and specialists who appraise one type of property. People who buy and sell property, such as automobile or antique dealers, can also give appraisals.

The valuation of some new property, such as retirement benefits and businesses, poses special problems. These things have value, but there is no marketplace in which their value can be fixed. After all, you can't very well sell your pension to someone else. You may be able to sell a small business, but the market is often faulty and you won't get what it's really worth. Despite these problems, there are ways to assign value to new property so it can be divided in divorce cases.

Before you can value retirement benefits, you must know what kind of benefit it is. There are two basic kinds of plans providing retirement benefits:

Defined benefit plan. In a defined benefit plan, or pension plan, the employer promises to pay stipulated benefits at retirement or death. These benefits are paid according to formulas which are usually based on a combination of the employee's age, years of service and earnings.

What an employee with a defined benefit plan has is the employer's promise of benefits; there is no retirement account reserved for the employee. Instead, the employer's retirement contributions (typically only the employer contributes) are pooled in a common fund, and retirement benefits are drawn from the fund as needed.

Most large private- and public-sector employers have defined benefit plans, although some are now discontinuing them in favor of defined contribution plans, especially the popular 401(k) plan.

Other employers have adopted a new kind of defined benefit plan, called a cash balance plan, which resembles a 401(k) plan. In a cash balance plan, employers make hypothetical contributions to employees' retirement "accounts," like defined contribution plans. But in reality, these accounts are merely bookkeeping entries, and all retirement benefits are drawn from a common fund. Thus, a cash balance plan remains a defined benefit plan.

Defined contribution plan. In some ways, a defined contribution plan is the opposite of a defined benefit plan. With a defined contribution plan, the employer's contributions, instead of the retirement benefits, are fixed. Each employee has a separate retirement account earmarked for him/her, to which s/he may also contribute. The money in the employee's retirement account is invested (usually by the employer), and any investment income is added to the account. At retirement, benefits are paid from the account as the employee directs.

There are many types of defined contributions plans: 401(k), profit-sharing, ESOP and saving/thrift plans (provided by employers), and IRA, SEP and Keogh (HR-10) plans (individual plans). Typically, small businesses have defined contributions plans, although the giant TIAA-CREF (the Teachers Insurance and Annuity Account-College Retirement Equity Fund), which provides retirement benefits to public school teachers, is a defined contribution plan.

The value of a defined benefit plan lies in the benefits the plan will pay in the future. These future benefits can be reduced to a current lump-sum value, called present value. Figuring present value isn't easy, but an accountant or pension specialist can do it for you. To value a defined contribution plan, you simply take the current account balance. You can get this figure from a recent benefit statement or by requesting it from the retirement plan administrator.

Valuing a business is also difficult. If the business cannot be sold as a going concern, the book value of the business (tangible business assets minus business liabilities) may be used. But if the business is marketable, consider valuing the business by multiplying the average annual net earnings (before taxes) by a multiplier (1, 1½, 2, etc.) customary for that type of business. If you own a business jointly with others, you may have a buy-sell agreement with the co-owners fixing the value of your share, and you can use this value.

Dividing Property

All real property must be divided by separate property division provisions in the divorce judgment. Some personal property, including valuable things like motor vehicles and new property (retirement benefits, businesses, etc.) must also be divided individually. But you can divide most personal property, such as household goods, clothing, and personal items, by just splitting it up. "Property Division Provisions" in Appendix F has more information and sample provisions for all kinds of property divisions.

Does My Property Need Protection?

Divorce sometimes puts property at risk. Spouses may try to transfer property to others, before or during the divorce, to keep it out of the property division. If the divorce is bitter, spouses may take out their frustrations on the property. A while ago, a Macomb County woman got back at her husband by destroying his collection of rare Frank Sinatra records (when Sinatra read about the incident he graciously offered to replace some of the discs). But that's nothing compared to a Seattle husband who, to spite his wife, took a bulldozer and demolished their $90,000 house!

Michigan courts have the power to prevent this kind of mischief. They can issue orders protecting property from transfer or destruction. Regrettably, this book doesn't have the instructions and forms to get these orders, so see a lawyer if you need one.

Debts can also jeopardize property and wealth during divorce. Financial stability often breaks down amid a divorce, as spouses are tempted to run up debts on joint accounts. Both spouses are liable for these joint debts regardless of which spouse incurred them. Thus, it's a good idea to close or at least freeze all joint accounts (credit card, charge accounts, etc.), if possible, immediately after separation.

You can close a joint account quickly if no debts remain in the account. If debts exist, you can pay these off or sometimes transfer them to individual accounts. Another option is to freeze the account, so no new debt is added, followed by payment later.

Do I Need to Change My Estate Plan?

Married couples often have estate plans mirroring each other. The husband's will may give all his property to the wife, and name her as personal representative, with her will doing the same. Or they may have living (*inter vivos*) trusts with each other as trustee and beneficiary. Their financial and health care powers of attorney may appoint the other spouse as agent. Spouses may also be the beneficiaries of life insurance and retirement benefits.

Even without an estate plan, spouses are entitled, by law, to many estate rights. These include the right to a share of a spouse's estate, dower (an estate that widows have in their husbands' real property) and other allowances from the spouse's estate.

As explained in "After Your Divorce" on page 101, a divorce terminates all these estate rights. But there is always a risk that one spouse may die or become incapacitated *during* the divorce, giving the other control of the property. If you're in good health, this risk is small and probably not worth worrying about. But if you're in poor health, you may want to do some quick estate planning during the divorce.

There are a few things you can do yourself without a lawyer. You can revise your will or living trust naming a new personal representative in the will or a new trustee/beneficiaries in the trust. If you've appointed your spouse as agent under a financial or health care power of attorney, you can make a new one with another agent. And unless you and your spouse have agreed otherwise, you can change the designation of your spouse as beneficiary of your life insurance and retirement benefits.

To do more, you're going to need legal help. In Michigan, you normally cannot totally disinherit your spouse by will, since spouses are guaranteed a minimum share of the estate. However, a lawyer can prepare a will for you reducing your spouse's share to that legal minimum. In exceptional cases, spouses can lose their estate rights by marital misconduct (bigamy, absence, desertion, neglect for one year or more). A lawyer can tell you whether you qualify for this exception, and how to disinherit your spouse if you do.

A lawyer can also advise you about releasing estate rights. You may have already done that in a prenuptial agreement. The lawyer can tell you whether the release was effective. It's also possible to release estate rights in a postnuptial agreement (signed after marriage), especially during a separation leading to divorce. A lawyer should prepare that kind of agreement. After any release of estate rights, you are free to benefit whomever you like in your will.

With a lawyer's help, you could also convert any joint tenancy property (also known as tenancy by the entirety property) into tenancy in common ownership. Unlike other forms of property, tenancy in common doesn't have rights of survivorship. So when a spouse-owner dies, the surviving spouse doesn't get everything. Instead, the deceased spouse's estate and the surviving spouse split the property. This division makes tenancy in common ideal for estranged spouses who want to keep their shares of joint property separate.

Do I Need "Preliminary Relief"?

In most lawsuits, you normally don't get any relief (the things you're asking for in your lawsuit) unless and until you win the case. But in divorce cases it's possible to get some relief before the end of the divorce.

As mentioned in "Alimony" on page 11, courts may decide alimony on a temporary basis. And as pointed out previously in this part, courts can do some emergency property division/protection during divorces. If a court grants such preliminary relief, the issue is decided until the end of the case when the court makes a final decision in the divorce judgment.

Preliminary relief is important in contested cases, both for practical and tactical reasons. But the relief can be useful in uncontested ones as well. The trouble is, the legal procedures for getting preliminary relief are complicated, so this book doesn't have instructions or forms for this type of relief.

As useful as preliminary relief is, it isn't required in divorce cases, and you can often get by without it. When you are self-sufficient, you may not need any preliminary alimony or property. Or if the defendant is unavailable or unable to provide any support, it may not even be worth seeking.

<table>
<tr><td>

More Information

On adjusting to life during and after divorce:

The New Creative Divorce, Mel Krantzler, et al., Holbrook, MA: Adams Media Corp., 1998

The Good Divorce, Constance Ahrons, New York: Harper Collins, 1994

</td></tr>
</table>

If you believe preliminary relief is necessary, you may be able to improvise a substitute. You and the defendant can arrange to have the equivalent of preliminary relief provided privately out of court. For example, you both could divide property informally and/or have alimony paid without a court order, while your divorce is pending. This arrangement would resemble what you might obtain in preliminary relief from the court, except that it wouldn't be legally enforceable.*

If this substitute won't work, and you believe you must have preliminary relief, see a lawyer. The lawyer can prepare the necessary papers to seek the relief from the court.

Can I Socialize during the Divorce?

As couples split up, they often wonder whether they can start new social or sexual relationships. What you do during separation and divorce ought to be your own business. But regrettably, extramarital activity can be interpreted as marital fault, which could hurt you.

In a contested divorce, marital fault from extramarital activity may influence property division and alimony. Marital fault usually doesn't cause problems in uncontested cases as long as everything remains agreeable. But the fault can become an issue if your agreement over the divorce falls apart.

As a result, use your common sense as you begin your single life. You don't have to live like a hermit. But you should be discreet in your new social and sexual relationships. That will prevent any possible legal trouble.

---

*   Another problem with paying alimony informally out of court is that the payer won't be entitled to an income tax deduction for the payments, since they're not being paid in a divorce document.

Can I Keep the Divorce Secret?

Although court files are public records, courts have the power to restrict access to the contents of files by sealing them. In fact, courts once routinely sealed divorce cases between wealthy or influential people.

In 1991, new court rules were adopted governing court secrecy. Now one must file a motion to seal a file and convince the court that there is "good cause" for sealing.* Because of these rules, it's difficult to have divorce files sealed. If you want to try to get your file sealed, contact a lawyer for help.

Some local newspapers cover legal news and publish lists of divorces granted by the courts in their area. There is really no way to keep that information out of the papers, since the completion of a divorce is a matter of public record even if the divorce file itself has been sealed.

Will I Have Tax Problems from the Divorce?

At one time, divorce was a tax nightmare. Not only were the tax rules for divorce complex, divorce itself had many negative tax consequences. These rules were changed by the Tax Reform Act of 1984 (TRA). The TRA is a rare example of a tax law that actually made the law simpler and fairer.

The TRA defined which divorce-related payments qualify as alimony (see "Alimony" on page 11 for more about these alimony tax rules). But the TRA didn't alter how alimony is taxed. It's still income for the recipient and a deduction (technically an adjustment to gross income) for the payer.

> ## More Information
>
> On taxes and divorce, obtain "Tax Information for Divorced or Separated Individuals" (Pub. 504), which is available from any IRS office, by calling the agency at (800) 829-3676 or by accessing the publication at www.irs.gov/formspubs.

The most far-reaching change wrought by the TRA was to make all transfers of property between divorcing spouses nontaxable. Previously, spouses could gain or lose income from the property divisions of their divorces. Such gain or loss from a divorce is no longer possible under the new law, although income tax problems can still crop up later when a spouse sells property obtained in the divorce.

What If My Spouse Is Mentally Incompetent?

If your spouse has been declared mentally incompetent by a probate court, s/he must be specially represented in the divorce. After a declaration of mental incompetency, the probate court may appoint a conservator (a rep-

---

*   A related problem is editing papers, which the defendant must receive, to keep selected personal information out of the hands of a defendant-spouse abuser. See "Keeping Personal Information away from a Spouse-Abuser" on page 42 for more about this issue.

resentative like a guardian) to manage the incompetent's affairs. A conservator has the authority to represent the incompetent in a divorce.

If you have been appointed as your spouse's conservator, you won't be able to represent him/her in the divorce because of the obvious conflict of interest. But you can ask the probate court for appointment of another person as conservator, and the new conservator could handle the divorce.

An alternative is to have a *guardian ad litem* (GAL) appointed for your mentally incompetent spouse. While a conservator has broad powers to manage affairs, a GAL's authority is limited to representing the incompetent in a single lawsuit. In a divorce, the court handling the divorce, not a probate court, can appoint a GAL for a spouse after the divorce is filed.

Whatever arrangements are made for your incompetent spouse, they should be completed before or soon after you file your divorce. Then you can serve the spouse's conservator or GAL with the divorce papers, and the divorce can proceed normally.

What If I Need to File for Bankruptcy?

Divorce and bankruptcy seem to go together because financial problems often cause divorce. According to one study, divorced people file for bankruptcy at three times the rate of the nondivorced population. Despite this link, divorce and bankruptcy aren't as compatible as they ought to be. Each procedure requires a separate case, filed in different court systems (divorce in state court; bankruptcy in federal court), using different laws and rules.

Because of these problems, if you're considering both a divorce and a bankruptcy, seek legal advice. The lawyer can advise you about the relationship between divorce and bankruptcy, which type of bankruptcy to file (there are several), and whether to file singly or jointly (even separated spouses are permitted to file joint bankruptcies).

Don't wait to get legal help, because the timing of a divorce and bankruptcy can be important. In some cases, it's better to file the bankruptcy before completion of the divorce to protect exempt marital property. In other cases, the divorce should be finished before the bankruptcy is started so that some debts and obligations can be wiped out (a new 2005 bankruptcy law now protects most intra-family divorce obligations (child support, alimony and property division debts) from elimination; but some nonfamily divorce obligations are still dischargeable in bankruptcy). There are no firm rules about the sequence of cases; the timing will depend on the nature of your property and debts. Your lawyer should be able to explain what's best in your situation.

What If I Want to Dismiss the Divorce?

According to one estimate, 20-30% of all divorces are voluntarily withdrawn and dismissed. No one knows the exact reason for all these dismissals, but it's reasonable to assume that most cases were dropped after the spouses reconciled.

There's no penalty for withdrawing your divorce after you start it. On the contrary, Michigan law encourages reconciliation and dismissal at every step of a divorce. That's what the statutory waiting period is for. If you and your spouse decide to reconcile, see Appendix E for instructions and the form to dismiss your divorce.

What If My Spouse Abuses Me?

The physical abuse of one spouse by the other—usually, but not always, a wife at the hands of her husband—has been a constant problem with marriage and divorce. It's been estimated that spouse abuse is a problem in one out of three marriages. Sometimes this domestic violence becomes deadly. According to recent FBI figures, nearly a third of all female homicide victims are murdered by either their husbands or boyfriends.

For years, the legal system offered abused spouses little protection. It often seemed that family violence was a private matter into which the legal system wouldn't intervene. But that attitude has changed, and Michigan's spouse abuse laws have been toughened recently. Today it's possible to get personal protection orders (PPOs) preventing your spouse from:

- assaulting, attacking, beating, wounding or molesting you or someone else
- threatening to kill or physically injure you or someone else
- any act or conduct interfering with personal liberty or causing a reasonable apprehension of violence, such as stalking, harassment or unwanted contact
- interfering with you at work or school
- having access to your personal records or those of your children to get information about you
- purchasing or possessing a firearm
- entering property (so that your spouse can be ordered away from your home, even when it's the joint marital home)
- interfering with your removal of personal property or children from your spouse's property
- removing minor children from the person with legal custody, except as allowed by a court order

You don't have to wait until a divorce to get a PPO. They're available anytime there's domestic abuse, even before you file. After filing, you can get a PPO while the divorce is pending. It's also possible to get a permanent PPO in your divorce judgment, which can remain in effect for any specified period of time.

> **More Information**
>
> About spouse abuse, get:
>
> *Getting Free: You Can End Abuse and Take Back Your Life*, 4th ed., Ginny Nicarthy, Emeryville, CA: Seal Press, 2004
>
> Call the **National Domestic Violence Hotline** at (800) 799-7233 for information, support or referral to a spouse abuse shelter in your area.
>
> A list of abuse shelters in Michigan is also available at the Michigan Coalition to End Domestic & Sexual Violence's Web site at www.mcedsv.org, then to Members, to Our Members.

When a spouse violates a PPO, s/he can be immediately arrested by the police, even if they didn't see the offense. Violation of a PPO is both a civil and criminal contempt of court, punishable by a maximum fine of $500 and 93 days in jail.

For all the protection it offers, Michigan's PPO law is complicated, making it difficult for nonlawyers to use. That's why it's best to have a lawyer when you're facing spouse abuse. If you have a low income, contact legal aid. The legal aid offices are very busy, but they usually give priority to spouse abuse cases. Or you can rely on a private lawyer for help. If you're determined to represent yourself, you can obtain PPO forms and instructions from the clerk of your circuit or family court. Since 1994, all Michigan circuit and family courts must make these materials available.

Whatever you do, keep in mind that a PPO cannot guarantee your safety. A court order is only a piece of paper; it won't stop someone bent on violence. If you believe your spouse is determined to harm you, take whatever precautions are necessary to protect yourself—with or without a PPO. This may even mean moving to a safe place. You may be able to find refuge with a friend or relative. There are also special shelters for abused spouses (and their children). Michigan has around 50 shelters serving every part of the state.

Keeping Personal Information away from a Spouse-Abuser

Several divorce papers contain personal information about you, where you live and sometimes your employment. During the divorce, the defendant gets copies of these papers.

If there's a danger of spouse abuse from the defendant, and you're keeping a distance, you may not want to reveal your current address and employment to the defendant. In exceptional cases like this, you can receive permission to withhold personal information from the divorce papers, and provide it separately and confidentially to the court. Ask the clerk about withholding personal information this way.

Where Can I File If My Spouse or I Am Native American?

Did you know that Michigan has the largest Native American population in the Eastern United States? Michigan has 12 federally-recognized Indian tribes and 4 which are recognized by the state. These tribes keep tribal rolls listing all members of the tribe (persons not on these rolls aren't regarded as members). The tribes often have their own reservations (these reservations plus satellite Indian communities are known as "Indian country") with separate tribal court systems which can grant divorces.

The jurisdiction rules for divorces involving at least one Native American spouse are still being worked out. It seems clear that when both spouses are Indian and living in Indian country, the tribal court has complete control of the divorce. If one or both

More Information

About divorce in tribal courts, contact:

Michigan Indian Legal Services
814 S. Garfield Ave.
Suite A
Traverse City, MI 49686
(877) 968-6877

Indian spouses are living in non-Indian country, a state court divorce is an option, but so is a tribal divorce because many tribal courts allow access based on tribal membership without strict regard to residence.

The far more difficult cases are when just one spouse is Native American and the other isn't. In these cases, jurisdiction depends on where the spouses are living (in or outside Indian country), which spouse (plaintiff or defendant) is Native American and what the tribal legal code says about jurisdiction. Another complication is division of tribal trust land, which state courts cannot do. If you're facing a complicated situation like this, you should talk to a lawyer who knows about Indian law.

What If My Spouse or I Am an "Alien" (Noncitizen)?

If you or your spouse are aliens, your foreign nationality probably won't prevent you from getting a divorce in Michigan (see below about aliens and jurisdiction). But your alien status can have all kinds of hidden effects on the divorce, which are also explained below.

Can an Alien Get a Divorce in Michigan?

In the United States, divorce jurisdiction is based on residence. If you reside here you can get a divorce, regardless of your nationality. But in other countries, particularly civil law areas (basically the non-English speaking world), divorce jurisdiction is usually determined by nationality, not residence. In these countries, you must be a citizen to get a divorce. A few countries, such as the Philippines, don't bother with divorce jurisdiction at all because they refuse to permit divorce.

If you're a citizen of one of those countries, a divorce you get in Michigan might not be recognized in your country. This won't be a problem if you have broken all ties with the country. But it could spell trouble if you intend to return to the country, or have children or property there. To find out how a Michigan divorce will be treated in your native country, check with your embassy or consulate.

Glossary
Immigrant—an alien who intends to settle in the country permanently.
Nonimmigrant—an alien who is staying in the country temporarily.

Divorce by a Plaintiff-Alien

An alien living in Michigan can usually file for divorce here, and the divorce will go through. What an alien must consider is the impact the divorce will have on his/her residence rights. The impact is different for two types of aliens:

Immigrant. Aliens married to U.S. citizens typically apply for permanent residence here as spouses of citizens, becoming "lawful permanent residents." Aliens married two years or more quickly gain permanent residence. But aliens in shorter marriages usually get conditional residence, because of a suspicion that the marriage might be a sham.

A divorce during the two-year conditional residence period can be a problem for an immigrant. The divorce itself doesn't prove that the marriage is a sham (that's judged by the parties' intentions when they got married). But a divorce makes it more difficult to prove the marriage is real, especially without the help of an estranged spouse.

Nonimmigrant. A divorce can jeopardize the residence rights of a nonimmigrant, here temporarily, particularly if admission status depends solely on marriage. After the marriage is terminated by the divorce, this status is gone and the nonimmigrant may face deportation (there are some exceptions if there has been spouse/child abuse or in cases of extreme hardship).

Plaintiff-Citizen Filing against a Defendant-Alien

As a U.S. citizen filing for divorce, your citizenship is secure and won't be affected by the divorce. The divorce could have an impact on the defendant-alien's residence rights, as described above. Nevertheless, the divorce could also have an unforeseen effect on you.

Typically, U.S. citizens marrying aliens seek residence rights for them by filing an Affidavit of Support. The affidavit promises to support the alien-spouse or else reimburse the government for any public assistance the alien might receive until the alien: 1) becomes a U.S. citizen 2) establishes an earnings record in the U.S. This obligation to support, which is actually a contract, survives divorce. So if you divorce an alien, and the alien receives public assistance, you could be liable for reimbursement.

Do You Need Legal Help?

If your divorce looks too complicated for you to do yourself, you need legal help. How do you find a good lawyer? The best way is by recommendation from someone you trust. But if you can't find a lawyer by word of mouth, legal services and referrals are available from:

Legal aid. Those who meet federal poverty guidelines are eligible for legal aid from one of the legal aid organizations located throughout the state. The problem is, these programs are often so understaffed that they can help only a fraction of those eligible for their services. To find the legal aid office in your area, look under "Attorneys" or "Social Service Organizations" in the yellow pages or go to the State Bar of Michigan's Web site at www.michbar.org/public_resources/legalaid.cfm, then to Legal Aid Programs and Services.

Legal clinics and services. Newspapers often carry advertisements for low-cost uncontested divorce services. Some of these services are offered by local attorneys doing business as clinics, while others may be branches of national legal service companies.

Lawyers. These days lawyers aren't shy about advertising, and you can find their ads in newspapers and the yellow pages. County bar associations in several of the larger counties provide lawyer referral services. To obtain lawyer referrals in other counties, call the state bar referral service at (800) 292-7850.

On the other hand, you may have decided that your divorce isn't too complicated. If that's true, you're ready to move on to Chapter 2 and begin your divorce.

Chapter 2

Legal Basics

Overview of Divorce Procedure

Doing Your Divorce

After Your Divorce

Legal Basics

For lawyers, an uncontested divorce isn't much more than a clerical task, which they usually assign to their secretaries. But nonlawyers are often stumped by the simplest things: How do I fill out the divorce papers? Where do I file them? When do I file them? How do I find the right court? This section deals with these legal basics and more, so you will be as well-prepared as any lawyer.

Court System

Before 1998, divorce cases were handled by the general circuit courts of Michigan. On Jan. 1, 1998, Michigan's court system was reorganized and new family courts (which are actually divisions of the circuit courts) went into operation. Michigan family courts deal with all kinds of family-related cases: divorce (including after-divorce matters), annulment, separate maintenance, family support, custody, parenting time, paternity, domestic violence, child abuse and neglect, juvenile delinquency, guardianship/conservatorship, adoption, emancipation of minors and name change cases.

The philosophy of the family court system is to specialize in family law matters, unlike the general circuit courts which deal with all kinds of civil and criminal cases. Michigan family courts also have a "one-family, one-

judge" policy, which brings all of a family's cases before the same judge, who is familiar with the family and its problems.

Family courts may be fairly new, but the court personnel haven't changed. The following people have responsibility for your divorce case:

Judge. Your divorce is handled by a family court judge, who is either a circuit court or probate court judge on assignment to the family court. You cannot choose the judge for your case. Ordinarily, when you file the clerk randomly assigns a judge to your case. But if you or members of your family have other family law cases pending in the court, the clerk will try to assign your divorce to the judge hearing the other case(s). With this assignment, the same judge will handle all the family's cases. If you dislike the judge, you cannot get another unless you can prove that the judge is actually biased or prejudiced against you.

Clerk. The family court clerk receives all your divorce papers and maintains a case file for them. Throughout this book, the family court clerk is simply called the clerk. In most counties, the county clerk is the clerk of the family court. But some counties have a special family court clerk, separate from the county clerk.

To find out who does the family court clerking in your county, call the county clerk and ask for information. Or simply look up the county government listing in the telephone book, and see if there is a separate listing for a clerk of the family division of the circuit court.

Courtroom clerk. The courtroom clerk sits in the courtroom next to the judge while the court is in session. During a trial, the courtroom clerk is responsible for marking and receiving exhibits. In an uncontested divorce case, the courtroom clerk has a smaller role, but in some counties s/he may receive and file papers during the final hearing.

Assignment clerk. Several larger counties use special assignment clerks to schedule court hearings. In these counties, final hearings in uncontested divorce cases may be scheduled through the assignment clerk.

Court reporter. The court reporter sits below the judge and records the court proceedings. In an uncontested divorce case, the court reporter makes a record of the final hearing, although it's unlikely that a transcript of the hearing will ever be needed.

Judge's secretary. Working in the judge's office, the judge's secretary may help in submitting papers to the judge for review.

Law clerk. Most judges have law clerks, who are often law students or new lawyers. Law clerks help judges with a number of tasks, including review of papers.

In many counties, these court personnel are conveniently located under one roof, usually in a courthouse or county building. But in other counties, whose court systems have outgrown their courthouses, court personnel may be scattered among several buildings. Before you begin your divorce, make sure you know where the court personnel are located.

The first person you want to find is the clerk, because you will begin your divorce in the clerk's office by filing the initial divorce papers there.

Papers

Many divorce-filers are surprised to find that courts won't do the divorce paperwork for you. Instead, it's your responsibility to prepare all the divorce papers. Don't try to do this all at once; prepare the papers as you need them, during each step of your divorce.

Preparing Papers

Whenever possible, type the divorce papers. But if you can't, it's permissible to print by hand in ink. Either way, make sure that the papers are neat and legible.

The divorce papers you file must also be accurate and honest. Judges can penalize those who intentionally or even carelessly file false legal papers. Ordinarily, these penalties are payments of money to opponents hurt by the false papers.

But for some false papers the penalties are severe. When you sign an affidavit, you swear to the notary public that the contents are true. You do much the same when you sign papers with a verification declaration ("I declare that the statements above are true to the best of my information, knowledge, and belief"). According to Michigan law, it's a crime to knowingly file a false affidavit; the intentional falsification of a verified document is a contempt of court. Don't be alarmed by these penalties; just make sure that your papers are accurate and honest.

> ### More Information
>
> An affidavit is a legal paper stating facts that must be sworn to under oath before someone, such as a notary public, who can give oaths.
>
> To obtain notary services, look in the yellow pages under "Notaries Public," or contact insurance agencies, banks or mailing/shipping stores, which often have notary services available.

Among your divorce papers are several forms issued by the State Court Administrative Office (SCAO). These state forms include Michigan court forms and friend of the court forms, which are coded in the lower left corner by type (MC or FOC), number and date of release. Besides these state forms, a few counties, notably Wayne (number-coded), have local forms.

Added to the state forms are several Grand River Press forms (code: GRP/number/date). The Grand River Press forms include most of the important divorce papers, such as the complaint, default and judgment. The state used to publish these forms, but discontinued publication in 1989. The Grand River Press forms have been created to replace them.

You may notice a difference in the type-size of the papers. On Jan. 1, 2004, a new court rule went into effect requiring that all court papers, except the state-issued (SCAO) forms, must be in 12-point type. Thus, the printing on all the GRP forms was increased to 12-point size. Also, when you fill in the papers, try to print or type in a larger size (no fine print) matching the printing on these forms.

The new court rule also specifies that all court papers must be 8½ x 11." Previously, this was the maximum size, but papers could be a little smaller. Prior editions of this book were 8½ x 11," making the perforated forms .25" smaller after detachment from the book (perforation of the forms causes a .25" loss in the binding margin). Now, the book has been increased in overall width by .25" to make up this difference.

Caption of Papers

Every form has a special purpose and each is prepared differently. Yet all the forms share similar captions which are filled in as follows:

STATE OF MICHIGAN Circuit Court - Family Division OJIBWAY COUNTY	JUDGMENT OF DIVORCE Page 1 of pages	CASE NO. 89-00501-Do JUDGE TUBBS
Plaintiff (appearing *in propria persona*):		**Defendant:**
DARLENE ANN LOVELACE 121 S. MAIN LAKE CITY, MI 48800 772-0000	v	DUDLEY ERNEST LOVELACE 900 S. MAPLE LAKE CITY, MI 48800 773-5004

STATE OF MICHIGAN Circuit Court - Family Division OJIBWAY COUNTY	JUDGMENT OF DIVORCE Page 2 of pages	CASE NO. 89-00501-Do
Plaintiff:		**Defendant:**
DARLENE ANN LOVELACE	v	DUDLEY ERNEST LOVELACE

As you can see, the papers have either a long or short caption. In a long caption, you must put the county where the divorce is filed in the upper left corner. The names, addresses and telephone numbers of you, as plaintiff, and your spouse, as defendant, go in the two large boxes.

Some state-issued forms have slightly different captions. In the upper left box, the MC forms may ask for the judicial circuit of your family court (in Michigan, the judicial circuits are numbered (1st (Hillsdale County), 2nd (Berrien County), 3rd (Wayne County), etc.). You can get the number of your local circuit court (of which the family court is a division) in a telephone book (look under the "County Government" listing in the blue (government) pages) or county directory. Some MC forms may also ask for the court's or friend of the court's address and telephone number. This extra information is also available in the telephone book or county directory.

Incidentally, the italicized Latin phrase in the caption of many of the forms signals that this is a self-help divorce. *In propria persona* (sometimes abbreviated to *in pro per*) means "in your own person," indicating that you are doing the case yourself without a lawyer. Some of the state-issued forms, such as the Summons and Complaint (MC 01), have caption boxes for lawyer representatives. You can leave these boxes blank, or insert in them: "In Pro Per."

Your case number goes in the upper right corner. This number starts with a two-digit number for the year followed by several other numbers. It ends with a two-letter case-type code. All cases in Michigan have codes according to their type: A divorce with minor children bears a DM code and divorces without minor children have a DO code. Because a case number isn't assigned until filing, you won't have it for your initial divorce papers, so leave the case number spaces blank on them. But include your case number in the captions of all your other papers.

If you're in a larger county that has more than one family court judge, write the name of your judge below the case numbers on all the papers you file after the initial divorce papers. This will help direct the papers to the correct case file and judge.

With a short caption, you can omit much of the above information. All you need for a short caption is the court, case number, and your and your spouse's names as plaintiff and defendant.

Oakland and Wayne Counties, which have the state's largest court systems, have a bar-coded caption-labeling system to prevent mishandling of court papers. When you file a divorce in these two counties, the clerk prints sheets of caption labels for both parties. Notice how the clerk takes several labels and affixes these to the captions of your initial divorce papers. As you file other papers, use labels from your sheet to label them in the same way. Save the other sheet of caption labels because you must have it served on the defendant later.

To Obtain

Extra copies of Wayne County forms, call the Wayne County Friend of the Court's call center at (313) 224-5300.

The Wayne County circuit court system also has a Web site, www.3rdcc.org, from which you can view and/or download many forms.

You should have enough caption labels for all your papers. But if you run out, you can get more in the clerk's office in room 201 of the Coleman A. Young Municipal Center (CAYMC) (formerly the City-County Bldg.) at 2 Woodward Ave. in Detroit.

Copying Papers

As you prepare divorce papers, you must make several photocopies. Except for the Summons and Complaint (MC 01), make two photocopies of each divorce paper. This gives you enough divorce papers and copies to distribute as follows:

- original - court (clerk)
- 1st copy - plaintiff
- 2nd copy - defendant

When you photocopy divorce papers, copy both sides of any two-sided forms because some papers have important information on the reverse. Most two-sided forms are tumble-printed, with their reverse sides upside down. This makes it possible to read the reverse sides while the papers are fastened to a file folder by simply lifting them up. When you photocopy these two-sided forms, you might not be able to run your copies through the photocopier again to make a tumble-printed form. If so, just make the paper into a two-page form and staple the pages together.

With all these papers and copies, it's easy to get disorganized. To keep track of everything, prepare a file for all your divorce papers. Not only will this file keep you organized during the divorce, it will give you a complete record of the case afterward.

Filing Papers

When you file your divorce, the clerk will open a file for your case. As you file papers, the clerk will ordinarily use the following procedure:

- keep the original for your case file
- return a copy for the plaintiff
- return a copy for the defendant

Glossary

Return copies—that the clerk returns to you after filing original papers may be unstamped or stamped as "true copies." A true copy stamp is an informal way of saying that the copy is a duplicate of the original (a clerk can also provide official "certified copies," but there is a fee for certification).

Try to get true copies of all papers you file, especially court orders such as the judgment.

You can file papers with the clerk personally, by mail or sometimes even by facsimile (fax). Despite these options, it's usually best to file the initial divorce papers in person and the other papers this way whenever you can. By filing personally, you can pay any fees that are due and immediately get back copies of your papers for service on the other party.

For filing by mail, send your papers and any fees to the clerk along with a cover letter asking for filing and return of the copies you have enclosed. To get copies back quickly, include a self-addressed envelope with postage.

Filing by fax isn't allowed when filing fees are due (unless you have paid in advance by depositing money with the clerk), because the clerk won't accept a filing without payment of the filing fee. Moreover, the clerk won't send or fax back copies of the papers you file, so there's no way to get copies. Thus, fax-filing should be used in emergency, when you have to file in a hurry to meet a filing deadline.

So-called "e-filing," or transmitting papers to a court clerk by email through the Internet, is in its infancy in Michigan. E-filing is being tested in a few counties, but hasn't been adopted statewide yet.

Fees

You must pay several fees to get a divorce (see "How Much Will My Divorce Cost?" on page 29 for a description of the fees). Except for the service fee, you pay these fees to the clerk. Clerks usually accept cash, personal checks and money orders as payment. After you pay, the clerk may give you a receipt, which you should keep as proof of payment.

The service fee is paid outside of court. As mentioned before, you can choose from among several methods of service: 1) acknowledgment 2) mail 3) delivery. You can usually obtain service by acknowledgment for free. When you use service by mail, you pay the post office for the mailing. If you use service by delivery, you pay the server, who is usually a sheriff or commercial process server. Ordinarily, the server bills you for the service fee after service when s/he returns the proof of service to you. But if you use service by delivery out of town or out of state, it's a good idea to prepay the service fee. When you send the service papers to the server, include a check or money order for $30 or so, and a note asking the server to refund/bill you for the difference between your prepayment and his service fee.

If you qualify, you can get an exemption from payment of the court fees. You are exempt from payment if you are receiving public assistance or have a low income. Appendix A has more about qualifying for a fee exemption, and instructions and the affidavit to apply for the exemption.

If you've received a fee exemption, you won't have to pay any court fees during your divorce (although you might have to pay them at the end of the divorce). If the clerk tries to charge you a fee during your divorce, refer the clerk to the fee exemption affidavit, which will be in your case file.

Courtroom Etiquette

During a court hearing, you should follow these rules of courtroom behavior:

- Dress neatly and be well-groomed.

- Turn off your cellphone while in the courtroom.

- Be on time.

- Be courteous to the judge and others.

- Wait until called on to speak.

- Don't interrupt while the judge or others are talking; you will get your chance to speak.

- After the judge makes a decision, don't persist in arguing your view.

Time

During your divorce, you must deal with several important time periods and deadlines, including: 1) 180-day state residence requirement 2) 10-day county residence requirement 3) answering period (usually 21 or 28 days) 4) statutory waiting period (60 days for divorces without minor children) 5) filing deadlines for various papers.

The court rules have detailed provisions to figure periods of time. For a time period of days, the period begins on the day after the day of an act (filing, service, establishment of residence, etc.); the day of the act itself isn't counted. The last day of the period is counted, unless it falls on a Saturday, Sunday or court holiday. In that case, the period extends to the next day that isn't a Saturday, Sunday or court holiday.

Example: You serve a defendant by mail on May 1. The 28-day answering period after service by mail begins on May 2 (the day after the day of service) and ends on May 29 (which in this example is not a Saturday, Sunday or court holiday). The defendant has until May 29 to answer.

Example: You serve a defendant by mail on May 1. The 28-day answering period after service by mail begins on May 2 (the day after the day of service) and ends on May 29. But this year May 29 is Memorial Day, a court holiday, so the answering period extends to May 30. The defendant must answer by May 30.

To avoid time problems, you can simply estimate the time period and then add a little more time for safety. For example, if you figure that a time period ends sometime during the first week of a month, you could wait until the middle of the month to take action, avoiding any danger of acting too quickly.

Courthouse Appearances

During your divorce, you must appear once in court before the judge. You may also have to make an informal appearance at the courthouse, outside the courtroom.

Court Hearings

All divorce plaintiffs are expected to attend a final hearing, in court before the judge, at the end of the case. During the hearing, you must give some brief testimony to get a Judgment of Divorce (GRP 4).

For a formal court hearing, make sure you know the location of the hearing beforehand. Court hearings normally take place in the courtroom of the judge assigned to your case, which is usually in the county courthouse or similar county building.

Go to the place of the court hearing on the scheduled day and time. Try to arrive around 30 minutes before the hearing, to take care of any last-minute business. By arriving early, you can also observe other hearings. Be prepared to spend most of the morning or afternoon at the hearing, since it may not start on time.

When your case is called by the courtroom clerk, step forward and identify yourself. Mention that you are representing yourself. Take a seat at one of the tables inside the bar (gate) of the courtroom, and get ready to begin your presentation.

Other Courthouse Appearances

The clerk may also ask you to attend a case conference, for scheduling or other reasons, outside of the courtroom. These are informal sessions held by court personnel without the judge. As with a formal court hearing, know where the meeting is held, be on time and observe normal courtroom etiquette.

Special Arrangements for a Courthouse Appearance

If you have a handicap (mobility, visual, speech or hearing impairment), court personnel can make special accommodations for your courthouse appearance. For non-English-speakers, the court can appoint an interpreter to translate the proceedings into your language.

Handicapper and Prisoner Accommodations

Tell court personnel about the handicap by preparing a Request for Accommodations (MC 70) (see the sample MC 70 at the end of this section). File or send the form to the clerk well ahead of the scheduled appearance. Court personnel will contact you before the appearance, and discuss the accommodation you need.

In exceptional cases, special accommodations aren't enough and you may be excused from the court appearance. If so, you can give information, such as testimony for a final hearing, in written or electronic form (by telephone, for example). Persons with severe handicaps may qualify for this exception. Prisoners are also frequently excused from court attendance, and can give written or electronic testimony (see "What If My Spouse or I Am Imprisoned?" on page 27 for more about this procedure).

Foreign Language Interpreters

The court can appoint a foreign language interpreter if you can't speak English well enough to understand the court proceedings. Use the Motion and Order for Appointment of Foreign Language Interpreter (MC 81) (a sample MC 81 appears at the end of this section). The judge may skip a hearing on this motion and simply sign the order.

You could file the MC 81 any time during the divorce. Whenever you file, send a copy of the motion to the defendant, even if s/he has defaulted, at his or her last known mailing address.

Incidentally, there are special foreign language Summons and Complaint (MC 01) forms available in Arabic, Chinese, Hmong, Korean, Russian and Spanish. You can get these from the clerk and use the special forms if your spouse speaks one of these languages, but isn't fluent in English.

Local Rules and Forms

For years, there were variations in divorce procedures among Michigan's 83 counties. In 1993, the state tried to standardize procedures by abolishing all local divorce rules and forms. But little by little, several counties, Wayne in particular, have been permitted to re-adopt local rules and forms.

Don't panic if you encounter some local practices that aren't described in this book. Ask the local authorities what the local practice is and adapt to it. Luckily, variations tend to be minor. They typically concern scheduling the final hearing.

New Laws, Rules, Forms and Fees

These days, divorce laws, rules, forms and fees change regularly. Congress and the Michigan Legislature are constantly passing new divorce-related laws. Added to this are the thousands of decisions courts issue each year, some of which affect divorce.

As a result of this activity, parts of this book may become outdated. To keep the book current, Grand River Press offers an update about recent changes in divorce law. See the order form in the front of this book for update information.

To Obtain

Laws, court rules and other legal information, visit a law library. Most county courthouses have law libraries which are open to the public. The divorce laws are in the MCLAs (Michigan Compiled Laws Annotated) and MSAs (Michigan Statutes Annotated); the court rules are published in *Michigan Rules of Court - State* by Thomson/West (this volume also includes all the local court rules).

Online, you can access Michigan laws via www.michiganlegislature.org, using the search engine to search by section or by subject. The basic divorce laws are MCL 552.1 to 552.1803 and 722.21 to 722.31 (Child Custody Act of 1970).

For court rules, go to www.courts.mi.gov, select the Legal Community tab, then to the Court Rules quick link and choose: 1) under Michigan Court Rules, Chapter 3 Special Proceedings and Actions, for the divorce court rules of MCR 3.201 to 3.219 2) under Other Rules, Local Court Rules - Circuit Courts, for local court rules arranged by county.

Approved, SCAO

REQUEST FOR ACCOMMODATIONS

Court name and location
OJIBWAY COUNTY CIRCUIT COURT - FAMILY DIVISION
200 N. MAIN
LAKE CITY, MI 48800

Today's date   4-10-89

Instructions for completing form. *Provide your name, address, and telephone number. Check the boxes which apply to you and provide any necessary details. When you have completed this request, please return it to the court at the above address.*

1. Name   DARLENE A. LOVELACE

   Address   121 S. MAIN   State   Zip   Telephone no.
                                      MI   48800   772-0000
   City   LAKE CITY

2. Court activity you need accommodations for:

   ☒ Hearing 5-7-89   ☐ Mediation meeting _____
              Date   Date
   ☐ Jury duty _____   ☐ Other (specify): _____
               Date(s)   include dates if relevant

3. What is the nature of your disability?

   ☒ Physical mobility impairment (wheelchair, walker, crutches, etc.)

   ☐ Speech impairment (specify): _____

   ☐ Visual impairment

   ☐ Hearing impairment (specify): ☐ deaf   ☐ hard of hearing   ☐ deaf-blind

   ☐ Other (specify): _____

4. What type of accommodation are you requesting? _____

   ☐ Interpreter for deaf (specify whether ASL, tactile, oral, etc.): _____

   ☐ Assistive listening device (specify): ☐ headphones ☐ neckloop ☐ computer-assisted real-time captioning (CART)
                                            ☐ other: _____
   NOTE: To determine if other accommodations are available, contact the Division on Deaf and Hard of Hearing, 201 N. Washington Square, Suite 150, Lansing, MI 48913, telephone 517-335-6004, T/V toll free 877-499-6232, T/V fax 517-335-7773.

   ☒ Physical location accessible for persons with a physical mobility concern.

   ☐ Other (specify): _____

5. If the request for accommodation is denied or if the accommodation does not successfully establish effective communication, the applicant may file a grievance in accordance with the court's established grievance procedure. Upon request, the court shall provide the applicant a copy of the court's established grievance procedure.

   _____ For court use only _____

MC 70 (3/11) **REQUEST FOR ACCOMMODATIONS**   MCL 393.501 *et seq.*, 42 USC 12111 *et seq.*

Approved. SCAO

Original - Court file
1st copy - Assignment clerk/Extra
2nd copy - Friend of the court/Extra

3rd copy - Opposing party
4th copy - Moving party

STATE OF MICHIGAN
JUDICIAL DISTRICT
JUDICIAL CIRCUIT
COUNTY

**MOTION AND ORDER FOR APPOINTMENT
OF FOREIGN LANGUAGE INTERPRETER**

CASE NO.

Court address

Court telephone no.

Plaintiff's name(s)

☒ moving party

Plaintiff's attorney, bar no., address, and telephone no.

Defendant's name(s)

☐ moving party

v

Defendant's attorney, bar no., address, and telephone no.

MOTION

1   I state that I am unable to speak English sufficiently to understand and participate in the proceedings in this case.

2   ☐ I am represented by an attorney.   ☒ I am not represented by an attorney.

3   I request the court to appoint a foreign language interpreter to interpret for me

4   I request an interpreter who speaks the ___KOREAN___ language.

5   If required, place my request on the motion calendar.

___4-1-89___
Date

Signature   *Darlene A. Lovelace*

To be completed only if the court
requires a hearing on the motion

NOTICE OF HEARING

You are notified that a hearing has been scheduled on this matter for.

Judge			
Hearing location	Bar no.	Date	Time
☐ Court address above ☐			

THE CLERK WILL SCHEDULE A HEARING ON THE MOTION, IF NECESSARY.

If you require special accommodations to use the court because of a disability or if you require a foreign language interpreter to help you fully participate in court proceedings, please contact the court immediately to make arrangements.

_____
Date

Signature _____

CERTIFICATE OF MAILING

I certify that on this date I served a copy of this motion on the parties or their attorneys by first-class mail addressed to their last-known addresses as defined in MCR 2.107(C)(3).

___4-2-89___
Date

Signature   *Darlene A. Lovelace*

IT IS ORDERED the above motion is   **ORDER**

___4-2-89___   ☒ granted.   ☐ denied
Date

Judge   *Lester Jubbs*

MC 81 (3/08) MOTION AND ORDER FOR APPOINTMENT OF FOREIGN LANGUAGE INTERPRETER

Overview of Divorce Procedure

At first, divorce procedure may seem forbidding. But it's really not so mysterious when you break it down into steps and understand the purpose of each step.

Like any lawsuit, a divorce starts when the plaintiff files a paper known as a complaint. Despite its rather alarming name, a complaint is simply the document that starts a lawsuit. A divorce complaint contains facts about the parties and their marriage, and then asks for relief on the divorce issues. At filing, the clerk issues a summons in the case notifying the defendant that a divorce has been filed. These papers (and possibly others) make up the initial divorce papers.

The defendant must get notice of the divorce by receiving the initial divorce papers. Notice is provided by serving these papers on the defendant. There are three regular methods of service, plus a couple of alternate service methods for elusive or disappeared defendants.

After service, the defendant may respond to the plaintiff's complaint within an answering period. The defendant's response can be either by filing: 1) an answer to the complaint or 2) a motion objecting to the complaint.

In the vast majority of cases, defendants don't bother to respond, putting them in default. The plaintiff can then go to the clerk and have the defendant's default declared. With this declaration, the case is officially an uncontested divorce, or what lawyers sometimes call a *pro confesso* or "pro con" divorce case.

But if the defendant responds to the complaint within the answering period, the divorce is contested. In that case, the plaintiff should seek a lawyer to take over the case because it's difficult to handle a contested case without a lawyer.

After the 60-day statutory waiting period, the plaintiff can get the Judgment of Divorce, which decides all the divorce issues, during the final hearing. The plaintiff must appear at the hearing and give testimony or "proofs" in support of the judgment. This sounds scary, but the final hearing is usually very brief and easy to get through. After the final hearing, the plaintiff files the divorce judgment making the divorce final.

This book has organized the divorce procedure into four steps: "Filing," "Service," "Default" and "Final Hearing." The flowchart below summarizes these steps and the time to perform them.

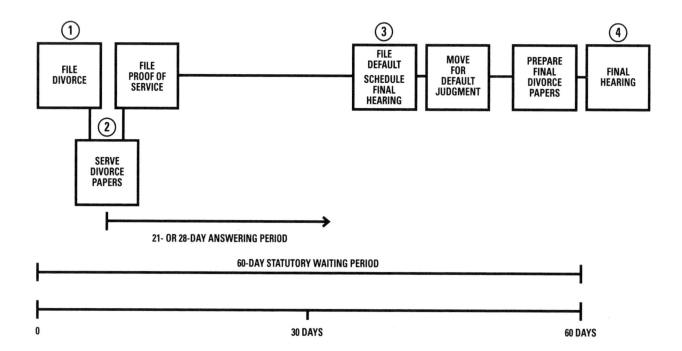

1 Filing

Preparing Your Initial Divorce Papers

You begin your divorce by preparing the initial divorce papers. These papers include the complaint and summons. The divorce complaint describes the basic facts of your marriage. It also tells the court that your marriage has broken down by citing the no-fault grounds for divorce. Finally, the complaint asks the court to decide the divorce issues. The purpose of the summons is to notify the defendant that you have filed a divorce complaint, and that s/he may respond to it.

The complaint and summons are contained in a set of forms: the Summons and Complaint (MC 01) and Complaint for Divorce (GRP 1). The Summons and Complaint (MC 01) includes the summons in the case along with the first part of the complaint. The Complaint for Divorce (GRP 1) is actually a continuation of this form and contains the main body of the complaint.

Optional and Local Forms

Your initial divorce papers will include the Affidavit and Order, Suspension of Fees/Costs (MC 20) when you want a fee exemption (see Appendix A for the form and instructions). You must file an extra paper and take other special steps if you seek alimony (see Appendix C for the details).

The blank forms for the initial divorce papers and all other divorce papers are located in the forms section in the back of this book. Optional forms like the Waiver/Suspension of Fees and Costs (MC 20), and local forms like the Certificate of Conformity for Domestic Relations Order or Judgment (1225) (filed at the end of Wayne County divorces) are located in a special section. All the forms are perforated so you can easily tear them out of the book.

There are filled-in samples of the initial divorce papers at the end of this section; other sample forms appear at the end of the sections they relate to by subject matter. For general information about form preparation, see "Papers" on page 51.

Ordinarily, you must make two photocopies of your divorce papers. The clerk gets the original, leaving copies for you and the defendant. But you will need an extra copy of the Summons and Complaint (MC 01),* giving you the following papers:

● Summons and Complaint	MC 01	3
● Complaint for Divorce	GRP 1	2
★ Waiver/Suspension of Fees and Costs	MC 20	2

Filing Your Divorce

Start your divorce by filing it with the clerk (see "Court System" on page 49 for information about finding the clerk). To file, you must have your initial divorce papers ready. And unless you receive a fee exemption, you must pay the filing fee (see "How Much Will My Divorce Cost?" on page 29 for the amount of the filing fee). In all, you should have the following items when you go to the clerk's office to file your divorce:

- ● Summons and Complaint   MC 01
  - original
  - 3 copies

- ● Complaint for Divorce   GRP 1
  - original
  - 2 copies

- ● money for the filing fee

- ★ Waiver/Suspension of Fees and Costs   MC 20
  - original
  - 2 copies

---

*   In Wayne County only, you can omit the MC 01 from your initial divorce papers because the Wayne County Clerk will print out summonses for you when you file the case.

When you arrive at the clerk's office, tell the clerk that you want to file a divorce complaint. The clerk should then do the following to file your divorce:

Obtain

If the clerk doesn't have Record of Divorce or Annulment (DCH-0838) forms, these are also available from:

Department of Community Health
Vital Records Office
201 Townsend St.
Capitol View Bldg. 3rd Floor
Lansing, MI 48913
(517) 335-8666

■ Take the Summons and Complaint (MC 01) and the three copies and: 1) assign a judge to the case and stamp his/her name on these papers 2) enter a case number on them 3) complete the summons boxes in the middle of the papers. File the Summons and Complaint (MC 01) and return three copies to you.

■ File the Complaint for Divorce (GRP 1) and return two copies to you.

■ Take the money for the filing fee

★ File the Waiver/Suspension of Fees and Costs (MC 20), if used, to suspend the fees immediately; or submit the form to the judge for consideration, and then return two copies to you.

✦ In Oakland and Wayne Counties only, prepare caption labels, label the captions of the initial divorce papers and give you two sheets of caption labels.

Before you leave the clerk's office, ask for a Record of Divorce or Annulment (DCH-0838). This form asks for personal and marital information. You complete and file it at the end of the divorce, when you get the judgment. After filing, the clerk sends the DCH-0838 to the Michigan Department of Community Health for addition to the state's vital records. Although you won't use the form until later, it's convenient to pick it up now while you're at the clerk's office.

	Original - Court 1st copy - Defendant	2nd copy - Plaintiff 3rd copy - Return
Approved, SCAO		CASE NO.

STATE OF MICHIGAN
JUDICIAL DISTRICT
JUDICIAL CIRCUIT
COUNTY PROBATE

SUMMONS AND COMPLAINT

Court ___ ___ ___ no.

Court address

Plaintiff's name(s), address(es), and telephone no(s).

v

Defendant's name(s), address(es), and telepho___

Plaintiff's attorney, bar no., address, and telephone no.

FILL OUT CAPTION ON THIS AND ALL OTHER PAPERS AS SHOWN IN "PREPARING PAPERS"

CLERK WILL COMPLETE SUMMONS BOXES

SUMMONS | **NOTICE TO THE DEFENDANT**: In the name of the people of the State of Michigan you are notified:
1. You are being sued.
2. **YOU HAVE 21 DAYS** after receiving this summons to **file a written answer with the court** and serve a copy on the oth___ **or take other lawful action with the court** (28 days if you were served by mail or you were served outside this state). (MCR ___
3. If you do not answer or take other action within the time allowed, judgment may be entered against you for the relief ___ in the complaint.

Issued 3-1-89	This summons expires 5-31-89	Court clerk _Martha Klee_

*This summons is invalid unless served on or before its expiration date.
This document must be sealed by the seal of the court

COMPLAINT | **Instruction:** *The following is information that is required to be in the caption of every complaint and is to be completed by the plaintiff. Actual allegations and the claim for relief must be stated on additional complaint pages and attached to this form.*

Family Division Cases
☒ There is no other pending or resolved action within the jurisdiction of the family division of circuit court involving the family or family members of the parties.
☐ An action within the jurisdiction of the family division of the circuit court involving the family or family members of the parties has been previously filed in _____ Court.
The action ☐ remains ☐ is no longer pending. The docket number and the judge assigned to the action are

Docket no.	Judge	B___

DESCRIBE ANY PRIOR FAMILY CASES INVOLVING YOU OR YOUR FAMILY, SO DIVORCE CAN BE DIRECTED TO FAMILY COURT JUDGE HANDLING PRIOR CASES

General Civil Cases
☒ There is no other pending or resolved civil action arising out of the same transaction or occurrence as alleged in ___
☐ A civil action between these parties or other parties arising out of the transaction or occurrence alleged in the ___ been previously filed in _____
The action ☐ remains ☐ is no longer pending. The docket number and the judge assigned to the act___

Docket no.	Judge

VENUE

Plaintiff(s) residence (include city, township, or village)	Defendant(s) residence (include city, township, or village)
(SEE CAPTIONS ABOVE)	

Place where action arose or business conducted

Darlene A. Lovelace

2-28-89	Signature of attorney/plaintiff
Date	

If you require special accommodations to use the court because of a disability or if you require a foreign language interpreter to help you fully participate in court proceedings, please contact the court immediately to make arrangements.

MC 01 (3/08) **SUMMONS AND COMPLAINT**   MCR 2.102(B)(11), MCR 2.104, MCR 2.105, MCR 2.107, MCR 2.113(C)(2)(a), (b), MCR 3.206(A)

STATE OF MICHIGAN
Circuit Court - Family Division
_____ COUNTY

COMPLAINT FOR DIVORCE

CASE NO.

INCLUDE FULL NAMES

Plaintiff: ☐ Husband ☒ Wife

DARLENE ANN LOVELACE

v

Defendant:

DUDLEY ERNEST LOVELACE

Plaintiff's name before this marriage:

DARLENE ANN ALBRIGHT

Defendant's name before this marriage:

SAME

1. Plaintiff's residence: at least
   ☒ 180 days in Michigan
   ☒ 10 days in this county — immediately before filing of th[is]
   and/or

   Defendant's residence: at least
   ☒ 180 days in Michigan
   ☒ 10 days in this county — immediately before filing of this co[mplaint]

SEE "CAN I GET A DIVORCE IN MICHIGAN?" FOR MORE ON RESIDENCE. CHECK BOXES AS THEY APPLY

2. Date of marriage _9-1-85_   Place of marriage _LAKE CITY, MICHIGAN_

3. The parties stopped living together as husband and wife on or about _1-15-89_

4. There has been a breakdown of the marriage relationship to the extent that the objects of matrimony have been destroyed and there remains no reasonable likelihood that the marriage can be preserved.

5. There are no children of th[e ...] marriage who are: a) minors (under 18)
   b) adults age 18-19½ entit[led ...]

CHECK IF YOU HAVE ALREADY DIVIDED ALL PROPERTY

SEE "DO I HAVE CHILDREN IN MY DIVORCE?" FOR MORE ABOUT CHILDREN

6. The wife ☒ is not pre[gnant ...]

7. There ☒ is ☐ is no property to be divided; ☐ division of property is controlled by the parties' prenuptial agreement attached as exhibit 1. [... and the estimated date of birth is ____]

CHECK IF YOU HAVE ALREADY DIVIDED SOME OR ALL PROPERTY

8. I request a judgment of divorce, and:

   a. property ☒ award to each party the [...]
             ☒ divide

   ☒ b. change wife's last name to _ALBRIGHT_

USE IF WIFE WANTS A NAME CHANGE

   ☐ c. spousal support for: ☐ plaintiff ☐ defendant
      plaintiff/defendant earns _____ monthly at _____ and [...]
      plaintiff/defen[dant ...] and ca[...]

   ☐ d. other: _____

CHECK BOXES AND ADD INCOME INFORMATION IF YOU SEEK SPOUSAL SUPPORT (ALIMONY)

IF YOU HAVE A PRENUPTIAL AGREEMENT CHECK THIRD BOX IN PARAGRAPH 7, MAKE PHOTOCOPIES OF THE AGREEMENT, WRITE EXHIBIT 1 AT TOP OF EACH, AND ATTACH COPIES TO ORIGINAL GRP1 AND ALL COPIES

Date _2-28-89_   _Darlene A. Lovelace_

GRP 1 (1/04)   COMPLAINT FOR DIVORCE, extension page to MC 01

2 Service

Due process requires that the defendant receive notice of the divorce so s/he can respond to it. Notice is provided by serving copies of the initial divorce papers on the defendant. You should begin service as soon as possible, within a few days after filing.

Although the purpose of service is notice, don't assume that you can skip it when the defendant already knows about the divorce. And don't try to serve the defendant by simply giving the divorce papers to him/her. No doubt your spouse would get informal notice of the divorce these ways. But the law requires that the defendant receive *official* notice of the divorce by service.

Official notice can only be accomplished by one of the service methods described below. With one of these methods, the court knows for sure that the defendant got notice of the divorce. For this reason, service is absolutely necessary. The service rules may seem artificial and even rather silly at times, but they must be followed carefully. If you omit service, or violate the service rules, there's a chance your whole divorce will be invalid.

There are three methods of serving defendants who are available to be served: 1) acknowledgment 2) mail 3) delivery.* Each method can be used anywhere in the state of Michigan. These service methods can also be used outside the state (including foreign countries), as long as there is Michigan jurisdiction over the nonresident defendant (see "Can I Get a Divorce in Michigan?" on page 24 for more about jurisdiction).

---

* Since 2007, legal papers can also be served among parties to a lawsuit by email. However, the parties must first stipulate to this form of service and follow strict service rules. This makes email service unsuitable for service of the initial divorce papers and difficult for uncontested divorces in which the defendant doesn't participate.

Despite service's wide reach, there are a few minor restrictions on serving papers. The court rules disqualify you from serving the initial divorce papers personally because you're a party to the case. Instead, you must have a neutral third party serve the papers for you. If you use service by delivery, a professional server, such as a sheriff or commercial process server, can serve for you. But when you choose either service by acknowledgment or service by mail, you must enlist a helper (who can be any mentally competent adult), such as a friend, to help with service. The helper acts as a straw man through whose hands the divorce papers pass to the defendant.

Whichever service method you choose, you mustn't have the divorce papers served on a Sunday, an election day, or on the defendant while s/he is: 1) at, en route or returning from a court appearance 2) attending a religious worship service, or going to or coming from the place of worship within 500 feet of the place. Michigan law gives people immunity from service in all these situations.

Preparing for Service

The defendant must be served with the papers listed below, which shall be referred to collectively as the "service papers:"

- • Summons and Complaint   MC 01

- • Complaint for Divorce   GRP 1

- ★ Waiver/Suspension of Fees and Costs   MC 20

- ✦ a sheet of caption labels (in Oakland and Wayne Counties only)

After the defendant is served with these papers, service must be proved in a proof of service. Each method of service (acknowledgment, mail, delivery) is proved differently. But all are proved in the Proof of Service on the reverse of your extra copy of the Summons and Complaint (MC 01). This paper will be referred to as the "proof of service copy of the Summons and Complaint (MC 01)." After service, you file it with the clerk so that your case file shows that the defendant was served.

Service by Acknowledgment

Service by acknowledgment is the simplest method of service. To use this method, you need the cooperation of the defendant and the assistance of a helper. If the defendant is in another county or state, you must find someone there to act as your helper.

Service is accomplished by having the helper hand the service papers to the defendant. You may be present during the transfer, but the helper, not you, must be the one who actually hands the service papers to the defendant. The day of service is the day the defendant receives the service papers from the helper.

Proving Service by Acknowledgment

Immediately after service, the helper should have the defendant date (with time and day) and sign the Acknowledgment of Service, which is at the bottom of the reverse of your proof of service copy of the Summons and Complaint (MC 01). Make two copies of this paper and save for filing later as your proof of service.

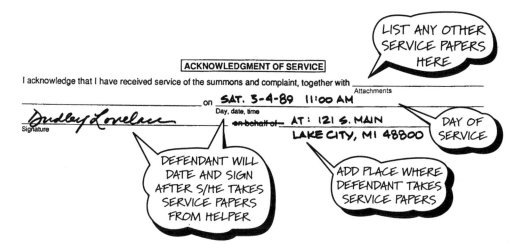

Service by Mail

Service by mail is a little more expensive than service by acknowledgment. But it's a very effective method of service because it goes anywhere U.S. mail is delivered—even overseas. The court rules permit service by mail through either registered or certified mail. Because certified mail is cheaper than registered mail, certified mail is the best choice.

When you serve by mail, you need the assistance of a helper and the U.S. Postal Service. Your helper mails the service papers to the defendant and the postal service delivers these to him/her by certified mail.

To prove service, you need several special services available with certified mail: 1) restricted delivery 2) return receipt service. By restricting delivery, the service papers are delivered only to the defendant personally or someone s/he has designated in writing to receive mail. The return receipt provides proof of who received the papers, the date of delivery and the address of delivery only if this is different from the address on the envelope. This receipt becomes a key part of the proof of service.

More Information

Service by mail can be carried out by certified mail inside the United States, its territories and possessions, and to military APOs and FPOs.

For service by mail in foreign countries, ask the post office about recorded delivery, which is similar to domestic certified mail and offers restricted delivery and return receipt services. The Recorded Delivery Receipt (PS Form 8099) explains this type of delivery. Recorded delivery with full restricted delivery and return receipt services isn't available in all countries.

These days, return receipt service is available in two varieties: 1) by mail using the postcard-like Domestic Return Receipt (PS Form 3811) 2) electronically by fax or email notification. Despite these options, for now stick with the old receipt-by-mail system using the PS Form 3811 since courts are used to seeing this form as part of the proof of service by mail.

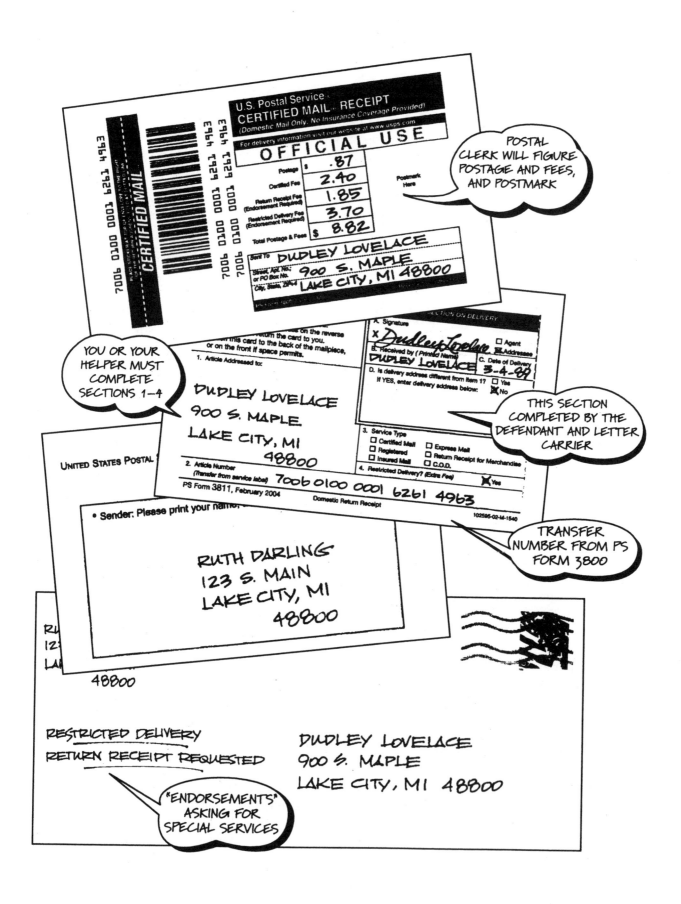

Before you have the service papers mailed, prepare the mailing by placing your service papers in an envelope addressed to the defendant with your helper's name and address as the return address. In addition to that, you or your helper must prepare two certified mail forms: 1) Certified Mail Receipt (PS Form 3800) 2) Domestic Return Receipt (PS Form 3811), which are available at any post office.

On the PS Form 3800, fill in the defendant's name and address at the bottom of the form. For the PS Form 3811, write your helper's name and address on the front of the card, and on the reverse complete boxes #1-4. In section #2, transfer the article number from the PS Form 3800. In section #3, check the certified mail box, and ask for restricted delivery in #4.

After you complete the postal forms, peel off the plastic strips on the ends of the PS Form 3811 and attach the card to the envelope (there probably won't be room on the front of the envelope, so attach it to the reverse side). On the front of the envelope, to the left of the defendant's address and below your helper's return address, write "Restricted Delivery" and "Return Receipt Requested" on the envelope. By making these notations (the PS Form 3800 calls this "endorsement"), you will remind the letter carrier to restrict delivery and provide a receipt.

Have your helper take the envelope containing the service papers, with the Domestic Return Receipt (PS Form 3811) attached, the Certified Mail Receipt (PS Form 3800) and money to pay for the mailing to a post office window. The helper should ask the postal clerk to mail the envelope by certified mail with the special services you have checked on the PS Form 3811. The clerk will prepare the certified mailing and return a postmarked Certified Mail Receipt (PS Form 3800) to your helper. Keep this receipt for your records.

Later, a letter carrier will deliver the mailing to the defendant, get his/her name (printed), signature and other delivery information on the reverse of the Domestic Return Receipt (PS Form 3811). Within a few days, your helper should get the PS Form 3811 back in the mail. You can then have your helper prove the service as described below. The day of service is the day the defendant receives the mailing from the letter carrier.

If your helper gets the whole envelope back, instead of the Domestic Return Receipt (PS Form 3811) alone, service by mail has failed. The defendant may have refused to accept the mailing, wasn't home or has moved without leaving a current forwarding order. Whatever the case, you will have to abandon service by mail because it only works when the defendant is ready and willing to take the certified mailing from the letter carrier. If service by mail fails, try service by delivery instead.

Proving Service by Mail

After your helper gets the Domestic Return Receipt (PS Form 3811) back in the mail, have him/her prove service on the reverse of your proof of service copy of the Summons and Complaint (MC 01). Complete the information about the service by mail under the Affidavit of Process Server, and have the helper sign the form before a notary public. For guidance, see the sample proof of service by mail on the next page.

As proof of the defendant's receipt of the mailing, staple the Domestic Return Receipt (PS Form 3811) to the reverse of your proof of service copy of the Summons and Complaint (MC 01). Make two copies of this paper and save one for filing later as your proof of service.

PROOF OF SERVICE	SUMMONS AND COMPLAINT Case No.

TO PROCESS SERVER: You are to serve the summons and complaint not later than 91 days from the date of filing or the date of expiration on the order for second summons. You must make and file your return with the court clerk. If you are unable to complete service you must return this original and all copies to the court clerk.

CERTIFICATE / AFFIDAVIT OF SERVICE / NONSERVICE

☐ **OFFICER CERTIFICATE**   OR   ☒ **AFFIDAVIT OF PROCESS SERVER**

I certify that I am a sheriff, deputy sheriff, bailiff, appointed court officer, or attorney for a party (MCR 2.104[A][2]), and that: (notarization not required)

Being first duly sworn, I ~~... ...etent~~ adult who is not a party/... ...nd that: (notarization req...)

LIST ANY OTHER SERVICE PAPERS HERE

☐ I served personally a copy of the summons and complaint,
☒ I served by registered or certified mail (copy of return receipt attached) a copy of the s... ...mons
together with _____
List all documents served with the Summons and Complaint

_____ on the defendant(s):

Defendant's name	Complete address(es) of service	Day, date, time
DUDLEY E. LOVELACE	900 S. MAPLE, LAKE CITY, MI 48800	SAT. 3-4-89

GET DATE FROM PS FORM 3811

DAY OF SERVICE

☐ I have personally attempted to serve the summons and complaint, together with a... ...llowing defendant(s) and have been unable to complete service.

Defendant's name	Complete address(es) of service	Day, date, time

I declare that the statements above are true to the best of my information, knowledge, and belief.

Signature Ruth Darling
Name (type or print) RUTH DARLING

Service fee $	Miles traveled	Mileage fee $	Total fee $

Subscribed and sworn to before me on ___3-7-89___,   Title OJIBWAY _____ County, Michigan
                                        Date
My commission expires: ___1-1-90___   Signature: _Loretta Smiley_
                        Date   ~~Deputy court clerk/~~Notary public
Notary public, State of Michigan, County of ___OJIBWAY___

Service by Delivery

You can also obtain service by having someone deliver the service papers to the defendant. Any mentally competent adult except you can do that. If the defendant is cooperative, you could have a helper perform service by delivery for you. But in that case it would be much easier to have the defendant simply acknowledge delivery of the service papers from your helper and get service by acknowledgment. Therefore, it's likely that you will use service by delivery for defendants who live out of town or state, or are otherwise hard to serve.

Service by delivery is usually carried out by a professional server, such as a sheriff or commercial process server. Whatever other service options you have, county sheriff departments will always serve papers for you. They often have a separate division or deputy in charge of service. In small towns or rural areas, the sheriff may be the only choice for service. Larger cities usually have commercial process servers as an alternative to the sheriff.

Both types of servers charge fees for service. By law, sheriffs charge a base service fee, currently $23, plus mileage billed at 1½ times the state civil service rate for travel during service (the travel distance is the shortest route between the court issuing the summons and the place of service times two (for going and returning)).

These fees can add up, but a service fee can be suspended if you get a fee exemption (see Appendix A for details). Even if you have to pay, sheriffs' service fees are normally cheaper than those of commercial process servers, who often charge around $30-50 for service. On the other hand, commercial process servers may be more persistent in finding and serving defendants.

Whomever you choose, you can often reduce the service fees by having the defendant pick up the service papers at the server's office. This saves the server's mileage fee. It also spares the defendant the possible embarrassment of being served with legal papers at home or work. If the defendant is willing, tell the server that the defendant will pick up the papers, and then have the defendant call the server to arrange for pick-up.

To obtain service by delivery in your area, take the service papers along with your proof of service copy of the Summons and Complaint (MC 01) to the server and ask for service on the defendant. The server will serve the defendant at the address in the captions of your papers. If the defendant can be found at another place, tell the server about the other address.

When the defendant lives in another county or state, you must find a server nearby. After you find one, mail the service papers and your proof of service copy of the Summons and Complaint (MC 01) to the server. Enclose a note asking for service and return of a proof of service (see also "Fees" on page 55 about prepaying an out-of-town server's service fee).

When you're seeking service outside the state of Michigan, you should mention in your note that the server must prove service in the Affidavit of Process Server, on the reverse of the proof of service copy of the Summons and Complaint (MC 01). An out-of-state process server must use the affidavit, instead of the Officer Certificate, because only Michigan court officers (such as Michigan sheriffs and their deputies) may use the certificate. In addition, ask the process server to have the notary public affix a seal on

More Information

To find sheriffs, look under the county government section for the sheriff department in a telephone directory. For commercial process servers, use a telephone directory for the defendant's area and search under "Process Servers" in the yellow pages.

Or you can find both kinds of process servers through process server trade associations, which provide referrals:

Michigan Court Officer, Deputy Sheriff & Process Servers Association (MCODSA) at (800) 992-4845 or www.mcodsa.com

National Association of Professional Process Servers (NAPPS) at (800) 477-8211 or www.napps.org

United States Process Servers Association (USPSA) at (314) 645-1735 or www.usprocessservers.com

the affidavit, since documents with out-of-state notarizations must be sealed.

If all goes as planned, the server will find the defendant and deliver the service papers to him/her. The day of service is the day the server delivers the service papers to the defendant.

Proving Service by Delivery

After service, the server will prove service on the reverse of the proof of service copy of the Summons and Complaint (MC 01) that you gave the server. For service by Michigan court officers, the proof of service will appear in the Officer Certificate; all other servers must use the Affidavit of Process Server.

After service is proved, the server will return your proof of service copy of the Summons and Complaint (MC 01) to you. Make two copies of this paper and save one for filing later as your proof of service.

Service Problems

In most cases, service by any of the three regular service methods goes smoothly. But certain service methods are best for particular defendants, such as prisoners and military servicemembers. And sometimes you may even have to use alternate service if the defendant is difficult to serve.

Serving Prisoners and Military Servicemembers

Service by mail seems to work best on incarcerated defendants. See "What If My Spouse or I Am Imprisoned?" on page 27 for tips on serving prisoners by mail. Service by mail is also the most effective way to serve military servicemembers, for reasons explained in "What If My Spouse or I Am in the Military?" on page 28.

Alternate Service

The regular methods of service work only if the defendant is available for service. But if the defendant is elusive (avoiding service) or has disappeared, you must resort to some form of alternate service. Appendix B has complete instructions and forms for serving elusive or disappeared defendants.

If you're convinced you need alternate service, don't wait too long to seek it. The summons in the Summons and Complaint (MC 01) lasts for 91 days after it's issued (this expiration date should have been inserted by the clerk on the front of the summons). If you fail to complete service within that time, the summons will expire and the clerk will dismiss your case (see below for more about the danger of dismissal).

There is a way to ask the judge for a new summons before the old one expires, but it's a lot of bother. The better way is to use alternate service as soon as it becomes apparent that regular service methods aren't working.

Filing the Proof of Service

Whatever method of service you use, be sure to file the proof of service soon after service is completed. This is important because delay in filing the proof of service can result in dismissal of your divorce.

As mentioned above, a summons expires after 91 days. When there's no proof of service on file after 91 days, the clerk will assume that service has failed and begin dismissal of the case for "no progress." (The clerk should give advance warning of dismissal by sending you a Notice of Intent to Dismiss (MC26).) After dismissal for no progress, you can file a motion asking the judge to reinstate the case. But reinstatement isn't guaranteed, and the judge may deny the motion. In that case, you would have to refile your divorce and start over.

Divorces without minor children are usually finished before the summons expires. But sometimes there can be unexpected delays. To avoid the risk of dismissal, make sure that you file the proof of service quickly, well before the 91-day summons expiration period elapses. Take/send the proof of service, which is on the reverse of your proof of service copy of the Summons and Complaint (MC 01),* plus two copies to the clerk. The clerk will file the original and return two copies to you.

---

* If alternate service was used, the proof of service is on the reverse of either the MC 304 or MC 307.

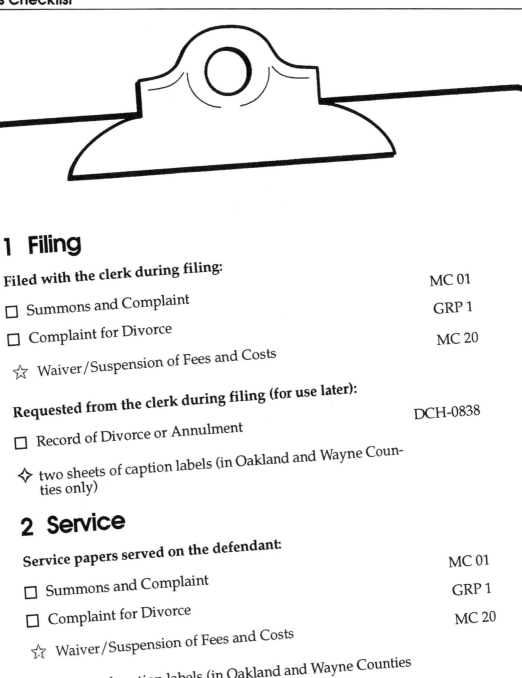

1 Filing

Filed with the clerk during filing:

☐ Summons and Complaint   MC 01

☐ Complaint for Divorce   GRP 1

☆ Waiver/Suspension of Fees and Costs   MC 20

Requested from the clerk during filing (for use later):

☐ Record of Divorce or Annulment   DCH-0838

✦ two sheets of caption labels (in Oakland and Wayne Counties only)

2 Service

Service papers served on the defendant:

☐ Summons and Complaint   MC 01

☐ Complaint for Divorce   GRP 1

☆ Waiver/Suspension of Fees and Costs   MC 20

✦ a sheet of caption labels (in Oakland and Wayne Counties only)

Filed with the clerk soon after service:

☐ proof of service   MC 01

Symbols
◻ regular paper
☆ optional paper
✦ local paper

3 Default

You've filed the divorce and served notice of the case. After several weeks, you're ready for the final part of your divorce, which begins with the default.

A default is important because it means that the defendant isn't contesting the divorce. Until then, you're relying on the defendant's word that the divorce is agreeable. But with the default, your divorce becomes *officially* uncontested, making it impossible for the defendant to re-enter and contest the case without special permission from the court.

Although you may be anxious to get the default, you must wait and see if the defendant responds to your divorce complaint. S/he can respond by filing with the court and sending you either: 1) an Answer to your complaint 2) a motion objecting to the complaint. If the defendant does neither, you can go ahead and apply for a default from the clerk.

To avoid default, the defendant must respond in one of those two ways within the applicable answering period. All answering periods begin the day after the day of service (see "Time" on page 55 for more on computing time periods). The length of answering periods depends on the method of service. The chart on the next page depicts this.

Your copy of the proof of service, which you should have filed earlier, shows the day of service. Use that and the chart to figure the answering period in your case. If the defendant hasn't responded by the end of that answering period, you're ready to get the default.

Answering Periods

Method of service	Day of service	Answering period
Service by acknowledgment	Day defendant takes the service papers from helper	21 days in Michigan or 28 days out of state
Service by mail	Day defendant takes the mailing of the service papers from letter carrier	28 days
Service by delivery	Day server delivers the service papers to defendant	21 days in Michigan or 28 days out of state
Alternate service:		
mailing	Day the service papers are sent	28 days
tacking	Day the service papers are tacked to door	28 days
household delivery	Day the service papers are delivered to person in defendant's household	28 days
publication	Day of final publication of advertisement	Set by judge in MC 307 (a minimum of 28 days after final publication date)
posting	Last day of posting period	Set by judge in MC 307 (a minimum of 28 days after last day of posting period)

Scheduling the Final Hearing

Although your divorce may only be several weeks old when you apply for the default, it's not too early to schedule the final hearing for your case. As required by law, you must appear in court at a final hearing to receive your divorce judgment. Final hearings in divorce cases are usually heard on special days, called motion days, which courts set aside each week or month. During these motion days, judges may hear many final hearings, often at 10- or 15-minute intervals. Nevertheless, judges' motion day schedules fill up quickly, so it's a good idea to schedule your final hearing at the time of the default. If you wait, you risk delaying the conclusion of your divorce.

As previously mentioned, Michigan imposes a 60-day waiting period on divorce cases without minor children (see "How Long Will My Divorce Take?" on page 28 for more on statutory waiting periods). This means that at least 60 days must elapse between the day you filed your divorce (this date is stamped on your Summons and Complaint (MC 01)) and the day of your final hearing.

Although you may want to get your divorce over with sooner, you must observe the waiting period. So when you schedule your final hearing, set it for a day at least 60 days after the day you filed your divorce (see "Time" on page 55 for more about figuring time in days).

Courts use several methods to schedule final hearings in uncontested divorce cases. In many counties, you can schedule a final hearing orally. When you get the default, ask the clerk to schedule a final hearing sometime after the statutory waiting period has expired. The clerk will reserve a time for you on the judge's motion day schedule or calendar (make sure that you make a note of the time and date).

In other counties, you must file a written request for a final hearing. In Wayne County, for example, you must request a final hearing on a special request form known as a praecipe. Wayne County's praecipe is a yellow slip of paper called the At Issue Praecipe for Default Judgment in Domestic Relations Action (#1121), which is available from clerk in room 201 of the Coleman A. Young Municipal Center (CAYMC) (formerly the City-County Bldg.) at 2 Woodward Ave. in Detroit. You file the praecipe with the docket management office in room 770 of the CAYMC. Docket management will schedule the final hearing and mail a notice of the time and date to you. Several other counties also use praecipes or similar written forms. If your county is among them, ask the clerk for the particular form and use it as directed.

> **Glossary**
>
> *Praecipe*–(pronounced "PRESS-uh-pee") is a request to a clerk for a court hearing on a motion or similar matter.

In some counties, such as Oakland, the clerk will schedule the final hearing for you. These counties typically have computerized case management systems that set final hearings automatically. After the hearing is set, a notice of the time and date will be sent to you.

As you can see, there is a great deal of variation when it comes to scheduling final hearings. In fact, there is probably more variation here than in any other part of divorce procedure. To find out the practice in your county, ask the clerk when you get the default.

After you schedule the final hearing, you must file a motion formally asking the court for a default judgment of divorce. The defendant must receive a copy of the motion which will include a notice of the place, date and time of the final hearing.

Getting the Default

When the defendant has failed to respond to your complaint within the applicable answering period, s/he has defaulted, allowing you to apply to the clerk for a default. The clerk declares or enters the default, but you must prepare the Default (GRP 2) form. You fill out the Request, Affidavit and (later after filing) Proof of Mailing sections. The middle Affidavit section must be signed by you before a notary public. During filing, the clerk will date and sign the Entry and Notice of Entry section of the GRP 2.

Default and the Military Relief Laws

As you prepare the Default (GRP 2) you'll see some business in the Affidavit section about the defendant's possible service in the military. Why do you have to concern yourself with this issue when you get an uncontested divorce? It's necessary because of a pair of military relief laws (one federal and one state) that protect some defendant-servicemembers from hard-to-handle lawsuits, including divorces.

Appendix D has lots more about the military relief laws and their legal impact. In general, the laws provide lawsuit protection to *active-duty* servicemembers in the five branches (Army, Navy, Marine Corps, Air Force and Coast Guard) of the U.S. military and the two branches of the Michigan National Guard (Army National Guard and Air National Guard). See "Military Relief Laws" on page 151 for more about the scope of these laws.

Because of these military relief laws, in uncontested divorces you must determine whether or not the defendant is in active-duty military service (see the sidebox for advice about how to find this out). After you know (or don't know) the defendant's (non)military status, you can deal with the military relief laws during default as follows:

Defendant isn't in active-duty military service. You know for a fact (by personal knowledge or a negative military status report from the DMDC) that s/he isn't an active-duty servicemember. As a result, you can check the first indented box in paragraph #3a of the Default (GRP 2) to that effect. This will let the court know that the military relief laws don't apply to the defendant.

Defendant is in active-duty military service. In this scenario, you know (by personal knowledge or a positive military status report from the DMDC) that s/he is in active-duty military service. You must check the second indented box in paragraph #3a of the Default (GRP 2). Before the divorce can go through, you must show how the military relief laws were satisfied (see "Satisfying the Military Relief Laws" on page 155 for more about ways to do this).

One easy way to satisfy these laws is to obtain a waiver of the laws' protections from the

More Information

With its enormous demands and responsibilities, active-duty military service isn't something you can easily keep secret. As a result, you should have personal knowledge (from observation of the defendant's activities and routines) about whether or not s/he is in the military.

But if the defendant is absent, disappeared or elusive, you may have to use the U.S. Department of Defense's Manpower Data Center (DMDC) to find out. The DMDC can tell you whether or not the defendant is in active-duty service in the U.S. military. You can contact the DMDC at:

Defense Manpower Data Center
Attn: Military Verification
1600 Wilson Blvd.
Suite 400
Arlington, VA 22209-2593
www.dmdc.osd.mil/appj/scra/scraHome.do

You can request information from the DMDC about the defendant's (non)military status by mail or via the Internet. You need the defendant's full name and social security number and/or date/year of birth for a search. With either type of request, your goal is to receive a written DMDC "military status report" which you can attach to your Default (GRP 2) so the judge knows the defendant's (non)military status. There is no charge for a mail or Internet request.

A DMDC military status report should be: 1) *positive* indicating that the defendant is on active duty by giving his/her branch of service and date the active duty began 2) *negative* stating that it does not possess any information that the defendant is on active duty 3) *inconclusive* in rare cases when the data submitted was incomplete, faulty or resulted in multiple matches.

A Request for Military Status Report* form is included in this book for a request by mail. Fill in the form and mail it to the DMDC (enclose a self-addressed stamped envelope for the reply), and you should get a military status report back soon.

For an Internet request, go to the DMDC's Web site cited above. If you get a security warning, ignore it by clicking "continue to this website (not recommended)" (it won't hurt your computer). Select a single record request and fill in the data field. After a few seconds, you will get an on-screen military status report, which you must print so you have written evidence of the report.

*A related Military Locator Request form is used when you know the defendant is in U.S. military service and you want to find out *where* for service of the divorce papers or other reasons.

defendant. You can get a waiver in the Appearance and Waiver of Military Relief Law Rights (GRP 6). In paragraph #3a of the Default (GRP 2), check the inside-the-paragraph box that defendant has appeared and waived all lawsuit relief rights, and attach the GRP 6 to the form. See "Waiver of Military Relief Law Rights by the Defendant" on page 156 for more about waiver.

If the defendant didn't waive, you'll have to respond to the military relief the defendant has sought (stay issued, stay application denied, no response, etc.). Check the "other" box in paragraph #3a of the GRP 2 and say what happened in the blank line. For example, the defendant may have received a 90-day stay, which has now expired, allowing the divorce to go forward. "Satisfying the Military Relief Laws" on page 155 has more about stay applications and unresponsive defendants.

Defendant's (non)military status is unclear. Sometimes, the defendant's (non)military status may be unclear. The defendant may be living far away, has disappeared or is elusive, so you don't know personally (hearsay (second-hand information) must be disregarded) whether s/he is in active-duty military service. Or maybe you know that the defendant is in the military, but aren't sure whether s/he is in active or inactive service (reservists frequently change status, especially during a call-up).

Try to clear up this uncertainty if you can. As explained in the sidebox, you should be able to use the DMDC to find out whether or not the defendant is in active-duty military service. You can then go forward under one of the scenarios described above.

But if for some reason your DMDC request results in an inconclusive military status report, check the box at #3b of the Default (GRP 2). The court will have to decide how to proceed when the defendant's military status is unknown. The SCRA provides several remedies in this situation, including requiring a bond from the plaintiff to protect the defendant's interests.

Symbols

- • regular paper
- ■ regular practice
- ★ optional paper or practice
- ✦ local paper or practice

Applying for the Default from the Clerk

You can apply to the clerk for the default personally or by mail. Applying in person is best because you can also schedule the final hearing orally or by written request during the visit. Either way, when you apply for the default you should have:

- • Default   GRP 2
    - • original
    - • 2 copies

- ★ special papers for dealing with a defendant-military servicemember, such as the Appearance and Waiver of Military Relief Law Rights (GRP 6), (see Appendix D)

- ✦ praecipe (if needed to schedule the final hearing)

While you're at the clerk office, it's often convenient to file the motion for a default judgment. You can do this if you are able to schedule a final hearing (orally or by praecipe) during your visit. Just in case, consider bringing the following motion materials with you when you file the default:

- Motion to Enter Default Judgment of Divorce (with   GRP 3
  caption-only completed)
    - original
    - 2 copies

- $20 motion fee

At the clerk's office, say that you want to file a default. The clerk should do the following things:

- Take the Default (GRP 2) and the two copies and complete the Entry section of these papers. File the original Default (GRP 2) and return two copies to you.

★ File any special papers for dealing with a defendant-servicemember and return two copies to you.

✦ After your oral or written request (by praecipe), schedule a final hearing for your case (unless you do it elsewhere or later).

If you can schedule a final hearing now, date, sign and complete paragraph #1 and the Notice of Hearing section in the Motion to Enter Default Judgment of Divorce (GRP 3) and copies at the clerk's office. The clerk will then:

- File the Motion to Enter Default Judgment of Divorce (GRP 3) and return two copies to you.

- Take the $20 motion fee.

As you fill out paragraph #1 of the Motion to Enter Default Judgment of Divorce (GRP 3), keep in mind what it says: You are seeking a divorce judgment granting the relief you asked for in paragraph #8 of your Complaint for Divorce (GRP 1). In fact, the relief you asked for in the complaint and the relief you plan to get in the judgment must match fairly closely so the defendant knows what the court is likely to order in the judgment. If they don't match up, you should check the box in paragraph #1 of the GRP 3 and describe the new or different relief in this paragraph. For example, you might not have asked for a name change in the complaint, but now want one. New or different items of relief like that should be described briefly on the blank line in paragraph #1.

After the Default

Despite the fact that the defendant is removed from the case when you get a default, s/he is entitled to a final notice about the default and default judgment. By giving this notice, the defendant can't complain later that s/he didn't know about the default or judgment.

If you were able to file the Default (GRP 2) and Motion to Enter Default Judgment of Divorce (GRP 3) together, send copies of each to the defendant. If the defendant has disappeared, send the papers to his/her last known address.

Take the remaining copies of the forms and use these for proof of service. Fill out the Proof of Mailing sections showing when the papers were mailed to the defendant. Make photocopies of these proof of service copies of the GRP 2 and 3. File/send to the clerk the original proof of service copies, keeping one set for yourself.

You may not be able to schedule a final hearing when you file the default, and cannot file the motion for default judgment then. If so, send the Default (GRP 2) to the defendant and prove service as explained above. A little later, after you get the final hearing date, complete and file with the clerk the Motion to Enter Default Judgment of Divorce (GRP 3), send a copy to the defendant and prove service, all as described above.

Typically, you will get the default and move for the default judgment mid-divorce, around halfway through the statutory waiting period. The timing is mostly up to you, as long as it's after the answering period.

But don't wait too long. You must act fairly quickly to schedule a final hearing. And more important, the court rules say that the Motion to Enter Default Judgment of Divorce (GRP 3) must be sent to the defendant no later than nine days (seven days' notice period plus two days for mailing) before the final hearing. Try to wrap up these default-related steps well before this final deadline.

Waiting for the Final Hearing

After the default, you must wait for your final hearing during the 60-day statutory waiting period. Not much will happen during this time, but the clerk may send a notice asking you to attend a pretrial, scheduling or other conference about your case. These case conferences give the clerk a chance to find out more about the progress of cases. They also provide you with practical information about the court's final hearing and judgment procedures. Case conferences are designed for contested cases, but some counties also hold them for uncontested divorce cases.

If the clerk schedules a case conference for you, make sure you go because the court can dismiss your case if you don't attend. Case conferences are usually held in a conference room at the courthouse, not in a courtroom. The defendant probably won't show up, and this should add to the relaxed and informal atmosphere. Nevertheless, court personnel might use the conference to ask you about the case or have you complete a questionnaire about the progress of your case.

STATE OF MICHIGAN Circuit Court - Family Division COUNTY	DEFAULT Request, Affidavit, Entry and Notice of Entry	CASE NO.

Plaintiff (appearing *in propria persona*):	v	Defendant:

(speech bubble) INSERT DAY OF SERVICE

REQUEST

1. As shown by the proof of service on file, defendant was served with a summons and complaint on __3-4-89__, but did not respond to the complaint within 21 days (28 days if served by mail or out of state).
I request the clerk to enter the default of defendant for failure to plead or defend as provided by law.
Date __4-10-89__   Plaintiff *Darlene A. Lovelace*

AFFIDAVIT

Plaintiff, being sworn, says:
2. Defendant is not a minor or an incompetent person.
3. Defendant's (non)military status:
☒ a. Based on ☒ my personal knowledge, ☐ attached military status report, defendant
　☒ is not in active-duty military service.
　☐ is in active-duty military service, and ☐ has appeared and waived all lawsuit relief rights under the Servicemembers Civil Relief Act and/or MCL 32.517 (or similar military relief law from another state) in the attached appearance and waiver form.
　☐ other: _____
☐ b. I am unable to determine whether or not defendant is in active-duty military service.

(speech bubble) PLAINTIFF MUST DATE AND SIGN AFFIDAVIT SECTION BEFORE A NOTARY PUBLIC

　　　　Plaintiff *Darlene A. Lovelace*
Date __4-10-89__ Subscribed and sworn to before me on __4-10-89__, __OTIBWAY__ County, Michigan
My commission expires __1-1-90__ Signature *Lovetta Smiley*
Notary public, State of Michigan, County of __OTIBWAY__

ENTRY AND NOTICE OF ENTRY

(speech bubble) CLERK WILL DATE AND SIGN

The default of defendant is entered for failure to plead or defend as provided by law.
Date __4-11-89__   Court clerk *Martha Gee*

TO DEFENDANT: Please take notice of this entry of default against you.

PROOF OF MAILING

On the date below, I sent a copy of this Default to defendant by ordinary first-class mail at his/her address in the caption above, which is defendant's last known address.
I declare that the statement above is true to the best of my information, knowledge and belief.
Date __4-12-89__   Plaintiff *Darlene A. Lovelace*

GRP 2 (3/07)   DEFAULT, Request, Affidavit, Entry and Notice of Entry

STATE OF MICHIGAN Circuit Court - Family Division COUNTY	MOTION TO ENTER DEFAULT JUDGMENT OF DIVORCE	CASE NO.

Plaintiff (appearing *in propria persona*):

v

Defendant:

1. After entry of defendant's default on __4-11-89__ , I request the court to enter a default Judgment of Divorce granting the relief I requested in my Complaint for Divorce; ☐ and grant the following new/different relief_____

I declare that the statement above is true to the best of my information, knowledge and belief.

Date __4-11-89__

Plaintiff __Darlene A. Lovelace__

NOTICE OF HEARING

A hearing on this motion will be held in the courtroom of the judge assigned to this case, located at (place) __OJIBWAY COUNTY COURTHOUSE__ on (date) __5-7-89__ at (time) __9:00 A.M.__

PROOF OF MAILING

On the date below, I sent a copy of this motion to defendant by ordinary first-class mail at his/her address in the caption above, which is defendant's last known address.

I declare that the statement above is true to the best of my information, knowledge and belief.

Date __4-12-89__

Plaintiff __Darlene A. Lovelace__

INSERT FINAL HEARING INFORMATION HERE

GRP 3 (3/07)   MOTION TO ENTER DEFAULT JUDGMENT OF DIVORCE

Request for Military Status Report

TO:

Defense Manpower Data Center
Attn: Military Verification
1600 Wilson Blvd.
Suite 400
Arlington, VA 22209-2593

RE:

Case name LOVELACE V. LOVELACE

Case number 89-00501-DO

Full name of defendant DUDLEY ERNEST LOVELACE

Defendant's date of birth 6-15-64

Defendant's social security number 379-10-5567

I am the plaintiff in the divorce case above seeking a default judgment of divorce against the defendant. I must know whether or not the defendant is currently in the active duty of the U.S. military service, to comply with the Servicemembers Civil Relief Act and/or Michigan Compiled Law 32.517 or a similar military relief law from another state.

Please respond by providing a military status report on defendant as soon as possible. A self-addressed stamped envelope is enclosed for your response.

Date 3-15-89

Signature *Darlene A. Lovelace*

Name DARLENE A. LOVELACE

Address 121 S. MAIN

LAKE CITY, MI 48800

Telephone: (517) 772-0000

4 Final Hearing

The final hearing comes at the end of your divorce. This hearing is held in court before the judge assigned to your case. You must attend the hearing and give some brief testimony to get a Judgment of Divorce (GRP 4), which decides all the divorce issues. Your divorce becomes final immediately after the hearing, when the judgment is filed.

Final Divorce Papers

The final hearing requires some preparation. A few days before the hearing, you should prepare the Judgment of Divorce (GRP 4) and any other final divorce papers you need. The Judgment of Divorce (GRP 4) is by far the most important divorce paper. The judgment ends the marriage, divides property, deals with alimony and may change a wife's name.

Although the Judgment of Divorce (GRP 4) is the court's order, you must prepare it for the court. For guidance, see the sample judgment at the end of this section and the additional judgment provisions in Appendix F.

Besides the Judgment of Divorce (GRP 4), your final divorce papers include the Record of Divorce or Annulment (DCH-0838). You probably got this form from the clerk when you filed the divorce. If not, you can obtain it from the clerk anytime. To prepare the Record of Divorce or Annulment (DCH-0838) for filing, answer questions #1-16 and #19-20. In Wayne County only, you must prepare an extra paper: the Certificate of Conformity for Domestic Relations Order or Judgment (1225). This paper tells the judge that your divorce judgment satisfies all legal requirements.

Preparing for the Final Hearing

Before you appear in court for your final hearing, you may want to prepare the testimony for the hearing. Since you don't have a lawyer to question you during the hearing, you must give the testimony in a monologue. This is a little more difficult than testifying by answering questions. Therefore, you might find it helpful to plan your testimony beforehand.

One way to do that is by using a script to organize your testimony. By preparing a testimony script, you should be able to memorize the bulk of your testimony. You can also take your testimony script with you to the final hearing and rely on it a bit if your memory fails while you're on the witness stand (using written materials to jog a witness' memory is called "refreshing the recollection" and is permitted by the rules of evidence).

Symbols

- regular paper

■ regular practice

★ optional paper or practice

✦ local paper or practice

Luckily, the testimony you give during a final hearing is usually quite brief. In most cases, it's simply a repetition of the information contained in your divorce complaint, adding factual detail when necessary about the marital breakdown, division of property or alimony, if granted.

You give all the testimony for your hearing; you don't need any testimony from the defendant or other witnesses. In fact, the defendant will probably be absent. Defendants have the right to attend final hearings, but cannot directly participate because of their default. Thus, defendants seldom attend final hearings in uncontested divorce cases.

On the other hand, having the defendant at the final hearing can be helpful to the judge. With the defendant present, the judge can ask him/her about such things as complicated or lopsided property divisions, payment of alimony or military issues, such as satisfaction of the military relief laws. Defendant-wives who want their names changed must also attend their final hearings to receive name changes.

Before the Final Hearing

When you attend the final hearing, it's a good idea to bring your file with all your divorce papers to the final hearing. If you haven't kept a file, at least bring the following items:

- Judgment of Divorce   GRP 4
  - original
  - 2 copies

- Record of Divorce or Annulment   DCH-0838

- testimony script

✦ Certificate of Conformity for Domestic Relations   1225
  Order or Judgment (in Wayne County only)
  - original
  - 2 copies

Attending the Final Hearing

When you go to the courthouse for the final hearing, arrive early so you can take care of any final details. Clerks often want you to check in with them to let them know that you are present and ready for the final hearing. In some counties, the clerk will give your case file to you to take to the courtroom. But in most counties the clerk will send the file to the courtroom ahead of time.

You should go to your judge's courtroom before the final hearing is scheduled to begin and wait in the visitor's section in back (see "Courthouse Appearances" on page 56 for more about how courts conduct hearings and how you should conduct yourself during a hearing in court). As your case is called, identify yourself, step forward and take a place at one of the tables. When the judge tells you to proceed, offer your Judgment of Divorce (GRP 4) and say you're ready to give the testimony.

After you take the witness stand and are sworn in, give the testimony as you have planned it. If you omit something important, the judge may question you briefly to complete the testimony. When your testimony is finished, ask the judge to enter your Judgment of Divorce (GRP 4), as you've requested in the Motion to Enter Default Judgment of Divorce (GRP 3). If the judgment is satisfactory, the judge will sign the original Judgment of Divorce (GRP 4) and maybe some copies.

If the judge objects to your judgment, s/he should tell you what the problem is. It may be something you can fix on the spot. If not, ask the judge for an opportunity to correct the judgment later. The court rules permit you to submit a corrected judgment to the judge within 14 days after the final hearing. If you get that chance, make any necessary modifications of your Judgment of Divorce (GRP 4) and take it to the judge's office. S/he should sign it there and you won't need another final hearing.

But if something really goes wrong at your final hearing, ask the judge for an adjournment of the final hearing to another day. There is an adjournment form, Order for Adjournment (MC 309), which the clerk might provide for the adjournment. After the judge signs the order and you file it, send a copy to the defendant at least seven days before the new final hearing takes place.

Filing the Final Divorce Papers

After the final hearing, file your final divorce papers with the clerk. Filing the papers quickly is important because, according to paragraph #12 of the Judgment of Divorce (GRP 4a), your divorce only becomes final when you file the judgment. At that time, your marriage is ended and all the other provisions of the judgment take effect.

In a few counties, you can file your final divorce papers (and pay the judgment fee) with the courtroom clerk during the final hearing. But in most counties, you must return to the clerk's office, where the clerk will:

■ File the Judgment of Divorce (GRP 4) and return two copies to you.

■ Take the Record of Divorce or Annulment (DCH-0838).

✦ In Wayne County only, file the Certificate of Conformity for Domestic Relations Order or Judgment (1225) and return two copies to you.

Before you leave the clerk's office you may want to obtain several *certified* copies of the Judgment of Divorce (GRP 4). These copies can be helpful in carrying out the judgment's property division or verifying a name change. See "After Your Divorce" on page 101 for more about these issues. Bring extra money for certified copies because the clerk charges $10 for issuing a certified copy plus $1 for each page of the document.

After the Final Hearing

Naturally, the defendant must know what the Judgment of Divorce (GRP 4) says because its provisions affect him/her. After the final hearing, the clerk should send the defendant a brief notice that a judgment was issued. However, the clerk doesn't send a copy of the Judgment of Divorce (GRP 4) itself to the defendant along with this notice. That's your responsibility.

You must send the judgment to the defendant within seven days of the final hearing. Send a true copy of the Judgment of Divorce (GRP 4) to the defendant by ordinary first-class mail at his/her last known mailing address. After mailing, prepare the Proof of Mailing (MC 302) and make two copies. Then file/send the original to the clerk.

STATE OF MICHIGAN
Circuit Court - Family Division
COUNTY

JUDGMENT OF DIVORCE
Page 1 of 2 pages

CASE NO.

Plaintiff (appearing *in propria persona*):

v

Defendant:

Judge LESTER TUBBS

Date of hearing 5-7-89

After the defendant's default, **IT IS ORDERED**:

1. **DIVORCE**: The parties are divorced.
2. **CHILDREN**: There are no children of the parties or born during their marriage who or adult and entitled to support.
☒ 3. **NAME CHANGE**: Wife's last name is changed to ALBRIGHT

☒ wife. ☒ husband.
☐ wife. ☐ husband.
☐ wife. ☐ husband.

4. **SPOUSAL SUPPORT**: Spousal support is
☒ not granted for
☐ reserved for
☐ granted later in the judgment for ☐ wife. ☐ husband.
is not being ordered.

A Uniform Spousal Support Order ☒ is not required because spousal support is g...ted.
☐ shall accompany and be incorporated into this judgment because spousal support is g...

5. **PROPERTY DIVISION**:
A. **Real property**:
(Land and buildings)
☐ The parties do not own any real property.
☒ Real property is divided elsewhere in this judgment.
☒ Real property owned by the parties in joint tenancy or tenancy by the entirety is converted t...

All real property owned by the parties in joint tenancy or tenancy by the entirety is converted t... cy in common, unless this judgment provides otherwise.

B. **Personal property**:
(All other property)
☒ Each party is awarded the personal property in his or her possession.
☒ Personal property is divided elsewhere in this judgment.
☒ Personal property is the property of the other, now owned or later

6. **STATUTORY RIGHTS**: All interests of the parties in the property of the other, now owned or later acquired, under MCL 700.2201-700.2405, are extinguish...d, including those known as dower under MCL 558.1-558.29.

7. **BENEFICIARY RIGHTS**: The rights each party has to the pro...ds or poli... ...ntracts of life insurance, endowments or annuities upon the life of the other as ...
ment during or in anticipation of marriage, are ☒ extinguished. ☐
8. **RETIREMENT BENEFITS**: Any rights of either party in any pens...
benefit of the other, whether these rights are vested or unvested, a...
☒ extinguished. ☐ awarded later in the judgment.
9. **DOCUMENTATION**: Each party shall promptly and properly execute a...
documents to carry out the terms of this judgment.
10. **PRIOR ORDERS**: Except as otherwise provided in this judgment, any nonfin...
tions entered in this action are terminated.
☐ 11. **SUSPENDED FEES AND COSTS**: The previously suspended fees and costs in this case of
_____ shall be ☐ paid by ☐ plaintiff ☐ defendant   to the clerk. ☐ waived finally.
12. **EFFECTIVE DATE OF JUDGMENT**: This judgment shall become effective immediately after it is
signed by the judge and filed with the clerk.

GRP 4a (3/07)   **JUDGMENT OF DIVORCE, page 1**

USE FOR WIFE'S NAME CHANGE

SEE "ALIMONY PROVISIONS" IN APPENDIX F FOR MORE ON SPOUSAL SUPPORT (ALIMONY)

SEE "PROPERTY DIVISION PROVISIONS" IN APPENDIX F FOR MORE ON PROPERTY DIVISIONS

CHECK BOXES AS THEY APPLY

SEE "PROPERTY DIVISION PROVISIONS" IN APPENDIX F FOR MORE ON DIVIDING RETIREMENT BENEFITS

		CASE NO.
STATE OF MICHIGAN Circuit Court - Family Division COUNTY	JUDGMENT OF DIVORCE Final of 2 pages	

Plaintiff:	v	Defendant:

IT IS ALSO ORDERED:

13.

14.

ETC.

INCLUDE ADDITIONAL JUDGMENT PROVISIONS HERE AS NEEDED

CHECK THESE BOXES TO CLOSE THE CASE

JUDGE WILL DATE AND SIGN AT FINAL HEARING

judgment ☒ resolves ☐ does not resolve the pending claim in this case, and ☒ closes ☐ does close   the case, except to the extent jurisdiction is retained by law.

Date 5-7-89   Judge *Lester Jubos*

GRP 4c (1/06)   JUDGMENT OF DIVORCE, final page

Testimony

1) My name is [full name] , my address is [address], and I am the plaintiff in this case.

2) I was married to the defendant on <u>SEPT. 1, 1985</u> at <u>LAKE CITY, MICHIGAN</u> by a person authorized to
   Date and place of marriage
   perform marriages.

3) Before the marriage, my/[my wife's] name was <u>DARLENE ANN ALBRIGHT</u>
   Wife's former name

4) I filed my complaint for divorce on <u>MARCH 1, 1989</u> . Before I filed the complaint, I had resided in Michigan since
   Filing date
   <u>1970</u> and in this county since <u>1970</u> .
   State residence   County residence

5) As I said in my complaint, there has been a breakdown in our marriage relationship to the extent the objects of matrimony
   have been destroyed because <u>WE COULD NEVER GET ALONG TOGETHER</u> and there remains no
   Brief facts to support grounds
   reasonable likelihood that our marriage can be preserved because <u>WE ARE TOTALLY INCOMPATIBLE</u>
   Brief facts to support grounds

6) The defendant and I have no minor children, and I/[my wife] am not now pregnant.

7) I am working at <u>A RESTAURANT AS A WAITRESS</u> and am able to support myself. As a
   Source of support
   result, no alimony is being ordered.

8) We own some <u>CLOTHING AND HOUSEHOLD GOODS</u> that we have split between us. We have also agreed that
   General description of personal property
   the defendant is to give me <u>A 1984 DODGE ARIES</u> and I will pay off the debt on it.
   Specific items of personal property transferred in judgment

9) We also own <u>A HOUSE IN LAKE CITY</u> worth around <u>$35,000</u>
   Description of any real property   Value
   We have agreed to <u>SELL IT, PAY OFF THE MORTGAGE AND SPLIT THE REST</u>
   Manner of division

   USE WHEN APPLICABLE

10) I would like my former name of <u>ALBRIGHT</u> back.
    Wife's name change

11) My court fees were suspended when I filed this divorce. Since then, <u>I AM STILL GETTING FIP PAYMENTS AND MY HUSBAND IS UNEMPLOYED.</u>
    Current financial condition

12) Does the court have any questions?

STATE OF MICHIGAN
THIRD JUDICIAL COURT
WAYNE COUNTY
Penobscot Bldg. 645 Griswold Ave. Detroit, MI 48226

CERTIFICATE OF CONFORMITY
FOR DOMESTIC RELATIONS
ORDER OR JUDGMENT

CASE NO.

313-224-5372

PLAINTIFF'S NAME

v

DEFENDANT'S NAME

I certify the attached Order of Judgment as presented for entry to be in full conformity with the requirements set forth by statute, INCLUDING A PROVISION FOR IMMEDIATE INCOME WITHHOLDING (WHICH SHALL BE IMPLEMENTED BY THE FRIEND OF THE COURT), THE PAYER'S SOCIAL SECURITY NUMBER AND THE NAME AND ADDRESS OF HIS/HER SOURCE OF INCOME, IF KNOWN, UNLESS OTHERWISE ORDERED BY THE COURT, and with Michigan Court Rules 3.201 and following and if applicable, includes all provisions of the Friend of the Court recommendation or is in conformity with the decision of

_____

_____ rendered on the _____

_____ , 20_____ . _____ day of

5-5-89
Date

Darlene A. Lovelace

Instructions: Please sign and present this certificate to the Court Clerk when the Order or Judgment is presented for entry. If an ex parte interim order is being presented to the Judge, please complete the "Certificate on behalf of Plaintiff regarding Ex Parte Interim Support Order: and follow Local Court Rule 3.206.

#1225(11/04) CERTIFICATE OF CONFORMITY FOR DOMESTIC RELATIONS ORDER OR JUDGMENT

USE THIS FORM
IN WAYNE
COUNTY ONLY

Approved, SCAO

STATE OF MICHIGAN JUDICIAL DISTRICT JUDICIAL CIRCUIT	PROOF OF MAILING	CASE NO.
		Court telephone no.

Court address

Plaintiff(s)		Defendant(s)
	v	

On the date below I sent by first class mail a copy of _____ **JUDGMENT OF DIVORCE**

to: Names and addresses

DUDLEY LOVELACE
900 S. MAPLE
LAKE CITY, MI 48800

I declare that the statements above are true to the best of my information, knowledge and belief.

5-8-89
Date

DARLENE A. LOVELACE
Name (typed)

Darlene A. Lovelace
Signature

MC 302 (5/88) PROOF OF MAILING

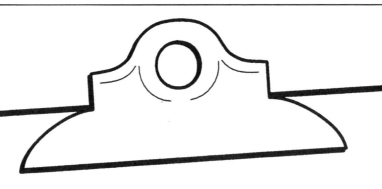

3 Default

Filed with the clerk around the time the default is received:

GRP 2

☐ Default

☆ Appearance and Waiver of Military Relief Law Rights, if defendant is in active-duty military service and is willing to waive military relief law rights

GRP 6

✧ praecipe or other written request for a final hearing

GRP 3

☐ Motion to Enter Default Judgment of Divorce

Filed with the clerk after the default:

☐ copies of the Default and Motion to Enter Default Judgment of Divorce with proof of service on defendant

GRP 2 & 3

4 Final Hearing

Filed with the clerk after the final hearing:

GRP 4

☐ Judgment of Divorce

DCH-0838

☐ Record of Divorce or Annulment

✧ Certificate of Conformity for Domestic Relations Order or Judgment (in Wayne County only)

1225

Filed with the clerk after service of the final papers on defendant:

MC 302

☐ Proof of Mailing

Symbols
☐ regular paper
☆ optional paper
✧ local paper

After Your Divorce

Although your divorce is over, there's still some work to do. The Judgment of Divorce (GRP 4) takes legal effect at filing, but you must carry out several judgment provisions. What's more, the end of your marriage may require changes in your will, powers of attorney, insurance, retirement benefits, etc.

Transferring Property

The Judgment of Divorce (GRP 4) divided your property, but it's your responsibility to transfer ownership of the property.

Ownership of real property must be transferred by deed. For transfers between ex-spouses, a simple form of deed called a quit claim deed is customarily used. Lawyers or real estate brokers can prepare these for a small fee.

If your ex-spouse is uncooperative or unavailable for transfer, you can sometimes use the divorce judgment to transfer ownership of real property yourself. To use the judgment this way, it must describe the property in detail (see "Property Division Provisions" in Appendix F for more about describing property using legal descriptions or identification numbers). You must also have an official certified copy of the judgment for the transfer. These are available from the clerk for a small fee.

You can transfer Michigan real property by recording a certified copy of the divorce judgment with the register of deeds for

> ### To Obtain
>
> A certified copy of your divorce judgment, go to the clerk of the court that granted your divorce.
>
> There is a $10 fee for issuing a certified copy, plus $1 for each page of the document.

the county where the property is located. This transfer method isn't available for out-of-state real property.

As mentioned in "Will I Have Tax Problems from the Divorce?" on page 39, real property transfers between ex-spouses aren't subject to income taxation. Nevertheless, the transferee (party receiving ownership) must report the transfer in IRS Form 1099-S and file this form with the IRS and give a copy to the transferor.

Within 45 days of a divorce property transfer, the transferee should also file a Property Transfer Affidavit (L-4260) with the local city or township tax assessor. Check the box near the bottom indicating that it is a "transfer creating or ending a joint ownership if at least one person is an original owner of the property (or his/her spouse)," and the assessor cannot adjust the taxable value of the property.

Personal property without titles (clothing, household goods, etc.) can be transferred by simply changing possession of the items. But both possession and title must be transferred for personal property with titles (stocks, bonds, motor vehicles, etc.). Stocks and bonds can be transferred through the designated transfer agent (usually a bank but sometimes the issuing company itself).

Transfer titles to motor vehicles through a secretary of state office by applying for a new title after the current owner has signed off on the back of the old certificate of title.

If the owner refuses to cooperate, you can use a certified copy of the divorce judgment for transfer of title. When you apply for a new title, submit a certified copy of the judgment, and you won't need your ex's signature on the old certificate of title.

Debts

You may have already closed or frozen joint accounts (see "Does My Property Need Protection?" on page 36 for more about handling joint accounts during divorce). If you haven't, do this at once. Otherwise, your ex can add new joint debt after the divorce for which you may be liable.

Estate Planning

Several judgment paragraphs extinguish rights and claims you and your ex-spouse have against each other's property (unless you choose to preserve these in the judgment). For example, paragraphs #7 and #8 of the Judgment of Divorce (GRP 4a) extinguish life insurance and retirement benefits, and paragraph #6 cuts off will and estate rights.

In 2000, Michigan adopted a new will, inheritance and probate law, called the Estates and Protected Individuals Code (EPIC). The EPIC says that divorce revokes all property transfers to and appointments of (as agent, beneficiary, trustee, personal representative, etc.) an ex-spouse and his/her relatives, such as your stepchildren, in all sorts of estate planning devices including:

- life insurance
- all kinds of retirement plans
- power of attorney
- trust
- will
- miscellaneous (such as payable-on-death (POD) bank accounts)

Despite this helpful provision in the EPIC, it's still necessary to follow up after divorce and review or revise many estate planning documents.

It's particularly important to contact your insurance agent and/or retirement plan administrator and revoke any designations of your spouse as beneficiary. Because of a peculiarity in the law, neither the judgment's nor EPIC's revocations are always effective, making individual revocation necessary. As you make the revocations, it's a good time to designate new beneficiaries.

The EPIC revokes appointments of an ex-spouse (and relatives) as agent under two popular kinds of powers of attorney: 1) durable power of attorney (DPA) for financial affairs 2) patient advocate designation (PAD) for health care decision-making, often including the power to terminate life-sustaining treatment.

With both kinds of powers of attorney, revocation of your ex as agent often means promotion of successor agents to first-choice status (frequently, spouses designate each other as first-choice agents, with successors named as back-ups). Nevertheless, it's a good idea to make new powers of attorney with new sets of first-choice and successor agents after divorce.

More Information

If they don't have good health care coverage of their own, ex-spouses should look into these options:

COBRA-coverage. A 1985 law, the Consolidated Omnibus Budget Reconciliation Act, or COBRA for short, can provide health care coverage. Immediately after divorce, COBRA allows you to obtain health care coverage for you and/or dependent children from your ex's employer-provided group plan (if the employer has 20 or more employees), which can last for a maximum of three years. What's more, you don't have to show medical insurability to get COBRA-coverage, so for example, you can get coverage immediately when you have high medical risks or pre-existing conditions.

One drawback to COBRA: You may have to pay the plan premiums (both the employer and employee shares) yourself. But fortunately, the premiums must be charged at group rates, which are usually lower than individual rates.

County health plans. Ingham County has devised a health plan for those without health care coverage. It provides coverage for doctor visits and prescription drugs, but not hospitalization. Other counties have signed onto Ingham's plan extending it all over the state.

Individual policy. Under the new Affordable Care Act, affordable health insurance policies should be avaialble at state health insurance marketplaces or exchanges after Oct. 1, 2013. For more about the act, go to HealthCare.gov.

Health savings plans. These savings plans, similar to 401(k)s, include: 1) Health Savings Account (HSA) into which you (and your employer) can put pretax money and withdraw it later tax-free to pay for uninsured health care expenses left by a high-deductible policy 2) Health Reimbursement Account (HRA) funded by employers only, which can also pay for uninsured health care expenses 3) Flexible Spending Account (FSA) resembling HRAs, but whose unused balances revert to the employer at the end of the year.

Trusts are another popular estate planning devices which come in two varieties: 1) living, or *inter vivos,* trust 2) testamentary trust in a will. The EPIC says that divorce revokes an ex-spouse (and relatives) as beneficiary of a trust and as trustee. Even so, it's still smart to amend the trust and remove your ex from the trust.

Both your divorce judgment and the EPIC revoke rights that your ex (and relatives) have in your will, including: 1) will gifts and other property transfers 2) appointments as personal representative, trustee (of a testamentary trust) or other roles.

But besides these selected will provisions, divorce doesn't touch other parts of a will. The will, minus the provisions benefiting an ex-spouse (or relatives), remains in force. Nevertheless, you should carefully review your

More Information

About the the COBRA law, go to the **U.S. Department of Labor's** Web site at www.dol.gov, then under Topics - Health Plans & Benefits, under Subtopics - Continuation of Health Coverage (COBRA).

For information about local county health programs like Ingham's, call your local county health department.

will after divorce. The removal of your ex from the will may have upset your scheme of property distribution and appointments. After review, you may decide that your will needs revision or even replacement.

You should also remove your ex as beneficiary of pay-on-death (POD) bank accounts, brokerage accounts and bonds. If you hold a safe deposit box jointly with your ex, you should terminate this arrangement. As with other estate planning devices, the EPIC terminates spousal rights in these things, but it's still advisable to do this in fact.

Health Care Coverage

With the high cost of health care these days, health care coverage is vital. The sidebox above describes some coverage options if you lack employer-provided or individual coverage.

If you decide to obtain COBRA-coverage through your ex-spouse's employer, contact his/her employee benefits office within 60 days after your divorce judgment is granted. Wait longer and you can lose the right to obtain health plan coverage this way.

Name Change

If you changed your name during the divorce, you must report the name change to the following agencies and offices, so documents issued by them can be revised:

- Michigan Secretary of State (driver's license and voter registration)
- Social Security Administration (social security card)
- passport acceptance agency (U.S. Post Office, county clerk, etc.) (passport)
- financial institutions (bank accounts, credit cards, etc.)
- insurance companies (life, disability and health insurance policies and documents)
- heath care providers (health care files and documents at doctor, dentist, etc.)
- utilities (accounts with utilities, telephone companies, cable television, etc.)
- employer (employee benefits documents)
- schools and alumni associations (school records, alumni directories, etc.)
- airlines (frequent flier programs)

Typically, you must visit many of these offices and agencies in person to change your name; it's difficult to make the change over the telephone or Internet. Many of these agencies and offices also require evidence of your name change. For proof, bring certified copies of the Judgment of Divorce (GRP 4).

You must also give a special notice of your name change to the Michigan Department of Community Health. This notice allows the department to add the GRP 4 with the name change to your birth records. When you get copies of the GRP 4, ask the clerk for an Application to Record Court-Ordered Legal Name Change to a Michigan Birth Record (DCH-0850). File the form according to the instructions in the form.

Credit Problems

Today, in our consumer economy credit is more important than ever. As always, lenders look at credit reports (tracking a person's borrowing and payment habits) when making lending decisions. But more and more, automobile and homeowner insurance companies are using credit histories to determine insurability and premiums, and mortgage companies base interest rates on creditworthiness.

After divorce, many women suddenly discover that they can't get credit because they have no credit history. A woman may lose credit if her credit was reported in her previous married name. Even women who don't change their names may suffer a loss of credit if they got credit through their husbands' credit reports.

The solution to these credit woes is building a credit history in your own name. If you had credit under your former married name, you can add this information to your credit file. Joint accounts with your husband may have been reported in your husband's name only (all joint accounts opened after June 1, 1977, are supposed to reported in both spouses' names). If so, you can sometimes persuade credit reporting agencies to add these credit references to your file.

In addition, you can apply for new credit from banks, retailers and other creditors to build a credit history. A federal law, the Equal Credit Opportunity Act (ECOA), bars creditors from canceling old credit accounts you had during marriage if you still meet their lending standards (you may have to submit new information to prove your creditworthiness). The ECOA also guarantees creditworthy persons access to credit regardless of sex or marital status, and outlaws various discriminatory credit practices.

As you build a credit history, make sure you pay your bills on time, because this factor has the biggest impact on credit. It's also smart to have a

---

More Information

Credit agencies receive credit information from lenders and merchants, compile this information into credit reports and sell these to lenders and others. To check on your credit status, get copies of your credit reports from the three main credit reporting agencies:

Equifax: P.O. Box 740241, Atlanta, GA 30374, (800) 685-1111 or www.equifax.com

Experian: P.O. Box 9595, Allen, TX 75013, (888) 397-3742 or www.experian.com

TransUnion: P.O. Box 1000, Chester, PA 19022, (800) 888-4213 or www.transunion.com

Each report is around $10, but consumers are entitled to one free report per year from each company under the new Fair and Accurate Credit Transactions Act. You can request the free reports from:

Annual Credit Report Request Service
P.O. Box 105281
Atlanta, GA 30348
(877) 322-8228
www.annualcreditreport.com

This is the official free credit report service. Watch out for look-alike or sound-alike for-profit companies that charge fees for the available-for-free credit reports.

For more information about credit and credit reporting, go to the **Federal Trade Commission's** Web site at www.ftc.gov, then to Consumer Protection, to Consumer Information, to Credit & Loans, to Credit Reports & Scoring and choose from publications on credit, credit reporting and credit and divorce.

good mix of credit, with both revolving (credit cards, charge accounts) and installment (mortgages, loans) debt.

One thing to avoid are credit repair services. These firms often charge a lot for meager results. Even worse, they can sometimes commit illegal practices for which you can be liable.

Enforcing or Modifying the Divorce Judgment

Divorced people face all kinds of after-divorce problems, mostly in cases with minor children. There are far fewer of these problems in cases without minor children, except when alimony has been ordered during the divorce. But no matter what type of case it is, all these after-divorce problems really amount to just two things: *enforcement* of the judgment or *modification* of the judgment.

Enforcement

By far the most important document from your divorce is the judgment of divorce. Examining the divorce judgment, you'll see that the document contains several provisions or orders, arranged by subject: end of marriage (the actual divorce), property division and alimony (also called spousal support), if ordered. These orders must be observed and obeyed by the parties.

If all goes well, you and your ex cooperate and carry out the judgment of divorce without much fuss. But if your ex disobeys any judgment order, you must enforce the order against your ex, usually with the help of the court that granted the divorce.

Grounds for Enforcement

It's simple: Violation of a divorce judgment provides grounds for enforcement. The various orders inside the judgment tell the ex-spouses to do various things: divide their property or pay alimony, if ordered. If one of the parties disobeys any of these orders, the other party has grounds for enforcing the judgment.

Methods of Enforcement

You can sometimes enforce a divorce judgment yourself, without going to court. For example, a well-crafted judgment should authorize you to carry out the property division by recording the judgment with the register of deeds to transfer ownership of property.

You will need the help of the court system for other kinds of enforcement. For enforcement of the property division in the divorce, you can ask the court to hold your ex in contempt of court, or seek execution (seizure) of property or garnishment of money.

If you received alimony in your divorce, and there's been nonpayment, your first stop is always the friend of the court. By law, the friend of the court is supposed to enforce alimony orders. If your ex isn't paying on time or in full, notify the friend of the court, in writing, and it might take care of the problem for you.

These days, the friend of the court possesses a number of powerful enforcement remedies. The friend of the court can collect alimony by withholding money from the payer's income, threaten contempt or revocation of driver's, occupational or sporting/recreational licenses, reporting the nonpayment to consumer reporting agencies, such as credit bureaus, or adding surcharges to the debt. State agencies teamed with the friend of the court have other even more powerful remedies, such as seizure of state and/or federal income tax refunds.

If the friend of the court won't intervene, you will have to seek enforcement yourself. Most of the friend of the court's enforcement remedies aren't available to you. But you can collect alimony by a contempt-of-court proceeding or normal debt collection methods, such as execution against property or garnishment of money. It's also possible to enforce alimony obligations by invoking state or federal criminal nonsupport laws.

Modification

Of the three issues in a divorce without minor children, two, end-of-marriage and property division, are normally closed by the divorce and cannot be modified later. There is an exception to this rule when the divorce judgment is legally defective (because of fraud, duress, serious legal irregularity, etc.). In that case, the end-of-marriage and property division issues can be reopened.

Alimony may or may not be open to modification after a divorce. Alimony is only modifiable if the alimony order is "live" (still in effect) or can be revived. In addition, the alimony must be the kind that is modifiable, since these days some types are nonmodifiable.

Effectiveness of Alimony Order

In most cases, divorce judgments "bar" or deny alimony for one or both parties. If the judgment denied alimony for you, you cannot ask for it later, unless you can show that the judgment is defective.

If the divorce judgment contained an alimony order, the alimony may be modified as long as the order is in effect. But the order may have expired by its own terms or because of the occurrence of conditions.

As explained in "Alimony" on page 11, alimony is often subject to conditions that can terminate it. These conditions can be imposed by law (for example, in Michigan alimony automatically ends when the alimony recipient dies). Or conditions can be attached by the divorce judgment (death of the alimony recipient or payer and remarriage of the recipient are popular ones). When these conditions are triggered, alimony terminates and cannot be modified.

There's a third possibility: reservation of alimony, intentionally or by omission. If the divorce judgment reserved alimony for you, you can ask for it after divorce. Reservation can also happen by accident. The court rules say that divorce judgments must grant, deny or reserve alimony for both parties; failure to do any of these results in reservation for the omitted party or parties.

Either way, when alimony is reserved for you, you may ask for an original alimony order after divorce. This doesn't guarantee that you will get alimony. But the court will look at the issue anew, as it would have during the divorce. Without reservation of alimony, you would have to show a change of conditions or circumstances for such a post-judgment modification.

Modifiability of Alimony Order

Keep in mind that not every type of alimony is modifiable. As explained in "Types of Alimony" on page 12, alimony-in-gross is really part of property division and is therefore nonmodifiable, except when the judgment of divorce is defective.

For years in Michigan, true alimony was always modifiable. This is no longer so. Since Michigan law was changed in 2000, divorce parties can negotiate and agree to make alimony nonmodifiable. Few older divorce judgments do this. Newer ones (after-2000) may, but the alimony order must clearly say that the alimony is nonmodifiable. See "Alimony" on page 11 for more about the different kinds of modifiable and nonmodifiable alimony.

In a modification request, you can ask the court to change the amount of the alimony. This could raise, lower or even terminate the alimony.

One thing you can't normally do is modify past alimony. Michigan law generally bans so-called retroactive modification of support, preventing an alimony recipient from asking for more past alimony or a payer's seeking reduction or cancellation of past-due amounts. All the law allows is modification of future alimony, effective the date the modification motion is served.

There are a few exceptions to the full-payment rule. Past-due alimony can be modified or even canceled when: 1) there is a court-approved retroactive modification agreement between the parties 2) one party has hidden income, then the debt can be modified to compensate for the fraud.

And a few years ago, a support debt relief law went into effect allowing a payer to seek court approval for a debt payment plan which can modify or cancel alimony arrearages. The provisions of this law are complicated with all sorts of restrictions and consents (from the alimony recipient and/or state) necessary before a plan may be approved. Contact the friend of the court for more information.

These days, most alimony is paid by immediate income withholding. According to this method, the alimony is deducted from the payer's source of income (usually an employer) and sent to the SDU, which forwards it to the alimony recipient.

Income withholding is popular with alimony recipients and courts because it's reliable. But some alimony payers may dislike this payment method since it means more paperwork for their employers. They may want to avoid immediate income withholding and set up a different method of payment.

For alimony, the only issue modifiable after divorce, the customary grounds for modifying the amount of alimony are change of conditions or circumstances in the lives of you and your ex. To modify an existing alimony order, the changed conditions or circumstances must concern the short-list of amount-of-alimony factors described on page 14. For example, an alimony recipient may ask for more alimony because her financial needs have increased or her earning ability has been diminished. An alimony payer could plead loss of income or financial hardship in seeking a decrease in alimony.

When the motion concerns an original alimony order, after reservation of the issue in the divorce judgment, both sets of alimony factors must be used (some of these factors overlap). The long-list of alimony factors cited on page 13 must be invoked to convince the court that alimony should be ordered. Then, the short-list of factors on page 14 is used to determine the amount of alimony.

If you want to ask for a different method of paying alimony, it's best to do this through a limited opt-out from the friend of the court system. See Appendix C for more about opt-outs.

Methods of Modification

Modification of alimony must be court-ordered to be binding legally. An informal modification where you and your ex informally agree to a change, outside of court, works while you abide by the agreement. But when there's a violation, courts will refuse to enforce your agreement, making an informal modification practically worthless.

If you and your ex agree on the modification, you can stipulate to a modification order, without appearing in court. The court, which has the final say on all modifications, could reject your proposed modification, but will usually approve it.

No agreement? Then you must file a motion for modification. The court may refer the matter to the friend of the court for mediation or refereeing, and the issue may be settled there. If not, the motion must be heard by the judge during a court hearing. The judge decides the motion and signs an order either accepting or rejecting the proposed modification.

Updating Your Personal Information

When alimony has been ordered in your case, and the case is still in the friend of the court system, you have an obligation to notify the friend of the court, in writing, of any changes in your personal information within 21 days of a change. Paragraph #6 of the Uniform Spousal Support Order (FOC 10b) imposes this obligation and cites the kind of information (address, employment, health care coverage, etc.) that must be kept up to date. This obligation lasts until the alimony terminates.

To make a change, use the Change in Personal Information (FOC 108). Insert the new information in the form and file it with the friend of the court.

The duty to keep your personal information up to date may be affected by an opt-out from the friend of the court system. After a limited opt-out, you must still give the friend of the court updates because your case stays within the friend of the court system (see paragraph #3 of the Agreement Suspending Immediate Income Withholding (FOC 63) and Order Suspending Immediate Income Withholding (FOC 64) about this duty to notify after a limited opt-out).

With a total or partial opt-out, you must still give notice, in writing, of changes in your personal information within 21 days of a change. But the notice goes to your ex, not the friend of the court, which has been removed from your case. Paragraph #5 of the Uniform Spousal Support Order, No Friend of Court Services (FOC 10c) imposes this obligation and says which information must be updated. There's no form for this notice. Just make sure it's in writing and keep a copy for your records.

Original - Friend of the court
Copy - Filing party

CASE NO.

Telephone no.

Approved, SCAO

STATE OF MICHIGAN
JUDICIAL CIRCUIT
COUNTY

CHANGE IN PERSONAL INFORMATION

Friend of the court address

Please type or print information. Complete only those sections that apply. You can only file changes for yourself or those minor children of whom you have physical custody. Use another form when making changes for more than one person. **You must sign this form and send it to the friend of the court.**

☐ for party and minor child(ren)   ☒ for party only
☐ for minor child   no longer living with custodial parent

1. New Address and/or Telephone Number ___ Name

| Street address 4ol LAKE | State MI | Zip 48800 | Area code and telephone number |
| City LAKE CITY | | | |

I understand that by filing this change of address, it will be used to automatically update address information on any other child-support cases I have in Michigan. This change is effective for (check all that apply)

☒ all addresses you have listed for me.
☐ residence address only (where I live).
☐ an address that is confidential by court order and which remains confidential with this change.
☐ the single mailing address to which all notices and papers will be served.

2. Alternate Address
The court has entered an order making my address confidential under Michigan Court Rule 3.203(F). The following is an alternate address for the court, the friend of the court office, and the other party to use in serving me with notice and other court papers. I will retrieve all my mail regarding this case from this alternate address.

| Street address | City | State | Zip |

3. Name Change (Attach order changing name or certificate of marriage.)
New name

4. New Employer   ☐ Employer information is confidential by court order.

| Employer name | Street address | | Area code and telephone number |
| City | State | Zip | |

5. New Driver's License

| Issuing state | License number | Expiration date |

6. New Occupational License

| Issuing state | Type of occupation | License number | Expiration date |

7. New Social Security Number ☐ for you   ☐ for minor child ___ Name
Social security number

8. Health Care Insurance Provider

| Provider name | Provider address and telephone number | Group number | Policy number |

9. Other Information: (To be provided as ordered by the court.) (Attach separate sheet.)

	Social security number 380-1b-1010	Date of filing 10-31-90
Name of party filing the change (type or print) DARLENE A. LOVELACE	Name of other party (type or print) DUDLEY E. LOVELACE
Signature of party filing the change _Darlene A. Lovelace_	

FOC 108 (5/10) **CHANGE IN PERSONAL INFORMATION**

Appendices

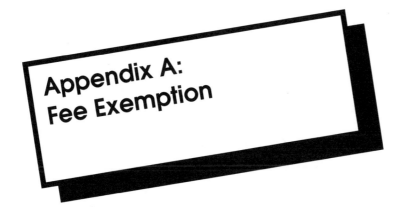

Appendix A:
Fee Exemption

Michigan law exempts some poor people from payment of the court fees of their divorces (see "How Much Will My Divorce Cost?" on page 29 for a description of these fees). If you qualify, you can get an exemption from payment of the filing and motion fees. You can also get an exemption from the service fee when you must use: 1) an official server (such as a sheriff for service by delivery; or a sheriff, policeman, or court officer for alternate service by posting) 2) publication for alternate service. Otherwise, you must pay the service fee yourself for service by mail or service by delivery using a commercial process server.

Who can qualify for a fee exemption? The court rules say that persons receiving "any form of public assistance" are automatically entitled to a fee exemption. According to instructions on the reverse of the exemption form (MC 20), public assistance includes any help from the Michigan Department of Human Services (DHS), including Medicaid (a joint state-federal program) and federal Supplemental Security Income (SSI). Public assistance doesn't include veterans or unemployment benefits.

In addition, the court rules say that indigent persons may qualify for fee exemptions. Indigent is just another word for poor. In Michigan, judges determine indigency on a case-by-case basis after they have reviewed applicants' financial information(income and assets versus obligations).

The fee exemption rules apply to all types of lawsuits, but there is a special rule for divorce cases. Although you and your spouse may be separated and financially independent, you're still treated as a family unit for fee exemption purposes. If you cannot pay the fees, but your spouse can, s/he may be ordered to pay them for you. If neither of you can pay the fees, because of: 1) receipt of public assistance 2) indigency, both of you are exempt from payment.

Obtaining a Fee Exemption

Obtaining a fee exemption is a two-step procedure: 1) initial suspension of fees when a divorce is filed 2) final waiver (or payment) of the fees at the end of the divorce. To get fees suspended initially, prepare the Affidavit section of the Waiver/Suspension of Fees and Costs (MC 20), and submit it to the clerk when you file your initial divorce papers.

A fee exemption request itself is a kind of motion for which a motion fee would normally be paid. However, the court rules say that no motion fee is due for fee exemption requests.

The clerk gives automatic fee exemptions to plaintiffs receiving public assistance. If you claim indigency, the clerk will pass the Waiver/Suspension of Fees and Costs (MC 20) onto the judge for review (the MC 20 should provide enough facts for the judge, but s/he could hold a hearing on the issue when the claim of indigency is in doubt). If the judge agrees that you're indigent, s/he will order a fee suspension at the bottom of the Waiver/Suspension of Fees and Costs (MC 20). A denial of your application would be indicated in the same place.

If your application is successful, you won't have to pay any fees during your divorce. However, the court will review your fee exemption at the end of the divorce. At that time, it will take another look at your financial condition and make a final decision about the fees.

During your testimony at the final hearing, you must mention that your fees were suspended at the beginning of the divorce. The judge will then re-examine your financial condition and either: 1) order you or your spouse to pay the fees 2) give you and your spouse a final waiver from payment of the fees. The same standards apply then as before; those on public assistance get an automatic exemption, while those claiming indigency must cite facts to prove it. To prove indigency, you should give extra testimony about your present financial condition.

Whatever the judge decides, you can provide for payment of the suspended fees (by you or the defendant) or a final fee waiver in paragraph #11 of the Judgment of Divorce (GRP 4a). Insert the amount of the suspended fees and check the correct box.

Approved, SCAO

| | Original - Court
1st copy - Applicant | 2nd copy - Friend of the court
(when applicable)
PROBATE JIS CODE: OSF |

STATE OF MICHIGAN
JUDICIAL DISTRICT
JUDICIAL CIRCUIT
COUNTY PROBATE

WAIVER/SUSPENSION OF FEES AND COSTS
(AFFIDAVIT AND ORDER)

CASE NO.

Court telephone no.

Court address

Plaintiff/Petitioner name   v   Defendant/Respondent name

Plaintiff's/Petitioner's attorney and bar no.   Defendant's/Respondent's attorney and bar no.

☐ Probate   In the matter of _____

NOTE: Requests for waiver/suspension of transcript costs or mediation fees must be made separately by motion.

COMPLETE 1a. IF YOU ARE RECEIVING PUBLIC ASSISTANCE

AFFIDAVIT

1. I ask the court to waive/suspend fees and costs for the following reason: (check either a or b)
☒ a. I am currently receiving public assistance: My DHS case number is VI 33609213 .
(MCR 2.002[C] requires the court to suspend payment of fees and costs.)

OR

☒ b. I am unable to pay fees and costs because of indigency, based on the following facts:
My average gross income is about $ 250 every ☒ week. ☐ two weeks. ☐ month.
☐ I am receiving unemployment benefits.
☐ I am not employed.
☐ I have a vehicle: Year: 1984 Make: DODGE Model: ARIES Amount Owed: $ 900
The total amount in all my bank accounts is: $ 1,000
Write down any other assets and how much they are worth. If you need more space, attach a separate sheet.

I pay $ 250 in rent/mortgage every month. I pay $ 100 in utilities (water, electricity, gas) every
month. I pay $ _____ for court-ordered child support. I pay $ _____ for court-ordered _____ .
Write down any other obligations and how much you pay. If you need more space, attach a separate sheet.

COMPLETE 1b. INSTEAD IF YOU ARE CLAIMING INDIGENCY

PRISONERS CLAIMING INDIGENCY SHOULD CHECK BOX 1b., SKIP REST OF THE SECTION, AND ATTACH CERTIFIED COPY OF THEIR INSTITUTIONAL ACCOUNT FOR PRIOR YEAR

2. The number of people living in my household is 1
☐ 3. I am signing this affidavit for a person who ☐ is a minor. ☐ has the following disability _____

Darlene A. Lovelace
Applicant signature
DARLENE A. LOVELACE
Name (type or print)

and sworn to before me on 2-28-89
Date

_____ County, Michigan.

ssion expires: 1-1-90 Signature: Loretta Smiley
Date   Deputy clerk/Register/Notary public

Notary public, State of Michigan, County of OJIBWAY

JUDGE WILL SUSPEND FEES OR DENY FEE SUSPENSION BELOW

ORDER

IT IS ORDERED:
☒ 1. The applicant has shown by ex parte affidavit that he/she is
☒ a. receiving public assistance, and payment of fees and costs are waived/suspended pursuant to M
☐ b. indigent and payment of fees and costs are waived/suspended pursuant to MCR 2.002(D).
The applicant is required to notify the court if the reason for waiving/suspending the fees and costs no l
☐ 2. The application is denied.

3-1-89   Lester Jubbs
Date   Judge

IF YOU MUST USE AN OFFICIAL SERVER, OR MUST GET ALTERNATE SERVICE BY PUBLICATION, EXPLAIN THAT ON A SHEET ATTACHED TO THIS FORM

MC 20 (8/12) **WAIVER/SUSPENSION OF FEES AND COSTS (AFFIDAVIT AND ORDER)**   MCR 2.002

JUDGE WILL DATE AND SIGN

Appendix B:
Alternate Service

The regular service methods of service by acknowledgment, mail and delivery are very effective when defendants are available for service. But if the defendant is hiding from service (an elusive defendant), or has disappeared entirely (a disappeared defendant), you must use another method of service.

Luckily, the court rules authorize alternate service on elusive and disappeared defendants. By using alternate service, your divorce can go ahead normally, just as if you had served the defendant by one of the regular service methods.

Forms of Alternate Service

Alternate service can take several forms including: 1) mailing 2) tacking (attaching papers to a door) 3) household delivery (delivering papers to an adult in the defendant's household) 4) publication (with or without an accompanying registered mailing) 5) posting (with or without an accompanying registered mailing) 6) any combination of #1-5 7) something completely different (by itself or in combination with any of #1-5).

The judge picks from among these options to devise a method of alternate service for the defendant. The method is designed to give the defendant *actual* notice of the divorce. But if the alternate service doesn't give actual notice, that's all right. Elusive and disappeared defendants are legally entitled to whatever notice alternate service provides, even if this means no actual notice.

When the defendant is elusive, the judge will probably order either mailing, tacking, household delivery or a combination of these. But these things won't work on disappeared defendants whose whereabouts are unknown. For them, judges normally order publication or posting. With either method, judges can order registered mailing of the service papers to the defendant's last known address. If that address appears to be outdated, the judge can skip the mailing and order publication or posting alone.

Whatever form alternate service takes, keep in mind that you cannot perform it yourself because you're disqualified from serving as a party to the divorce. Like regular service, you must have a server—a helper or professional server—to carry out alternate service. You can apply for and help with the alternate service, but the helper or server must serve the service papers for you (see "Preparing for Service" on page 70 for which papers make up your service papers).

Alternate Service for an Elusive Defendant

With an elusive defendant, you know his/her home and/or business address. Before you apply for alternate service, you must try service by delivery on the defendant at those or other places. For service by delivery, use the procedure described in "Service by Delivery" on page 74. Since the service will probably be difficult, use a professional server, such as a sheriff or commercial process server. Tell the server to attempt delivery not once but three or four times.

You must also ask the server to describe each attempt in the Verification of Process Server section of the Motion and Verification for Alternate Service (MC 303), which you should give to the server along with the service papers. The server's description of each delivery attempt must include specific information about the date, place and result of the attempt, as shown in the sample form at the end of this appendix.

If the server succeeds in serving the defendant during those attempts, you have obtained service on the defendant by delivery, and don't need alternate service. But if service by delivery fails, the server will return the service papers to you and you can apply for alternate service.

Make sure that the server has completed the Verification of Process Server section in the Motion and Verification for Alternate Service (MC 303), and then pay the server for the attempted service. You must complete the top portion of the Motion and Verification for Alternate Service (MC 303), above the verification section. Because you are trying to serve an elusive defendant, complete paragraph #2a of the motion showing that you know the defendant's current home and/or business address. You should also complete the caption and paragraph #1 of the Order for Alternate Service (MC 304), and return to the clerk with:

- Motion and Verification for Alternate Service   MC 303
  - original
  - one copy

- Order for Alternate Service   MC 304
  - original

- $20 motion fee

File the Motion and Verification for Alternate Service (MC 303) with the clerk. After filing, go to your judge's office and submit a copy of the Motion and Verification for Alternate Service (MC 303) and the original Order for Alternate Service (MC 304) to the judge's secretary. The judge will review your motion in his/her office (although probably not while you wait), so a court hearing on the motion won't be necessary. If the judge grants your motion for alternate service, get the papers back from the judge's office and make three photocopies of the Order for Alternate Service (MC 304). Return to the clerk and file the original.

Examine the Order for Alternate Service (MC 304) to see which method of alternate service the judge has designed for the defendant. It will probably be either mailing, tacking, household delivery or a combination of them. (If the judge has ordered several things, prepare multiple sets of the service papers and the Order for Alternate Service (MC 304) because you will need separate sets of these papers for each form of alternate service ordered.) However, the judge could order another method of alternate service, which would be described in paragraph #2d. If the judge orders publication or posting, see the sections on these below.

Mailing

For this type of mailing, ordinary first-class mailing is permissible. Have your helper or server mail the service papers and a copy of the Order for Alternate Service (MC 304) to the person named by the judge in paragraph #2a of the order. The recipient might be the defendant personally or a friend or relative of the defendant. The day of service is the day the mailing is sent, not received. After the mailing is sent, have the helper or server complete paragraph #1 in the Proof of Service section on the reverse of one of your copies of the Order for Alternate Service (MC 304).

Tacking

When tacking has been ordered, have your helper or server take the service papers and a copy of the Order for Alternate Service (MC 304) to the address indicated at paragraph #2b of the order, and attach them to the front door at this address. The day of service is the day the papers are tacked to the door. After tacking, the helper or server must complete paragraph #2 in the Proof of Service section on the reverse of the copy of the Order for Alternate Service (MC 304) that you're using to prove service.

Household Delivery

To use this service method, your helper or server takes the service papers and a copy of the Order for Alternate Service (MC 304) to the defendant's house and delivers them to any adult living there. The helper or server must also tell that person to give the papers to the defendant. The day of service is the day the papers are delivered to the person in defendant's household. After delivery, the helper or server must prove service on the reverse of your proof of service copy of the Order for Alternate Service (MC 304). In this case, proof of the household delivery is made in paragraph #3 in the Proof of Service section of that paper.

Proof of Service by Mailing, Tacking or Household Delivery

After service by mailing, tacking or household delivery has been proved on the reverse of a copy of the Order for Alternate Service (MC 304), make two copies of this paper and save one for filing later as your proof of service.

Alternate Service for a Disappeared Defendant

If you don't know the current home or business address of the defendant, you might be able to convince the court that the defendant has disappeared and obtain alternate service by publication or posting. But before you ask for that, you must prove the defendant's disappearance by searching for his/her current home and business addresses.

Your search will be shaped by the information you have about the defendant. If you don't know much, start with one of the general sources of information listed below, moving to specific sources as you find out more.

¶ *Telephone directories.* If you know the city where the defendant lives, look in the telephone book for that city. Many libraries keep large collections of telephone books. You can also get the same information by calling 411 for directory assistance (there is a fee for this service). For free directory assistance, go to a telephone directory Web site like www.switchboard.com, www.anywho.com or www.whitepages.com.

¶ *City/suburban directories* Libraries frequently have these "reverse" directories, such as Polk's and Bresser's, which cross-index names, addresses and telephone numbers in various ways (Polk: names, addresses and telephone numbers; Bresser: addresses and telephone numbers). So for example, if you have someone's telephone number, Polk's will give you that person's name and street address. Polk's is also online at www.citydirectory.com.

¶ *Internet.* The Internet has revolutionized searching for people. Some of the best ways are:

- *Search engines.* Look for items about the defendant on search engines like Google, Bing, Ask or multiple compiler engines like Dogpile. If s/he has a common name, put the name inside quotation marks or you'll get too much unsorted information. Also, try variations in the first name. Search via several search engines because they have different data.

- *Social media.* Check Facebook, Twitter, MySpace, LinkedIn or other social media sites.

- *People search sites.* There are specialized people search sites like ZabaSearch.com or Intelius.com offering free or fee-based search packages.

¶ *News database.* The defendant may have been in the news recently. Check the Web site of the newspaper(s) in the defendant's area. Nexis (also available through Lexis) compiles a lot of this material. Nexis is expensive to subscribe to, but some libraries offer free access. Factiva is another service with similar data.

¶ *Motor vehicle records.* Like most states, Michigan provides information about licensed drivers and vehicle registration/ownership (title). This information isn't given out as freely as it used to be (you once could get it over the telephone). Now you have to submit an application and have a good reason to receive the information.

In Michigan, driver's license and motor vehicle registration/ownership information is available from the Secretary of State's record lookup service. Call (517) 322-1624 and ask for a record request form. Information is also available at www.michigan.gov/sos, then to Other Business Services, to Driving and Vehicle Record Request, to Requesting a Driving or Vehicle Record, to Requesting Another Person's Record. You can download a record request form from this site. In sec. 4D of the request form, say that you are making the request in connection with a civil proceeding. The fee is $7 for each record lookup.

In other states, record lookup requests are typically handled by department of motor vehicles (DMV) offices. The Johnson and Knox book lists these offices nationwide. Or go to www.dmv-department-of-motor-vehicles.com for links to every state DMV.

¶ *Voter registration.* If the defendant is registered to vote, you can obtain address information from the voting registrar, which is the city or township clerk in Michigan.

¶ *Real property records.* The defendant may have been involved in a real property transaction as a seller, buyer, mortgagor (mortgage-borrower), etc. You can get this information from:

- *County register of deeds.* At the register of deeds office there are indexes listing sellers or mortgagors (grantors) and buyers (grantees) of property. Some counties have put this information online; try the Web site of the county where you think the defendant's real property is located.

- Several private Internet companies provide real property information nationwide:
  Public Records Online at www.netronline.com/public_records.htm
  Search Systems at www.searchsystems.net

¶ *Association memberships.* If you know or believe the defendant is engaged in a trade or profession or belongs to a trade, professional or social organization, contact the organization for information.

- *Association directories.* These directories list associations which may have directories of members:
  Directories in Print, 35th ed., Detroit: Thomson Gale, 2013
  Encyclopedia of Associations, Detroit: Thomson Gale; available in international, national and state and local editions
  National Trade and Professional Associations Directory, Buck Downs, et al., eds., Bethesda, MD: Columbia Books, and the *State and Regional Associations Directory,* various eds.

¶ *State licensing bureau.* In Michigan, 33 trades and professions are regulated by the Bureau of Commercial Services. You can find out if someone is licensed to practice a trade or profession in the state by calling the bureau's licensing verification unit at (517) 241-9288, or go to www.michigan.gov/lara, then to Online Services, to Verify a License/Registration.

¶ *School directories.* If the defendant is a student or faculty member at a school, get the school directory.

Has the defendant graduated from a school? Schools, especially colleges and universities, keep extensive data on their alumni. Contact the school directly for information or try www.alumni.net. Classmates.com and Reunion.com provide alumni information about their millions of registered members.

¶ *Contact friends, relatives, etc.* Contact the defendant's friends, relatives, former neighbors, landlords and employers to see if they know where s/he is now.

¶ *Postal search.* The U.S. Postal Service has discontinued the release of change-of-address information. But you can often get the equivalent by:

1) Sending a first-class letter to the defendant's last known address. On the envelope, put your return address and just below that write: "Do not forward—Address correction requested"

2) If the defendant has an active change-of-address card on file (they last for one year), the letter will come back to you with the defendant's new address.

The defendant may have special characteristics or circumstances which will influence the search.

¶ *Military servicemember.* If the defendant is an active-duty servicemember, reservist or veteran, there are special ways to search for the defendant. See "Divorcing a Defendant-Servicemember" on page 154 in Appendix D for more about locating active-duty servicemembers. The Johnson and Knox book on locating military personnel cited in that section also has tips on locating reservists and veterans.

¶ *Prisoner.* Do you know or suspect the defendant is an inmate at a state or federal prison? If you do, see "What If My Spouse or I Am Imprisoned?" on page 27 for more about finding prisoners through state or federal prison locator services.

¶ *Overseas resident.* The U.S. Department of State has visa information about expatriates, but normally can't release the information without a privacy waiver from the expat. You can call the state department's Overseas Citizens Services office at (888) 407-4747 and see what information about the defendant is available.

If you know the foreign country where the defendant is residing, call the American Citizen Service section of the U.S. embassy or consulate in that country and see if it can help (they sometimes have public domain telephone books or directories for finding people). Or you can try to locate the defendant yourself using Infobel.com, an international telephone directory.

¶ *Professional search.* If you can afford it, hire a private investigator to find the defendant. They have access to special databases which are very effective. The cost is around $30-200 to do a basic search of five databases. For a PI in your area, look in the yellow pages or ask for a referral from:

Michigan Council of Private Investigators
(800) 266-6274
www.mcpihome.com

National Association of Investigative Specialists
(512) 719-3595
www.pimail.com/nais

During your search for the defendant, keep a written record of when and what you did. For example, if you contact relatives or friends of the defendant, record the date, person with whom you spoke and what s/he said. Keep any written evidence of your attempts to find the defendant, such as return-to-sender letters to him/her or correspondence with others about the defendant's disappearance. All this information is valuable because you will use it later when you apply for alternate service.

If you find the defendant's home and/or business address during your search, attempt service on him/her using one of the regular service methods.* But if you cannot locate the defendant, the failure will show that the defendant has disappeared, allowing you to apply for alternate service by publication or posting.

Complete the top portion of the Motion and Verification for Alternate Service (MC 303) above the Verification of Process Server section, which you can leave blank. Since you're trying to serve a disappeared defendant, complete paragraph #2b of the motion saying that you don't know the defendant's current home and business addresses.

After you complete the Motion and Verification for Alternate Service (MC 303), attach any written materials (undelivered letters, correspondence with the defendant's friends and relatives, etc.) showing that you failed to discover the defendant's whereabouts. Then complete the caption and first two lines of the Order for Service by Publication/Posting and Notice of Action (MC 307). After you prepare these papers, return to the clerk with:

- Motion and Verification for Alternate Service   MC 303
    - original
    - one copy

- Order for Service by Publication/Posting and Notice   MC 307
  of Action
    - original

- $20 motion fee

File the Motion and Verification for Alternate Service (MC 303) with the clerk. After filing, go to your judge's office and submit a copy of the Motion and Verification for Alternate Service (MC 303) and the original Order for Service by Publication/Posting and Notice of Action (MC 307) to the judge's secretary. The judge will review your motion in his/her office (although probably not while you wait), so a court hearing on the motion won't be necessary. If the judge grants your motion for alternate service, get the papers back from the judge's office and make two photocopies of the Order for Service by Publication/Posting and Notice of Action (MC 307). Return to the clerk and file the original.

Examine the Order for Service by Publication/Posting and Notice of Action (MC 307) to see which method of alternate service the judge has devised for the defendant. It's probably either publication (paragraph #2) or posting (paragraph #3), and possibly a registered mailing (paragraph #4). If registered mailing has been ordered, make an extra photocopy of the Order for Service by Publication/Posting and Notice of Action (MC 307).

---

*   If you discover the defendant's current home or business address, but fail to have him/her served there, see above on serving an elusive defendant.

If the judge has ordered publication as the alternate service in your case, you must publish a legal advertisement in a newspaper. Maybe you have seen fine-print legal advertisements in your local newspaper. This is the kind of ad you must have published.

The court rules say that the legal advertisement must be published in a newspaper in the county where the defendant resides when you know the defendant's residence. If you don't know where the defendant is residing, the court rules permit advertisement in the county where the case is filed. Since your defendant has disappeared, you can advertise in the county where you filed for divorce, which is probably your county.

See which newspaper the judge has chosen as the publisher of your advertisement in paragraph #2 of the Order for Service by Publication/Posting and Notice of Action (MC 307). Take/send a copy of the MC 307 to that newspaper and ask it to prepare a legal advertisement for you. The newspaper will create an advertisement using the caption and paragraph #1 of the Order for Service by Publication/Posting and Notice of Action (MC 307). It will publish the advertisement as instructed in paragraph #2 of the order. Ordinarily, publication must be once a week for three consecutive weeks.

Once the advertisement has been published the required number of times, the newspaper will bill you for the cost of publication. After you pay the bill, the newspaper will complete the Affidavit of Publishing on the reverse of the copy of the Order for Service by Publication/Posting and Notice of Action (MC 307) that you gave it and return this paper to you.

If the defendant's last known address is out of date, the judge will probably omit registered mailing of the service papers to the defendant. But if the defendant's last known address is fairly recent, registered mailing may be required.

If the judge has ordered registered mailing, have a helper mail the service papers and a copy of the Order for Service by Publication/Posting and Notice of Action (MC 307) to the defendant at his/her last known address. This mailing must be by registered (not certified) mail, return receipt requested. The mailing must be sent sometime before the date of the last publication of the legal advertisement.

Afterward, have your helper complete the Affidavit of Mailing on the reverse of a copy of the Order for Service by Publication/Posting and Notice of Action (MC 307), and attach both the Receipt for Registered Mail (PS Form 3806) and the Domestic Return Receipt (PS Form 3811), signed or unsigned by the defendant, to it. Your helper can use the Affidavit of Mailing on the same copy of the Order for Service by Publication/Posting and Notice of Action (MC 307) that the newspaper used to prove publication, or you can use another copy. Either way, make two copies of the reverse of the order(s) and save one for filing later as your proof of service.

More Information

The cost of a legal advertisement depends on the size of the ad and frequency of publication. Since you really only need to publish the caption and paragraph #1 of the Order for Service by Publication/Posting and Notice of Action (MC 307), your advertisement should not be very large. The newspaper may want to print the entire order, but that is unnecessary and will cost you more.

Your advertisement will probably be published three times. In that case, there is a minimum charge of $59 (adjusted annually for inflation), but the cost will probably be slightly more, perhaps $60-100.

Posting

Judges seem to prefer publication as the method of alternate service for disappeared defendants, and posting is seldom ordered. But if posting was ordered in your Order for Service by Publication/Posting and Notice of Action (MC 307), look at paragraph #3 to see who was designated as the poster. That person might be a sheriff, policeman or court official, such as a bailiff. Take four copies of the Order for Service by Publication/Posting and Notice of Action (MC 307) to the person designated as the poster and request posting of the order.

The poster will post the order in the courthouse and the two other public places the court has specified in paragraph #3. Ordinarily, the order will remain posted for three consecutive weeks. After the posting period expires, the poster will bill you for posting services and prove the posting in the Affidavit of Posting on the reverse of the extra copy of the Order for Service by Publication/Posting and Notice of Action (MC 307).

Like alternate service by publication, alternate service by posting can be with or without registered mailing of the service papers to the defendant. If the judge has ordered registered mailing in paragraph #4 of the Order for Service by Publication/Posting and Notice of Action (MC 307), have your helper mail the service papers and a copy of the MC 307 to the defendant at his/her last known address. This mailing should be made by registered (not certified) mail, return receipt requested. The mailing must be sent sometime before the last week of the posting.

Afterward, have your helper complete the Affidavit of Mailing on the reverse of a copy of the Order for Service by Publication/Posting and Notice of Action (MC 307), and attach both the Receipt for Registered Mail (PS Form 3806) and the Domestic Return Receipt (PS Form 3811), signed or unsigned by the defendant, to it. Your helper can complete the Affidavit of Mailing on the same copy of the Order for Service by Publication/Posting and Notice of Action (MC 307) that the poster used to prove posting, or you can use another copy. Either way, make two copies of the reverse of the order(s) and save one for filing later as your proof of service.

Original - Court
1st copy - Serving Party
2nd copy - Extra

Approved, SCAO

STATE OF MICHIGAN	MOTION AND VERIFICATION	CASE NO.
JUDICIAL DISTRICT JUDICIAL CIRCUIT COUNTY PROBATE	FOR ALTERNATE SERVICE	Court telephone no.

Court address

Plaintiff name(s), address(es), and telephone no(s).

v

Defendant name(s), address(es), and telephone no(s).

In the matter of _____ DUDLEY E. LOVELACE _____ cannot reasonably be made

> COMPLETE 2b. INSTEAD FOR A DISAPPEARED DEFENDANT

1. Service of process upon as otherwise provided in MCR 2.105, as shown in the following verification of process server.

2. Defendant's last known home and business addresses are:

900 S. MAPLE	LAKE CITY	MI	48
Home address	City	State	
1000 SERVICE RD.	"	"	
Business address	City	State	

a. I believe the ☒ home ☒ business address shown above is current.

b. I do not know the defendant's current ☒ home ☒ business address. I have made the following efforts to ascertain the current

> COMPLETE 2a. FOR AN ELUSIVE DEFENDANT

address: 3-4-89 SEARCHED TELEPHONE AND CITY DIRECTORIES/3-7-89 REQUESTED ADDRESS CORRECTION FROM USPS/3-7-89 DID RECORD LOOKUP AT MICHIGAN SECRETARY OF STATE/3-7-89 WROTE TO MABEL LOVELACE (MOTHER) (SEE ATTACHED LETTER); ALL WITHOUT RESULTS.

3. I request the court order service by alternate means.

I declare that the statements above are true to the best of my information, knowledge and belief.

3-15-89
Date

Darlene A. Lovelace
Plaintiff/Plaintiff's attorney signature

DARLENE A. LOVELACE
Name (type or print)   Bar no.

Address

City, state, zip   Telephone no.

VERIFICATION OF PROCESS SERVER

1. I have tried to serve process on this defendant as described: State date, place, and what occurred on each occasion

3-4-89 TRIED TO SERVE DEFENDANT AT 900 S. MAPLE, LAKE CITY, MI, BUT A WOMAN THERE TOLD ME DEFENDANT WAS NOT AT HOME WHEN IT APPEARED HE WAS.

3-5-89 " " " "

3-7-89 TRIED TO SERVE DEFENDANT AT 1000 SERVICE RD, LAKE CITY, MI, BUT HIS EMPLOYER PREVENTED SERVICE.

3-8-89 TRIED TO SERVE DEFENDANT AT 1000 SERVICE RD, LAKE CITY, MI, BUT HE SPED AWAY IN HIS CAR.

I declare that the statements above are true to the best of my information, knowledge and belief.

3-14-89
Date

Chester Gunn
Signature

CHESTER GUNN
Process server (type or print)

MCR 2.105

> SERVER MUST COMPLETE VERIFICATION OF PROCESS SERVER FOR ATTEMPTED SERVICE ON AN ELUSIVE DEFENDANT

...N AND V...ATION FOR ALTERNATE SERVICE

Approved, SCAO

STATE OF MICHIGAN		
JUDICIAL DISTRICT		Original - Court 1st copy - Defendant 2nd copy - Plaintiff 3rd copy - Return
JUDICIAL CIRCUIT	ORDER REGARDING ALTERNATE SERVICE	CASE NO.
COUNTY PROBATE		
Court address		

Court telephone no.

Plaintiff name(s), address(es), and telephone no(s).

v

Defendant name(s), address(es), and telephone no(s).

Plaintiff's attorney, bar no., address, and telephone no.

THE COURT FINDS:

☒ 1. Service of process upon the defendant, _DUDLEY E. LOVELACE_

cannot reasonably be made as provided in   ☒ MCR 2.105   ☐ MCR 2.107(B)(1)(b) _____ and service of p

may be made in a manner that is reasonably calculated to give the defendant actual notice of the proceedings and an opp

to be heard.

IT IS ORDERED:

☒ 2. Service of the   ☒ summons and complaint

and a copy of this order shall be made by the following method(s).   ☐ other: _____

☒ a. First-class mail to _900 S. MAPLE, LAKE CITY, MI_

☒ b. Tacking or firmly affixing to the door at _____ "

☒ c. Delivering at _____ "

to a member of the defendant's household who is of suitable age and discretion to receive process, with instructions to

deliver it promptly to the defendant.

☐ d. Other: _____

_____

For each method used, proof of service must be filed promptly with the court.

☐ 3. The motion for alternate service is denied.

_3-17-89_
Date

Lester Jubbs
Judge

Bar no.

MC 304 (9/09)   **ORDER REGARDING ALTERNATE SERVICE**

MCR 2.103, MCR 2.105

(handwritten note callout: LIST ANY OTHER SERVICE PAPERS HERE)

(handwritten note callout: JUDGE WILL CHOOSE ONE OR MORE OF THESE METHODS)

A MICHIGAN COURT OFFICER CARRYING OUT SERVICE WILL USE THE OFFICER CERTIFICATE

DAY OF SERVICE

HELPER/SERVER MUST PROVE EVERY SERVICE METHOD ORDERED AND USED

IF SEVERAL SERVICE METHODS WERE USED ON DIFFERENT DAYS, USE LAST DAY AS DAY OF SERVICE (3-20-89 IN THIS CASE)

ORDER REGARDING ALTERNATE SERVICE
Case No.

PROOF OF SERVICE

TO PROCESS SERVER: You must serve the copies of the order regarding alternate service and file proof of service with the court clerk. If you are unable to complete service, you must return this original and all copies to the court clerk.

CERTIFICATE / AFFIDAVIT OF SERVICE / NONSERVICE

☐ OFFICER CERTIFICATE

I certify that I am a sheriff, deputy sheriff, bailiff, appointed court officer, or attorney for a party (MCR 2.104[A][2]), and that: (notarization not required)

OR

☒ AFFIDAVIT OF PROCESS SERVER

Being first duly sworn, I state that I am a legally competent adult who is not a party or an officer of a corporate party, and that: (notarization required)

I served a copy of the ☒ summons and complaint ☐ other:

and a copy of the order for alternate service upon DUDLEY E. LOVELACE _____ by

☒ 1. First-class mail to _900 S. MAPLE, LAKE CITY, MI_ , on _SAT. 3-18-89_ .
Date

☒ 2. Tacking or firmly affixing to the door at _____ " , on _SAT. 3-18-89_ .
Date

☒ 3. Delivering at _____ " , on _MON. 3-20-89_ .
Date

[...] age and discretion to receive process, w[...] instructions to deliver

to a member of the [...]

it promptly to the defe[...] , on _____
Date

☐ 4. Other: _____
specify

I declare that the statements ab[...] information, knowledge, and belief.

Ruth Darling
Signature
RUTH DARLING
Name (type or print)

Title

Service fee	Miles traveled	Fee	
$		$	TOTAL FEE
Incorrect address fee	Miles traveled	Fee	$
$		$	

Subscribed and sworn to before me on _3-21-89_ _OJIBWAY_ County, Michigan.
Date

My commission expires: _1-1-90_ Signature: _Loretta Smiley_
Date   Deputy court clerk/Notary public

Notary public, State of Michigan, County of _OJIBWAY_

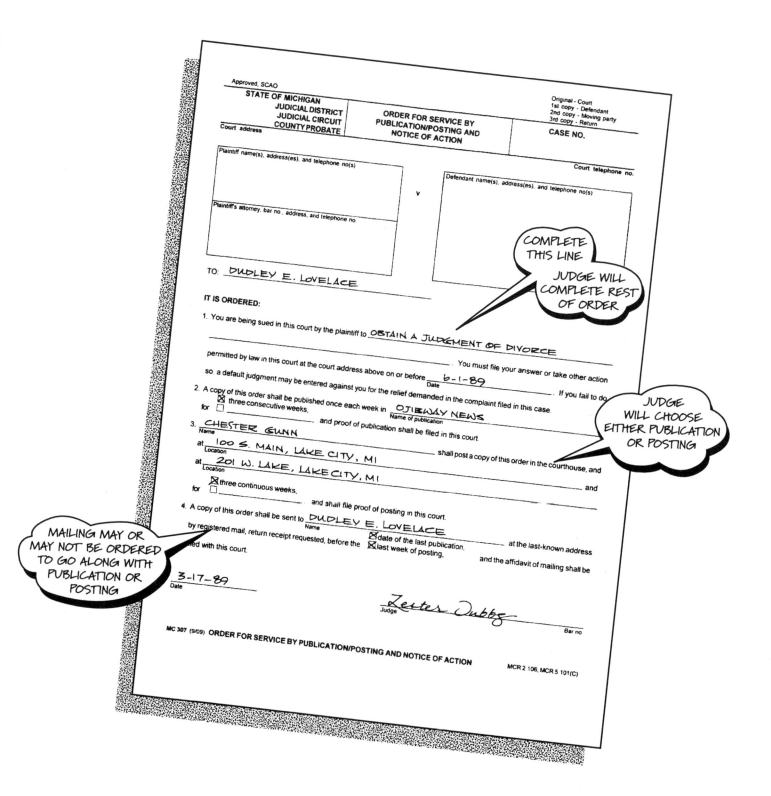

AFFIDAVIT OF PUBLISHING

Attach copy of publication here.

Name of ☒ publisher ☐ agent of publisher
ELTON BEAN

County where published
OJIBWAY

Name of newspaper
OJIBWAY NEWS

This newspaper is a qualified newspaper. The order for service was published in this newpaper at least once each week for three consecutive weeks on these dates:

3-25-89, 4-1-89, 4-8-89

4-15-89   *Elton Bean*
Date   Affiant signature

Subscribed and sworn to before me on 4-15-89   OJIBWAY   County, Michigan
                                      Date

commission expires: 1-1-90   Signature: *Loretta Smiley*
                    Date   Court clerk/Notary public

Notary public, State of Michigan, County of OJIBWAY

NEWSPAPER WILL ATTACH A COPY OF THE ADVERTISEMENT

POSTER WILL COMPLETE

NEWSPAPER WILL COMPLETE

AFFIDAVIT OF POSTING

I have posted this order in a conspicuous place in the OJIBWAY COUNTY courthouse and the following places as ordered by this court: 100 S. MAIN AND 201 W. LAKE, LAKE CITY, MI

It has been posted for ☒ three continuous weeks ☐ _____ continuous weeks as ordered by this court.

4-15-89   *Chester Gunn*
Date   Affiant signature

Subscribed and sworn to before me on 4-15-89   OJIBWAY   County, Michigan.
                                      Date

My commission expires: 1-1-90   Signature: *Loretta Smiley*
                       Date   Court clerk/Notary public

Notary public, State of Michigan, County of OJIBWAY

AFFIDAVIT OF MAILING

Attach mailing receipt and return receipt

ATTACH BOTH PS FORM 3806 AND PS FORM 3811

As ordered, on 3-18-89   I mailed a copy of the summons and complaint
               Date

and this order to DUDLEY E. LOVELACE
                  Name

at 900 S. MAPLE, LAKE CITY, MI
   Address

The mailing receipt and return receipt are attached at right.

3-18-89   *Ruth Darling*
Date   Affiant signature

Subscribed and sworn to before me on 3-18-89   OJIBWAY   County, Michigan.
                                      Date

commission expires: 1-1-90   Signature: *Loretta Smiley*
                    Date   Court clerk/Notary public

Notary public, State of Michigan, County of OJIBWAY

HELPER/SERVER WHO PERFORMED REGISTERED MAILING MUST COMPLETE

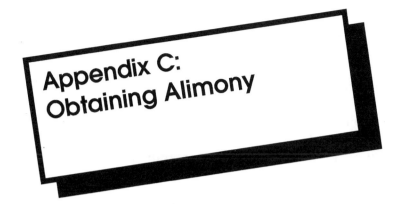

Appendix C: Obtaining Alimony

If you and the defendant have agreed on the payment of alimony, you must take several extra steps described in this appendix. At the beginning of your divorce, you must ask for alimony in paragraph #8c of your Complaint for Divorce (GRP 1),* and then show: 1) your need for the alimony 2) the defendant's ability to pay it. If you omit this request, you may not be able to get alimony later.

Alimony and the Friend of the Court

The friend of the court is a family court official with a number of duties in divorce cases. In cases with minor children, the friend of the court investigates and makes recommendations to the judge about divorce issues, referees and mediates disputes, reviews, modifies and enforces orders. The friend of the court used to collect and distribute support (child support and alimony), but these duties have been transferred to a new financial agency in Lansing, the state disbursement unit (SDU). Today, support payments are funneled through the SDU, which distributes the support to recipients all over the state.

    The friend of the court isn't normally involved in divorce cases without minor children. However, the friend of the court is supposed to take part in no-children cases *whenever alimony is sought*. Despite this rule, these days the friend of the court doesn't always participate in alimony cases, thanks to a law passed in 2002.

---

*   As mentioned in "Alimony" on page 11, the divorce papers call alimony by its real name: spousal support.

Friend of the Court: In or Out of Your Divorce Case?

According to the 2002 law, it's now possible to "opt out" of the friend of the court system. After opting out, the friend of the court never enters the case (for an opt-out from a new case) or withdraws from the case and closes its file (after an opt-out from an open case).

Is an opt-out worth considering? If your divorce is amicable with a willing and reliable alimony-payer, it may make sense. But don't underestimate the value of the friend of the court when alimony or other support is at stake. The friend of the court performs an important bookkeeping function, keeping track of support payments. Without a neutral third party like the friend of the court, it's one party's word against the other when a dispute breaks out. In this way, a dispute over payment of alimony could escalate, turning a once amicable divorce into a bitter one.

Staying in the Friend of the Court System

If you want to remain in the friend of the court system, add the friend of the court to your case by taking the following extra steps:

Notice to the friend of the court. The friend of the court must receive notice of your divorce by getting copies of all your divorce papers. To do that, make extra copies of the divorce papers (generally three instead of two) and mark the upper left corners of the copies with the notation "FOC." As you file your divorce papers with the clerk, give the extra marked copies to the clerk. The clerk will forward these to the friend of the court.

Information for the friend of the court. Although the divorce papers provide a good deal of information about your marriage, the friend of the court needs more personal and financial information. The friend of the court gets that extra information in the Verified Statement and Application for IV-D Services (FOC 23). This paper must be given to the clerk along with your initial divorce papers when you file for divorce. Unlike most other divorce papers, the clerk doesn't place the FOC 23 in your case file. Instead, the clerk forwards the statement to the friend of the court, without keeping a copy for itself. However, a copy of the Verified Statement and Application for IV-D Services (FOC 23) must be included in your service papers and served on the defendant.

A similar friend-of-the-court-only information form, the Domestic Relations Judgment Information form (FOC 100) is also filed at the end of a divorce when alimony is sought.

Friend of the court pamphlet. While you're at the clerk's office filing your divorce, ask the clerk for two copies of the friend of the court pamphlet. The pamphlet describes the office of the friend of the court and its role in divorce. Keep one pamphlet for yourself. The other must be served on the defendant with the service papers. After service, list the friend of the court pamphlet in the proof of service as having been served on the defendant.

Because you aren't contesting alimony, the friend of the court probably won't intervene in your divorce. But it could decide to investigate alimony and submit a recommendation to the judge on the issue. If so, you should take the recommendation into account when you prepare the alimony (spousal support) order in your final divorce papers. Some counties may also want the friend of the court to review and approve the final divorce papers when alimony is at stake.

Whatever happens, see "Alimony Provisions" in Appendix F for more about the special steps that must be taken to provide for short- or long-term alimony in your divorce judgment.

Opting Out of the Friend of the Court System

Opting out of the friend of the court system takes more than just notifying the friend of the court. There are in fact three types of opt-outs. And there are several restrictions on opting out, and automatic triggers for bringing cases back under friend of the court control.

Types of Opt-Outs

The 2002 opt-out law allows several kinds of opt-outs from the friend of the court system:

- *total* opt-out from all friend of the court services
- *partial* opt-out from all friend of the court services except collection and distribution of support through the state disbursement unit (SDU) (with or without immediate income withholding as the method of payment)
- *limited* opt-out from immediate income withholding only, but receipt of all other friend of the court services

Total Opt-Out

In some cases, you can opt out of the friend of the court system completely, giving up all friend of the court services in your divorce. Afterward, you are responsible for all future management of your case, including payment of alimony (you lose SDU-payment of alimony with a total opt-out). You must have the consent of the defendant to get (and keep) a total opt-out. And the judge must review and approve your opt-out request, which must be granted if the case is eligible for opting out (see below).

The timing of an opt-out is important. You can get a total opt-out at the beginning of a divorce (new case) or later while the case is pending (open case). The procedures for new- and open-case opt-outs are a little different, and these are described below.

Total Opt-Out in a New Case

You can opt out of a new-filed case, so the friend of the court never enters the case and never opens a file for the case. Not every case is eligible for this kind of opt-out. The opt-out law bars opting out of a new case when:

- a party is eligible for DHS services (services from the Michigan Department of Human Services; also known as title IV-D services) because of past or current receipt of public assistance
- a party is applying for DHS services
- a party requests friend of the court services
- there is evidence of 1) domestic violence, or 2) uneven bargaining position between the parties; and evidence that a party is opting out against the best interests of that party or any children
- the parties have not signed and filed a FOC 101, showing consent to the opt-out

If your case is eligible for opting out, you must request an opt-out at the start of your divorce, when you file. As you prepare your initial divorce papers (see "Filing" on page 63 for more about preparing these papers), make additions to one of these papers:

- Complaint for Divorce (GRP 1), in paragraph #8d check the "other relief" box, and then in the blank space insert: "I request an opt-out from all friend of the court services" (total opt-out)

You must also prepare two extra papers, which will be referred to as the opt-out papers:

- Advice of Rights Regarding Use of   FOC 101   2
  Friend of the Court Services

- Order Exempting Case from Friend of the   FOC 102   2
  Court Services

The FOC 101 warns you which services you lose by opting out. You and the defendant must receive separate copies of the FOC 101, and both of you must date and sign the original form, which will be filed with court. This tells the court that both parties consent to the opt-out.

The FOC 102 is the actual opt-out order. You select a total opt-out by leaving both boxes at paragraph #13a and b unchecked. The sample form shows you how to do this. Afterward, paperclip the signed FOC 101 to the FOC 102.

After you file your divorce, you must bring the opt-out request to the judge right away. By acting quickly, you can keep the friend of the court out of the case before it opens a file. The best way is to take your (unfiled) opt-out papers to the judge's office and ask the judge's secretary or law clerk to pass these onto the judge for review.

If the judge approves an opt-out, file the opt-out papers with the clerk (the friend of the court won't get copies since it has dropped out of the case), and serve another set of copies on the defendant with the service papers (see "Service" on page 69 for more about service). After receiving a denial (because of no consent from the defendant, ineligibility of the case for opting out or some other irregularity), you must withdraw your opt-out papers and the judge will note the denial on the Complaint for Divorce (GRP 1) or in the case file.

After a total opt-out, the friend of the court won't participate in your case. As a result, skip all the extra steps and papers (such as the FOC 23 and FOC 100) involving the friend of the court described in "Staying in the Friend of the Court System" above and "Alimony Provisions" on page 172 in Appendix F.

As the divorce continues, you may change your mind and want the friend of the court back in your case. All you have to do is submit a simple written request to the friend of the court; no motion is necessary. You can use the Request to Reopen Friend of the Court Case (FOC 104) for this purpose. The friend of the court will also intervene on its own when: 1) either party requests friend of the court services 2) a party applies for public assistance.

At the end of the divorce, you must decide whether you want the friend of the court in or out of your case during the after-divorce (called the post-judgment) period. During this time, which lasts until the alimony terminates, the friend of the court provides services for modification and enforcement of the divorce judgment (the FOC 101 has a good summary of these post-judgment duties).

If you still want the friend of the court out of the case, you must say so in your final divorce papers. Ordinarily, the opt-out order would expire according to paragraph #10 of the Judgment of Divorce (GRP 4a), as a nonfinal order. But you can extend the opt-out order in the blank space at paragraph #8 of the Uniform Spousal Support Order, No Friend of Court Services (FOC 10c) (this is the special alimony order used in total or partial opt-out cases), as follows:

> The previsously-ordered opt-out of this case from all friend of the court services shall remain in effect. Spousal support shall be paid directly to the payee without immediate income withholding.

Omit the Order Regarding Income Withholding (FOC 5) from your final divorce papers because this is unnecessary. Also, explain the opt-out to the judge during your testimony at the final hearing.

If you want the friend of the court back in your case post-judgment, you could file a Request to Reopen Friend of the Court Case (FOC 104) before the hearing. Or you could let paragraph #10 of the Judgment of Divorce (GRP 4a) terminate the prior total opt-out as a nonfinal order. This will reinstate friend of the court services and the normal method of alimony payment specified by the Uniform Spousal Support Order (FOC 10b) (use this instead of the FOC 10c, which is the opt-out version of the order): payment by immediate income withholding to the SDU. With this payment method back in place, you will also need the Order Regarding Income Withholding (FOC 5).

There's yet another choice: You want to change the opt-out, switching from a total opt-out to a partial or limited one. For a partial opt-out, see "Partial Opt-Out" for general information and "Partial Opt-Out in an Open Case" below about the steps for opting out at the end of a divorce. Likewise, see "Limited Opt-Out" and "Limited Opt-Out in an Open Case" below about limited opt-outs.

To switch opt-outs, let the previous opt-out order expire as a nonfinal order, as described above. Then provide for the different type of opt-out (partial or limited) as described in the relevant open-case section below.

Total Opt-Out in an Open Case

The friend of the court may have participated in your case while it was pending. But now you want to opt out totally from the friend of the court system for the after-divorce (called the post-judgment) period. It's possible to have the friend of the court withdraw from the case and close its file that way with the consent of the defendant and approval of the court, which must be granted if the case is eligible for opting out.

Not every open divorce case is eligible for total opt out. Like a new case, there are several open-case restrictions which are similar to but not the same as the ones for a new case:

- a party objects to opting out
- a party is eligible to receive DHS services (services from the Michigan Department of Human Services; also known as title IV-D services) because the party receives public assistance
- a party is eligible to receive DHS services because the party received public assistance and an arrearage is owed to the state
- no support arrearage or custody or parenting time order violation (for cases with children) has occurred in the last 12 months
- neither party has reopened a friend of the court case during the last 12 months
- there is evidence of 1) domestic violence, or 2) uneven bargaining position between the parties; and evidence that a party is opting out against the best interests of that party or any children
- the parties have not signed and filed a FOC 101, showing consent to the opt-out

If you want to opt out late in your case, the final hearing, when the divorce judgment is granted, is a convenient time. Otherwise, you must file a separate motion and schedule a hearing on your request. Before the final hearing, prepare two extra opt-out papers:

- Advice of Rights Regarding Use of   FOC 101   2
  Friend of the Court Services

- Order Exempting Case from Friend of the   FOC 102   2
  Court Services

The FOC 101 warns you which services you lose by opting out. You and the defendant must receive separate copies of the form, and both of you must date and sign the original form which will be filed with the court. This tells the court that both parties consent to the opt-out.

The FOC 102 is the actual opt-out order. You select a total opt-out by leaving both boxes at paragraph #13a and b unchecked. The sample form shows you how to make the correct choice. Afterward, paperclip the signed FOC 101 to the FOC 102.

You must also prepare your final divorce papers to go along with a total opt-out. You will use the Uniform Spousal Support Order, No Friend of Court Services (FOC 10c), which is the special opt-out version of the uniform spousal support order. At paragraph #8 of the FOC 10c, add an alimony payment provisions like this:

> Spousal support shall be paid directly to the payee without immediate income withholding.

Omit the Order Regarding Income Withholding (FOC 5) from your final divorce papers because this is unnecessary.

During the final hearing, include the FOC 101 and 102 among your final divorce papers (see "Final Hearing" on page 91 for more about preparing, filing and sending the final divorce papers to the defendant after the divorce). In your testimony, say that you want to opt out. It's also helpful to have the defendant on hand to confirm the opt-out; but the defendant's signing the FOC 101 is sufficient to show consent.

If the judge denies your opt-out request, replace the Uniform Spousal Support Order, No Friend of Court Services (FOC 10c) with the Uniform Spousal Support Order (FOC 10b) as your alimony order. The substitution will make alimony payable by immediate income withholding to the SDU. You will also need the FOC 5.

After opting out, the friend of the court won't help with any judgment modification or enforcement during the post-judgment period. But if you want the friend of the court back in, just file the Request to Reopen Friend of the Court Case (FOC 104). The friend of the court will also re-enter the case automatically if: 1) either party requests friend of the court services 2) a party applies for public assistance.

Partial Opt-Out

Ordinarily, when you opt-out totally from the friend of the court system you give up all friend of the court services, including payment of alimony through the SDU. SDU-payment is an efficient means of collecting and distributing support, and not everyone opting out wants to lose this.

Luckily, the 2002 opt-out law allows partial opt-outs: You give up all friend of the court services except payment of alimony to the SDU. If you choose this option, you also have two subchoices: 1) SDU-payment by immediate income withholding 2) SDU-payment without immediate income withholding, and payment from the payer directly to the SDU.

A partial opt-out is a lot like a total opt-out (they're really just different choices in the Order Exempting Case from Friend of the Court Services (FOC 102)), and they share similar procedures. And as with a total opt-out, you can opt out partially from a new case (before the friend of the court's entry into the case) or an open case (after the FOC has entered the case). However, new-case partial opt-outs aren't dealt with because they primarily concern payment of temporary alimony, which this book doesn't provide for (see "Do I Need 'Preliminary Relief?'" on page 37 for more about temporary alimony).

Partial Opt-Out in an Open Case

Partially opting out from an open case resembles an open-case total opt-out. And the same seven restrictions (objection, eligibility for DHS services, etc.) apply. See "Total Opt-Out in an Open Case" above for more about these procedures and restrictions.

There is a difference in the paperwork. When you prepare the FOC 102, pay close attention to paragraph #13 (unused in a total opt-out). This is where a partial opt-out occurs. Having opted out of the friend of the court system, you, in essence, opt back in for SDU-payment.

> ### More Information
>
> Ordinarily, the friend of the court helps set up payment of support to the SDU. If you opt out, the friend of the court won't do this and you have to contact the SDU yourself.
>
> To make payment arrangements, call the SDU at (800) 817-0805 or go to www.misdu.com, then to Registration, to as an Individual.
>
> The SDU will help you set up (or continue) immediate income withholding, if you chose that option, or issue a payment coupon book to the payer if you've selected direct payment to the SDU.

After you opt back for SDU-collection, you have a choice: Do you want the SDU to collect the alimony by immediate income withholding or by direct payment from the payer? By checking #13a of the FOC 102, you get SDU-payment by immediate income withholding. You have to set up the withholding yourself (or continue it), the friend of the court won't do this for you. With choice #13b, you elect payment from the payer to the SDU, without immediate income withholding.

Your final divorce papers must also follow the choices you made. In the Uniform Spousal Support Order, No Friend of Court Services (FOC 10c), which controls alimony in partial opt-out cases, add an alimony payment provision at paragraph #8 like this:

Spousal support shall be paid through the SDU by [immediate income withholding/direct payment from the payer.]

If you skip the immediate income withholding option, omit the Order Regarding Income Withholding (FOC 5) from your final divorce papers.

Limited Opt-Out

You may be comfortable with the friend of the court's management of your case; all you want is a different method of alimony payment. The law allows you to opt out of immediate income withholding only, which is the normal means of paying alimony, and choose another payment method. Other payment options include: 1) payment to the SDU directly 2) direct payment to the alimony payee/recipient.

After a limited opt-out, you will have access to the usual friend of the court services. You may or may not have SDU-collection and -distribution of support. But either way, the friend of the court will monitor payments and enforce the alimony order.

There are two ways to avoid immediate income withholding through a limited opt-out: 1) with the consent of the defendant 2) for "good cause," without the consent of the defendant. Either kind requires court approval.

As with total and partial opt-outs, there is a restriction on limited opt-outs. You can't opt for good cause if alimony is already past due. And like other types of opt-outs, you can get a limited opt-out from a new case or an open case. New-case limited opt-outs are omitted here becase they concern payment of temporary alimony, which this book lacks.

Limited Opt-Out in an Open Case

The final hearing is a good time to ask for a limited opt-out because you're going before the judge anyway. Prior to the final hearing, prepare one or two extra "opt-out papers." To opt out with the agreement of the defendant, you need both forms; opt-outs for cause use the order only:

- Agreement Suspending Immediate Income Withholding   FOC 63   3

- Order Suspending Immediate Income Withholding   FOC 64   3

You must obtain the consent of the defendant for an agreed-to opt-out. At a minimum, the defendant must sign the FOC 63. It's also helpful if the defendant can attend the final hearing and confirm that s/he agrees to alimony payment without immediate income withholding. But the defendant's signing the FOC 63 should be sufficient to show consent.

You must also prepare your final divorce papers to go along with a limited opt-out. You do this in the Uniform Spousal Support Order (FOC 10b), which controls alimony in limited opt-out cases. At paragraph #10 of the FOC 10b, add an alimony payment provision like this:

Notwithstanding other provisions of this order, spousal support shall be paid without immediate income withholding by the payer [to the SDU/directly to the payee.]

Also, omit the Order Regarding Income Withholding (FOC 5) since this goes along with immediate income withholding.

During the final hearing, include the FOC 63 and/or 64 among your final divorce papers (see "Final Hearing" on page 91 for more about preparing, filing and sending final divorce papers to the defendant). In your testimony, say that you want to avoid immediate income withholding and describe your alternate method of payment.

If the judge denies your opt-out request, just strike the alimony payment provision you added at paragraph #10 of the FOC 10b. The denial will make alimony payable by immediate income withholding to the SDU. You will also need the FOC 5.

If the judge approves your opt-out request, the alimony will be paid without immediate income withholding. The friend of the court will take steps to reinstate income withholding if past-due alimony equals one month of alimony. The payer can also agree to resume immediate income withholding or the payee can ask for this, although this takes a separate motion and hearing.

Approved, SCAO

STATE OF MICHIGAN JUDICIAL CIRCUIT COUNTY	VERIFIED STATEMENT AND APPLICATION FOR IV-D SERVICES	Original - Friend of the court 1st copy - Plaintiff/Attorney 2nd copy - Defendant/Attorney CASE NO.

1. Mother's last name	First name		

1. Mother's last name **LOVELACE**   First name **DARLENE**   Middle name **ANN**   2. Any other names by which mother is or has been known

3. Date of birth **5-1-65**   4. Social security number **380-16-1010**   5. Driver's license number and state **L 650 603 440 886 MICH.**

6. Mailing address and residence address (if different) **121 S. MAIN, LAKE CITY, MI 48800**

7. Eye color **BLUE**   8. Hair color **BLONDE**   9. Height **5'6"**   10. Weight **120**   11. Race **WHITE**   12. Scars, tattoos, etc.

13. Home telephone no. **772-0000**   14. Work telephone no. **772-0011**   15. Maiden name **ALBRIGHT**   16. Occupation **WAITRESS**

17. Business/Employer's name and address **10,000 PANCAKES, 111 M-78, LAKE CITY, MI 48800**

18. Gross weekly income **$250**

19. Has mother applied for or does she receive public assistance? If yes, please specify kind. ☐ Yes ☒ No   20. DHS case number

21. Father's last name **LOVELACE**   First name **DUDLEY**   Middle name **ERNEST**   22. Any other names by which father is or has been known

23. Date of birth **6-15-64**   24. Social security number **379-10-5567**   25. Driver's license number and state **L 649601402201 MICH.**

26. Mailing address and residence address (if different) **900 S. MAPLE, LAKE CITY, MI 48800**

27. Eye color **BROWN**   28. Hair color **BLACK**   29. Height **6'**   30. Weight **170**   31. Race **WHITE**   32. Scars, tattoos, etc.

33. Home telephone no. **773-3004**   34. Work telephone no. **773-0011**   35. Occupation **SALESMAN**

36. Business/Employer's name and address **WATERBED WORLD, 1000 SERVICE RD., LAKE CITY, MI 48800**

37. Gross weekly income **$375**

38. Has father applied for or does he receive public assistance? If yes, please specify kind. ☐ Yes ☒ No   39. DHS case number

40. a. Name of Minor Child Involved in Case	b. Birth Date	c. Age	d. Soc. Sec. No.	e. Residential Address

41. a. Name of Other Minor Child of Either Party	b. Birth Date	c. Age	d. Residential Address

42. Health care coverage available for each minor child

a. Name of Minor Child	b. Name of Policy Holder	c. Name of Insurance Co./HMO	d. Policy/Certificate/Contract/Group No.

43. Names and addresses of person(s) other than parties, if any, who may have custody of child(ren) during pendency of this case

If any of the public assistance information above changes before your judgment is entered, you are required to give the friend of the court written notice of the change.

☒ I request support services under Title IV-D of the Social Security Act.

I declare that the statements above are true to the best of my information, knowledge, and belief.

Date **2-28-89**

FOC 23 (3/12) **VERIFIED STATEMENT AND APPLICATION FOR IV-D SERVICES**

Signature *Darlene A. Lovelace*

MCR 3.206(B)

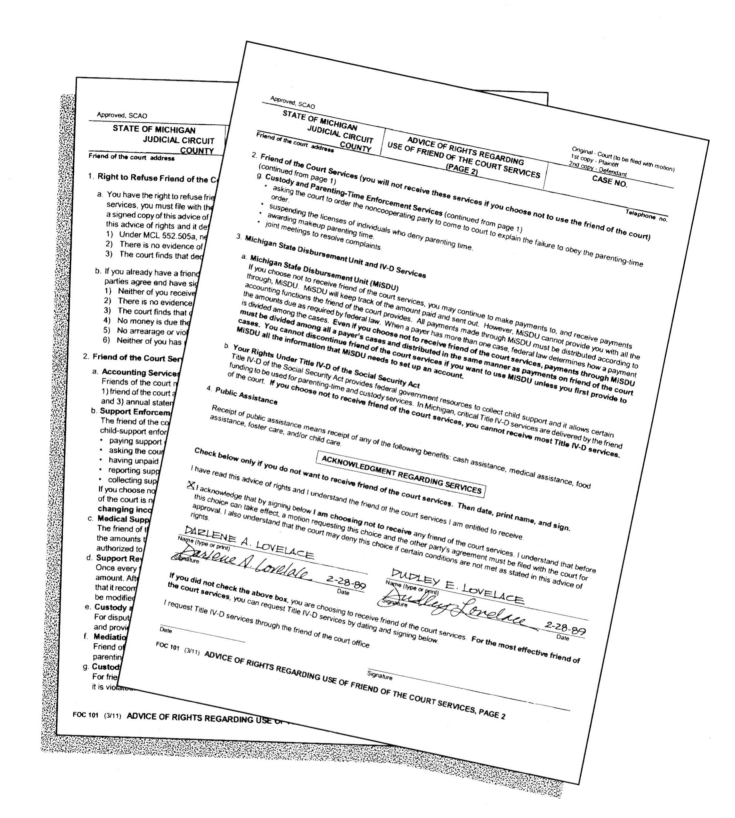

Approved, SCAO

STATE OF MICHIGAN
JUDICIAL CIRCUIT
COUNTY

Friend of the court address

1. **Right to Refuse Friend of the C...**

a. You have the right to refuse frie...
   services, you must file with th...
   a signed copy of this advice of...
   this advice of rights and it de...
   1) Under MCL 552.505a, n...
   2) There is no evidence of...
   3) The court finds that dec...

b. If you already have a friend...
   parties agree and have si...
   1) Neither of you receive...
   2) There is no evidence...
   3) The court finds that...
   4) No money is due the...
   5) No arrearage or vio...
   6) Neither of you has...

2. **Friend of the Court Ser...**

a. **Accounting Services...**
   Friends of the court...
   1) friend of the court a...
   and 3) annual staten...

b. **Support Enforcem...**
   The friend of the co...
   child-support enfor...
   • paying support...
   • asking the cou...
   • having unpaid...
   • reporting sup...
   • collecting sup...
   If you choose no...
   of the court is n...
   changing inco...

c. **Medical Supp...**
   The friend of t...
   the amounts t...
   authorized to...

d. **Support Rev...**
   Once every...
   amount. Aft...
   that it recom...
   be modified...

e. **Custody a...**
   For disput...
   and provi...

f. **Mediatio...**
   Friend o...
   parentin...

g. **Custod...**
   For frie...
   it is viola...

FOC 101 (3/11) **ADVICE OF RIGHTS REGARDING USE O...**

Approved, SCAO

STATE OF MICHIGAN
JUDICIAL CIRCUIT
COUNTY

Friend of the court address

**ADVICE OF RIGHTS REGARDING
USE OF FRIEND OF THE COURT SERVICES
(PAGE 2)**

Original - Court (to be filed with motion)
1st copy - Plaintiff
2nd copy - Defendant

CASE NO.

Telephone no.

2. **Friend of the Court Services** (you will not receive these services if you choose not to use the friend of the court)
(continued from page 1)
g. **Custody and Parenting-Time Enforcement Services** (continued from page 1)
   • asking the court to order the noncooperating party to come to court to explain the failure to obey the parenting-time order.
   • suspending the licenses of individuals who deny parenting time.
   • awarding makeup parenting time.
   • joint meetings to resolve complaints.

3. **Michigan State Disbursement Unit and IV-D Services**

a. **Michigan State Disbursement Unit (MiSDU)**
   If you choose not to receive friend of the court services, you may continue to make payments to, and receive payments through, MiSDU. MiSDU will keep track of the amount paid and sent out. However, MiSDU cannot provide you with all the accounting functions the friend of the court provides. All payments made through MiSDU must be distributed according to the amounts due as required by federal law. When a payer has more than one case, federal law determines how a payment is divided among the cases. **Even if you choose not to receive friend of the court services, payments through MiSDU must be divided among all a payer's cases and distributed in the same manner as payments on friend of the court cases. You cannot discontinue friend of the court services if you want to use MiSDU unless you first provide to MiSDU all the information that MiSDU needs to set up an account.**

b. **Your Rights Under Title IV-D of the Social Security Act**
   Title IV-D of the Social Security Act provides federal government resources to collect child support and it allows certain funding to be used for parenting-time and custody services. In Michigan, critical Title IV-D services are delivered by the friend of the court. **If you choose not to receive friend of the court services, you cannot receive most Title IV-D services.**

4. **Public Assistance**
   Receipt of public assistance means receipt of any of the following benefits: cash assistance, medical assistance, food assistance, foster care, and/or child care.

ACKNOWLEDGMENT REGARDING SERVICES

Check below only if you do not want to receive friend of the court services. Then date, print name, and sign.

I have read this advice of rights and I understand the friend of the court services.

[X] I acknowledge that by signing below **I am choosing not to receive** any friend of the court services I am entitled to receive. this choice can take effect, a motion requesting this choice and the other party's agreement must be filed with the court for approval. I also understand that the court may deny this choice if certain conditions are not met as stated in this advice of rights.

DARLENE A. LOVELACE
Name (type or print)
Darlene A. Lovelace   2-28-89
Signature   Date

DUDLEY E. LOVELACE
Name (type or print)
Dudley Lovelace   2-28-89
Signature   Date

If you did not check the above box, you are choosing to receive friend of the court services. **For the most effective friend of the court services,** you can request Title IV-D services by dating and signing below.

I request Title IV-D services through the friend of the court office.

Date _____

Signature _____

FOC 101 (3/11) **ADVICE OF RIGHTS REGARDING USE OF FRIEND OF THE COURT SERVICES, PAGE 2**

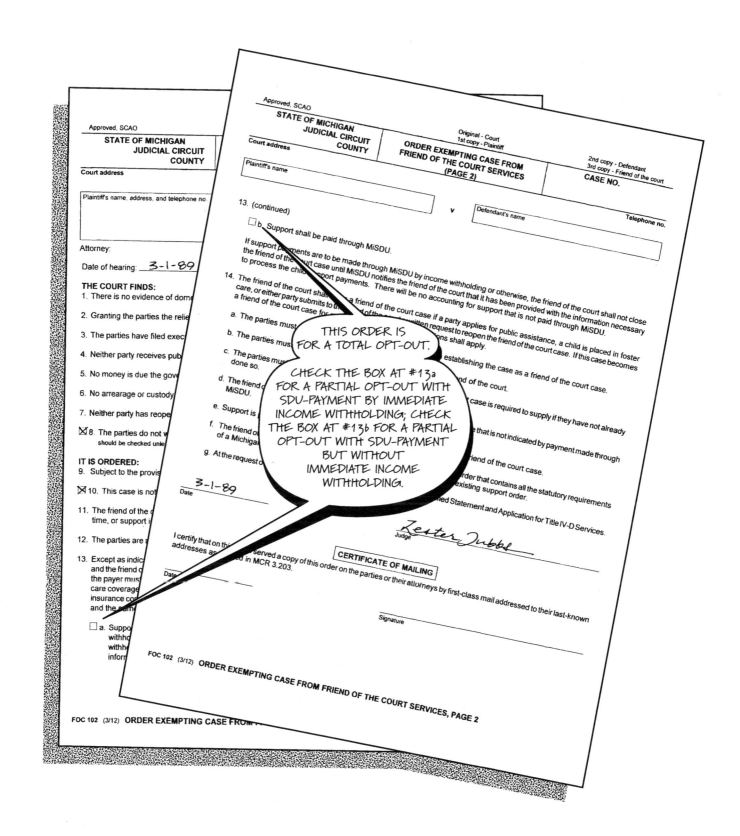

Approved, SCAO

Original - Court
1st copy - Friend of the court

2nd copy - Plaintiff
3rd copy - Defendant

STATE OF MICHIGAN JUDICIAL CIRCUIT COUNTY	REQUEST TO REOPEN FRIEND OF THE COURT CASE	CASE NO.

Telephone no.

Court address

Plaintiff's name, address, and telephone no.

v

Defendant's name, address, and telephone no.

Attorney:

Attorney:

1. On ___3-1-89___ an order was entered exempting this case from friend of the court services.
Date

I REQUEST that the friend of the court case be reopened upon filing of this request with the friend of the court office. Attached is a completed Verified Statement (form FOC 23).

☒ I request support services under Title IV-D of the Social Security Act.

___4-1-89___
Date

Darlene Lovelace
Signature

CERTIFICATE OF MAILING

I certify that on this date I served a copy of this request on the friend of the court and on the parties or their attorneys by first-class mail addressed to their last-known addresses as defined in MCR 3.203.

___4-1-89___
Date

Darlene Lovelace
Signature

FOC 104 (3/09) **REQUEST TO REOPEN FRIEND OF THE COURT CASE**

MCL 552.505, MCL 552.505a

Approved, SCAO

Original - Court
2nd copy - Friend of the court
3rd copy - Plaintiff
4th copy - Defendant

STATE OF MICHIGAN
JUDICIAL CIRCUIT
COUNTY

Court address

AGREEMENT SUSPENDING
IMMEDIATE INCOME WITHHOLDING

CASE NO.

Plaintiff's name, address, and telephone no.

Court telephone no.

v

Defendant's name, address, and telephone no.

NOTE: MCL 552.604(3) requires that all new and modified support orders after December 31, 1990, include a provision for immediate income withholding and that income withholding take effect immediately unless the parties enter into a written agreement that the income withholding order shall not take effect immediately.

We understand that by law an order of income withholding in a support order shall take effect immediately. However, we agree to the following.

1. The order of income withholding shall not take effect immediately.

2. An alternative payment arrangement shall be made as follows:

DEFENDANT SHALL PAY THE SUPPORT DIRECTLY TO THE SDU.

(DESCRIBE OTHER METHOD OF PAYMENT)

3. Both the payer and the recipient of support will notify the friend of the court, in writing, within 21 days of any change in
   a. the names, addresses, and telephone numbers of their current sources of income;
   b. any health-care coverage that is available to them as a benefit of employment or that is maintained by them; the names of the insurance companies, health-care organizations, or health-maintenance organizations; the policy, certificate, or contract numbers; and the names and birth dates of the persons for whose benefit they maintain health-care coverage under the policies, certificates, or contracts; and
   c. their current residences, mailing addresses, and telephone numbers.

4. We further understand that proceedings to implement income withholding shall commence if the payer of support falls one month behind in his/her support payments.

5. We recognize that the court may order withholding of income to take effect immediately for cause or at the request of the payer.

5-5-89
Date

Darlene A. Lovelace
Plaintiff's signature

5-5-89
Date

Dudley E. Lovelace
Defendant's signature

FOC 63 (3/08) AGREEMENT SUSPENDING IMMEDIATE INCOME WITHHOLDING

MCL 552.604

CHECK THIS BOX FOR A LIMITED OPT-OUT FOR "GOOD CAUSE" WITHOUT THE CONSENT OF THE DEFENDANT.

OR CHECK THIS BOX FOR AN AGREED-TO LIMITED OPT-OUT WITH THE CONSENT OF THE DEFENDANT.

Original - Court
1st copy - Friend of the court
2nd copy - Plaintiff
3rd copy - Defendant

Approved, SCAO

STATE OF MICHIGAN
JUDICIAL CIRCUIT COUNTY

ORDER SUSPENDING IMMEDIATE INCOME WITHHOLDING

CASE NO.

Court telephone no.

Court address

Plaintiff's name, address, and telephone no.

v

Defendant's name, address, and telephone no.

Date of hearing: 5-7-89   Judge: LESTER TUBBS   Bar no.

2. THE COURT FINDS:

☒ a. There is good cause for the order of income withholding not to take effect immediately as follows.
1) It is in the best interest of the child for immediate income withholding not to take effect for the following reasons:

DEFENDANT IS A SALESMAN WORKING ON COMMISSION WITH AN IRREGULAR INCOME, SO IMMEDIATE INCOME WITHHOLDING IS NOT PRACTICAL.

2) Proof of timely payment of previously-ordered support has been provided

☐ b. The parties have entered into a written agreement that has been reviewed and entered in the record as follows
1) The order of income withholding shall not take effect immediately.
2) An alternative payment arrangement has been agreed upon and is attached

3. Both the payer and the recipient of support shall notify the friend of the court, in writing, within 21 days of any change in income;
a. the names, addresses, and telephone numbers or that is maintained by them, the names of the
b. any health-care coverage that insurance companies, organizations; the policy, certificate, or contract numbers; and the names and maintain health-care coverage under the policies, certificates, or contr
c. their current residence, mai

IT IS ORDERED:

4. Income withholding shall not take effect as specified in law.
5. Income withholding shall take effect if the fixed amount of arrearage specified in law.

5-7-89
Date

Lester Tubbs
Judge

MCL 552.511, MCL 552.604, MCL 552.607

FOC 64 (3/08) **ORDER SUSPENDING IMMEDIATE INCOME WITHHOLDING**

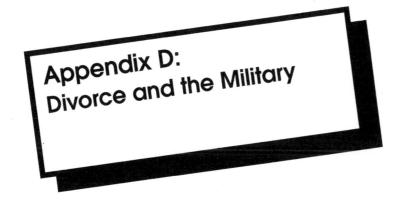

Appendix D: Divorce and the Military

Divorce by or against a spouse in active-duty military service creates several special problems. Right away, there can be practical problems with locating and serving papers on the servicemember who may be stationed at a distant military base. The military has its own retirement plan and health care system which are unlike civilian ones and often difficult to navigate. The military also has special benefits, like PX and commissary, that can be divided during divorce.

Military Relief Laws

By far the biggest problem posed by a divorce against a military spouse are the military relief laws protecting active duty servicemembers. There are actually two laws: the federal Servicemembers Civil Relief Act (SCRA) and a similar Michigan relief law.

Federal Servicemembers Civil Relief Act (SCRA)

The SCRA, which has the widest scope, covers servicemembers in the active duty of the U.S. military (see the sidebox for which personnel are covered by the SCRA). The act offers several forms of relief to servicemembers protecting them from some kinds of debts, taxes, installment contracts, lawsuits, etc. The intent of the SCRA is to protect servicemembers from these obligations so they can focus on their military duties.

It's the lawsuit relief protections of the SCRA that have an impact on divorce. In essence, these protections shield defendant-servicemembers

More Information

(1) The SCRA covers all five service branches of the U. S. military:

- **Army**
- **Navy**
- **Marine Corps**
- **Air Force**
- **Coast Guard**

The act also covers commissioned officers in the Public Health Service and National Oceanic and Atmospheric Administration.

The SCRA protects servicemembers in the *active duty* of the U.S. military which are made up of two components:

Active component. Members of regular units (Regular Army, Regular Navy, etc.).

Reserve component. Servicemembers *activated* from the two segments of the military reserve:

- *Reserves.* Each service branch has its own reserve unit (Army Reserve (Army), Naval Reserve (Navy), etc.), which is always under federal command.

- *National Guard.* State Army National Guard (attached to the Army) and Air National Guard (attached to the Air Force) units, including Michigan's army and air units.
  National Guard units fall under state control, unless they have been called to federal active duty by the president. After 30 consecutive days of federal service, guardmembers are protected by the SCRA.

The SCRA protects servicemembers lawfully away from active duty, such as during a period of leave or hospitalization. The act also covers military inductees after receiving induction orders. The act doesn't apply to civilians working for the military.

(2) Michigan's military relief law covers members in Michigan's two National Guard units:

- **Army National Guard**
- **Air National Guard**

This law protects guardmembers in *active duty* for more than seven days after activation by the governor: 1) to support civilian authority (such as during a riot, flood, etc.) 2) for a war or emergency of the state or nation.

The protections of the Michigan law extend beyond the period of active duty for some things, but not for lawsuit relief which is the focus here.

Note: Other states have similar military relief laws protecting their National Guardmembers, which could be an issue if a party is in the active duty of an out-of-state unit.

from hard-to-handle lawsuits, including divorces. There are two main lawsuit relief remedies:

Stay. During a lawsuit, a servicemember can ask for a stay or freezing of the case (see "Satisfying the Military Relief Laws" on page 155 for more about two kinds of stays and the grounds for issuing them). The court can grant a stay for 90 days or more, effectively stopping the case for this period. Typically, a stay will last only until the servicemember can get leave so s/he can deal with the lawsuit.

Reopening a default judgment. If a servicemember doesn't participate in the lawsuit, and a default judgment is ultimately issued, s/he can ask for reopening of the case. The request must be made no later than 90 days after the servicemember leaves military service. Reopening isn't guaranteed; the member must have a good defense and show that military service impaired his/her ability to take part in the case.

The SCRA's lawsuit relief remedies are really designed for different situations. But sometimes a servicemember can use both remedies; other times using one means loss of the other. The SCRA also allows a servicemember to waive (give up) these relief protections. The chart on the opposite page explains how these remedies fit together.

During peacetime, the SCRA's lawsuit relief protections seldom totally bar a divorce against a servicemember. At a minimum, the act requires a little extra paperwork and the divorce can go through as smoothly as one against a civilian. At most, the divorce will be frozen until the servicemember can respond, either by obtaining leave or by separation from the service.

In a war, the SCRA's stay remedy may be extended. For example, during the Persian Gulf War in 1990-91, stays were expanded effectively freezing all lawsuits against active-duty servicemembers until after the war. This kind of total-but-temporary freeze could be used again in a future war or crisis.

SCRA Lawsuit Relief Rights

	Right to request stay	Right to request reopening of default judgment
Defendant appears and signs a waiver of SCRA rights	No	No
Defendant asks court for a stay	Yes	No
Defendant doesn't respond in case:		
open case	Court must appoint a lawyer for servicemember who can ask for a stay or other relief	Yes
closed case	(2) Yes, if case is reopened	(1) Yes, then may ask for a stay

Michigan's Military Relief Law

Many people don't know it, but Michigan has a military relief law similar to the SCRA. The state law covers Michigan National Guardmembers in active duty (see the sidebox for the scope of coverage). Like the federal law, Michigan's law offers protection from some debt collection, foreclosures, utility shutoffs and lawsuits.

Unlike the SCRA, Michigan's relief law offers absolute protection from lawsuits without regard to hardship for the servicemember. After a seven-day activation of guardmembers, Michigan's law effectively freezes lawsuits against them until termination of their active-duty service for the state.

Divorce by a Plaintiff-Servicemember

Before filing, a plaintiff-servicemember must decide where to file. Choosing the correct state is known as jurisdiction (see "Can I Get a Divorce in Michigan?" on page 24 about jurisdiction), while choice of county inside Michigan is called venue (venue rules are covered in "Can I File the Divorce in My County?" on page 26). Both jurisdiction and venue are based on residence or one's permanent home.

Special residence rules apply to military servicemembers. Ordinarily, servicemembers keep their pre-enlistment state and county residence. So if you were a Michigan resident before enlistment, you're still a resident of Michigan and your home county regardless of where you are stationed now.

You may then file either in your old home county or the Michigan county where the defendant is residing now.

It is possible for servicemembers to change residence and adopt a new residence where they are stationed. Changing residence takes more than simply filing a military State of Legal Residence Certificate; it requires a combination of things in the new state (registration to vote, ownership or rental of real property, payment of taxes, etc.), showing an intent to regard the new state as a permanent home. If you have lost your Michigan residence that way, you can still file for divorce here, but only in the Michigan county where the defendant lives.

Wherever you file, you can file by mail and have the divorce papers served by any of the service methods. Later on, other papers can be filed by mail and the divorce conducted from afar.

Divorcing a Defendant-Servicemember

Before you begin the divorce, choose the correct state (this choice is known as jurisdiction and is covered in "Can I Get a Divorce in Michigan?" on page 24) and county (choice of county is known as venue; see "Can I File the Divorce in My County?" on page 26 for venue rules) for filing. Both jurisdiction and venue are based on residence or one's permanent home.

There are special residence rules for servicemembers which can affect jurisdiction and venue. Ordinarily, servicemembers keep their pre-enlistment state and county residence, no matter how far away they are stationed now. So if the defendant resided in Michigan with you during your marriage just before entry into the service, there should be full Michigan jurisdiction. For convenience, you will probably file in the Michigan county where you live.

More Information

About military retirement benefits, health care coverage and other benefits (such as PX and commissary) available to a divorced non-military spouse, contact:

Ex-Partners of Servicemembers for Equality (Ex-Pose)
P.O. Box 11191
Alexandria, VA 22312
(703) 941-5844
www.ex-pose.org

About division of military retirement pay from a servicemember's point of view, get:

Divorce and the Military II: A Comprehensive Guide for Service Members, Spouses, and Attorneys, 2nd ed., Marsha L. Thole and Frank W. Ault, Redlands, CA: The American Retirees Association, 2001

Before you can have the divorce papers served, you must know where the defendant is stationed. If you've lost touch, there are ways to find military servicemembers through a military locator service. The sidebox explains how to contact a base locator (when you know where the defendant is stationed) or a service branch locator (when you lack specific information).

The best way to serve a military spouse is by mail, since the U.S. Postal Service delivers mail (including certified mail necessary for service) to military bases all over the world. Military mail overseas can be a little slow, so allow extra time for service outside the country. See "Service" on page 69 for more about serving by mail and by the other service methods.

If a defendant is stationed at a stateside military installation and refuses to accept mailed service, contact the sheriff or a commercial process server in the county and arrange for service by delivery. Military personnel living off base can be served at home without a problem. But except for the Air Force, most service branches don't allow process servers to enter military bases and serve servicemembers there directly. Instead, the defendant-servicemember's commanding officer sets up a time and place for service, if the member agrees to accept the papers; if s/he refuses service, the commanding officer notifies the server of the refusal. Sheriffs and commercial process servers in areas with military bases should be familiar with these service procedures.

Oddly, service can be easier at a military base in a foreign country. Overseas, commanding officers can help carry out service, but are discouraged from acting as actual process servers. As a compromise, you can contact the defendant's unit commander and suggest service by acknowledgment (see "Service by Acknowledgment" on page 70 for instructions). The commander can hand the service papers to the defendant and ask for acknowledgment of service. If the defendant refuses service, the commanding officer cannot force service and will notify you of the refusal.

Satisfying the Military Relief Laws

After service, you must come to grips with the military relief laws. If the defendant-servicemember is protected by Michigan's military relief law, or if the SCRA has put a temporary ban on all lawsuits, you can only proceed with a waiver from the defendant (see below about getting a waiver).

But typically, the defendant will be protected by the SCRA's lawsuit relief remedies (stay and default judgment reopening). As explained before, these are flexible remedies which often allow divorces to go through. Here are several typical scenarios in which the SCRA is satisfied allowing completion of the divorce.

More Information

It can be difficult to find the address of active-duty servicemembers. But there are several resources that can help. For good general information, get:

How to Locate Anyone Who Is or Has Been in the Military: Armed Forces Locator Guide, 8th ed., Richard Johnson and Debra Knox, Spartanburg, SC: MIE Publishing, 1999

If you know where the defendant is stationed, call the base locator (often just the telephone information operator at the base). The Johnson and Knox book has a list of base locator telephone numbers for all military installations in the U.S. and worldwide. Or you can get the same information from Military OneSource at (800) 342-9647 or www.militaryonesource.mil, then to Military Installations. Besides finding the defendant, the base locator can also provide information about contacting the defendant's commanding officer for carrying out service.

You should know the defendant's service branch, either from personal knowledge or a military status report from the Defense Manpower Data Center (DMDC) (a DMDC report confirming the defendant's active-duty service should also show the defendant's service branch, but no actual location information).

To make a military locator request, you need the defendant's full name and date of birth or social security number; other information like rank, service number and last duty assignment/last known military address is helpful. The locators charge fees for requests, but these are usually waived for close family member-requesters.

The five military locators generally take requests by mail only (none has interactive Internet access). Recently, the Coast Guard began taking locator requests by telephone or email. For convenience, a Military Locator Request form, addressed to all five locators, is included in this book. Send your request to the correct military locator with a stamped self-addressed envelope and expect a response within two-four weeks.

One problem with all the military locators is that they typically won't release current military addresses or duty assignments of troops overseas, aboard ships or in a war zone, for security reasons. You may be able to get around this problem if you know the defendant's overseas base or ship. The Johnson and Knox book cited above has lists of all overseas military installations and Navy and Coast Guard ships and home ports. The book has suggestions about improvising addresses to servicemembers overseas or at sea using APO (Army Post Office serving Europe and the Middle East) and FPO (Fleet Post Office for the Pacific and Far East) addresses.

You might get lucky and contact the defendant that way. If not, you will have to use a form of alternate service (see Appendix D for more about alternate service). Be sure to attach the (failed) locator response to your motion for alternate service. The alternate service may involve service on the defendant's relatives who probably have his/her military address.

Waiver of Military Relief Law Rights by the Defendant

As with other legal rights, a defendant-servicemember can voluntarily waive (give up) the lawsuit relief rights provided by the military relief laws. The waiver cuts off these rights, allowing the divorce to go through normally.

Waiver is the only way to satisfy Michigan's military relief law and the SCRA when it has imposed a temporary wartime freeze on lawsuits. But even if the SCRA applies in its normal peacetime form, waiver always makes it easier for the divorce to proceed.

If the defendant is willing to waive, send the Appearance and Waiver of Military Relief Law Rights (GRP 6) to the defendant and have him/her sign the form. After you get the GRP 6 back, attach the form to the Default (GRP 2) as described in "Default and the Military Relief Laws" on page 84.

The Defendant Applies for a SCRA Stay

After receiving the divorce papers, the defendant may contact the court and apply for a stay under the SCRA. The application can be quite informal—just a letter or other communication—but must include:

- information from the servicemember showing: 1) how military duties materially affect the servicemember's ability to appear 2) a date when the servicemember can appear
- information from the servicemember's commanding officer confirming that: 1) military duties prevent the servicemember from appearing, and 2) military leave is not currently available

During a stay application, the primary issue is whether the servicemember's military service has a material effect on his/her ability to appear in the case. Courts have defined material effect in terms of two main factors:

Geographical distance. This is probably the most important factor. If the defendant-servicemember is at sea or stationed overseas, a good argument can be made that military service is hampering the defendant in the case. On the other hand, leave can cancel distance, since the servicemember can often use the leave to return home and participate in the case. Thus, the availability of leave is often the pivotal issue for a stay request. It's also important for determining the length of the stay, if one is issued.

Financial hardship. Courts want to know if military service has caused a financial hardship for the servicemember, which has impaired the ability to appear. Military service often means a loss of income and extra financial obligations. On the other hand, some large employers make up the difference in pay and offer extra benefits to activated employees, resulting in no net loss of income. Under- or unemployed servicemembers may actually see an increase in income from military service.

A servicemember's Leave and Earnings Statement (LES) can answer both issues. The LES, which the military provides twice a month, shows a servicemember's accrued leave and details his/her military pay (base pay, allowances and allotments). If the defendant hasn't submitted a recent LES with the stay application, s/he should be required to submit one to the judge reviewing the application.

When the defendant's stay application shows the four things enumerated in the list above, the court must grant the defendant's application. The SCRA says that a stay must be a minimum of 90 days, but can be longer. The court can also add even more time in an additional stay.

But typically, the stay will last only until the defendant has time to deal with the divorce. This could be until the next period of leave or when the defendant leaves the service, when discharge is imminent. You can wait until the stay expires and then resume the divorce where you left off.

If the stay is long, the clerk may try to dismiss the case for no progress. You can prevent dismissal by pointing out the stay to the clerk, and explain that this is the reason for delay in the case.

Whether a stay is granted or denied, the fact that the defendant applied for the stay is important. The stay request is regarded as the defendant's chief SCRA remedy and results in loss of the right to request reopening of any default judgment of divorce entered later.

As a result, when you the file the Default (GRP 2), describe the defendant's stay application on the blank line in paragraph #3a. Bring this to the judge's attention also during your testimony at the final hearing.

The Defendant Doesn't Respond

It's more difficult dealing with a defendant-servicemember who doesn't respond. The fact is, the defendant may have very good reasons for not responding, such as absence aboard a ship or service in combat. The SCRA recognizes these difficulties and has special protections for unresponsive defendants.

When a defendant doesn't respond, the SCRA says that the court must appoint a lawyer for the defendant. The appointed lawyer and the defendant don't have the usual lawyer-client relationship because the servicemember may not have ever spoken to the appointed lawyer or even know that s/he exists. Nevertheless, the appointed lawyer may ask for a stay for the defendant, which the court must grant for a minimum of 90 days if:

- the defendant has a defense to the divorce that can't be presented without the defendant; or
- the appointed lawyer has been unable to contact the defendant or determine if a good defense exists

Ordinarily, a stay application is significant because it results in loss of the right to request reopening a default judgment later. But this rule doesn't necessarily apply to an appointed lawyer's stay application because of the peculiar relationship between the appointed lawyer and the servicemember described above. As a result, the servicemember doesn't lose his/her right to request reopening a default judgment after the stay application.

If the divorce goes forward to a default judgment, the defendant can request reopening the judgment. The defendant can make the request anytime while in military service and even within 90 days after leaving the service. Reopening of the case isn't automatic. The defendant must show both a material effect from military service and a good defense to get back in the case.

If the case is reopened, the defendant may be able to participate right away. But if the defendant is still serving in the military, or just recently discharged, s/he can apply for a stay, to get extra time to defend. The application would be treated like a prejudgment stay request, as described in "The Defendant Applies for a SCRA Stay" on page 156.

Naturally, you'll want to describe this activity on the blank line in paragraph #3a of the Default (GRP 2). The judge should be familiar with this, but mention it at the final hearing.

STATE OF MICHIGAN Circuit Court - Family Division COUNTY	APPEARANCE AND WAIVER OF MILITARY RELIEF LAW RIGHTS	CASE NO.

Plaintiff (appearing *in propria persona*): **Defendant:**

v

Defendant says:

1. I am in the active duty of the following unit of the U.S. military:

333RD MILITARY POLICE COMPANY, MICHIGAN ARMY NATIONAL GUARD

2. I am currently stationed at:

FORT LEONARD WOOD
WAYNESVILLE, MO

3. I previously received copies of the summons and complaint for divorce and any other initial divorce papers in this case.

4. I make a general appearance and waive all lawsuit relief rights, including the right to request a stay or adjournment of proceedings, provided to me in this case by the Servicemembers Civil Relief Act (50 USC App. 501 et seq.) and/or Michigan's military relief law (MCL 32.517) (or similar military relief law from another state).

Date 4-1-89   Defendant *Dudley Lovelace*

GRP 6 (3/07)   APPEARANCE AND WAIVER OF MILITARY RELIEF LAW RIGHTS

Military Locator Request

TO:

Army
Army World Wide Locator Service
Enlisted Records and Evaluation Center
8899 East 56th Street
Indianapolis, IN 46249-5301

Navy
Bureau of Naval Personnel
PERS-312E
5720 Integrity Drive
Millington, TN 38055-3120

Marine Corps
Commandant of The Marine Corps
Headquarters, U.S. Marine Corps (MMSB10)
2008 Elliott Road, Suite 201
Quantico, VA 22134-5030

Air Force
Air Force Manpower and Personnel Center
ATTN: Air Force Locator/MSIMDL
550 C Street West, Suite 50
Randolph Air Force Base, TX 78150-4752

Coast Guard
Commander
Coast Guard Personnel Command
4200 Wilson Blvd., Suite 1100 (CGPC-adm-3)
Arlington, VA 20598-7200

RE:

Case name ___LOVELACE V. LOVELACE___

Case number ___89-00501-DO___

Full name of defendant ___DUDLEY ERNEST LOVELACE___

Defendant's date of birth ___6-15-64___

Defendant's social security number ___379-10-5567___

Defendant's rank and service number (if known) ___—___

Defendant's last duty assignment (if known) ___—___

Defendant's last military address (if known) ___—___

I am the plaintiff in the case above seeking a divorce against the defendant. I request information about the defendant's *current* rank, service number, unit of assignment and military address. I need this information for service of the divorce papers, to satisfy the military relief laws and other reasons related to this divorce case. A self-addressed stamped envelope is enclosed for your response.

As the defendant's spouse, I ask for waiver of the locator request fee.

Date ___3-6-89___

Signature ___Darlene A. Lovelace___

Name ___DARLENE A. LOVELACE___

Address ___121 S. MAIN___

___LAKE CITY, MI 48800___

Telephone: ___(517) 772-0000___

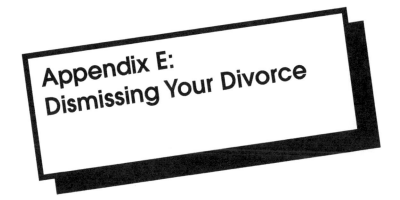

Appendix E: Dismissing Your Divorce

If you and your spouse reconcile during the divorce, you may be anxious to dismiss the divorce immediately. But this may not always be wise. It takes a lot of work to file a divorce, so why jeopardize all your effort with a hasty dismissal? Wait a while and see if the reconciliation lasts. If it does, go ahead and dismiss your divorce as described below. But if your reconciliation fails, pick up the divorce where you left off and finish it.

At one time, it was possible to let a divorce remain in court for months or even years while the parties attempted reconciliation. These days, courts are under pressure to move cases along quickly, so they won't tolerate very much delay. Nevertheless, you probably could let your divorce sit for a few months. Just make sure that your proof of service is on file with the clerk or else the clerk may dismiss the case for no progress after the 91-day summons expiration period (see "Filing the Proof of Service" on page 77 for more about this danger).

After you decide that your reconciliation is going to last, go ahead and dismiss your divorce. To dismiss your uncontested divorce, fill out the Notice of Dismissal by Plaintiff section of the Dismissal (MC 09). Choose dismissal "without prejudice" because this makes it easier to file another divorce later should your marriage break down again. After you prepare the Dismissal (MC 09), file it with the clerk and send a copy to the defendant.

Incidentally, if your fees were suspended at the beginning of the divorce, you must deal with the fees again before you file the Dismissal (MC 09). At that time, the court can order a final fee exemption or require payment of the fees (see Appendix A for more about the fee exemption procedure).

```
                                            Original - Court
                                            1st copy - Applicant
                                            Other copies - All appearing parties
 Approved, SCAO                                          CASE NO.
   STATE OF MICHIGAN
        JUDICIAL DISTRICT        DISMISSAL
         JUDICIAL CIRCUIT
         COUNTY PROBATE                          Court telephone no.

Court address

Plaintiff name(s) and address(es)        Defendant name(s) and address(es)

                               v

Plaintiff's attorney, bar no., address, and telephone no.    Defendant's attorney, bar no., address, and telephone no.
```

☒ **NOTICE OF DISMISSAL BY PLAINTIFF**　　　☐ with
　　　　　　　　　　　　　　　　　　　　　　☒ without　　prejudice as to:

1. Plaintiff/Attorney for plaintiff files this notice of dismissal of this case
　☒ all defendants.
　☐ the following defendant(s): _____

2. I certify, under penalty of contempt, that:
　a. This notice is the first dismissal filed by the plaintiff based upon or including the same claim against the defendant.
　b. All costs of filing and service have been paid.
　c. **No answer or motion has been served upon the plaintiff by the defendant** as of the date of this notice.
　d. A copy of this notice has been provided to the appearing defendant/attorney by ☒ mail ☐ personal service.

7-1-89　　　　　　　　　　　　　　_Darlene A. Lovelace_
Date　　　　　　　　　　　　　　　　　Plaintiff/Attorney signature

☐ **STIPULATION TO DISMISS**　　　☐ with
　　　　　　　　　　　　　　　　　　☐ without　　prejudice as to:

　I stipulate to the dismissal of this case _____
　☐ all parties.
　☐ the following parties: _____

_____　　　　Plaintiff/Attorney signature
Date

_____　　　　Defendant/Attorney signature
Date

☐ **ORDER TO DISMISS**　　　☐ with
　　　　　　　　　　　　　　　☐ without　　prejudice. Conditions, if any: _____

IT IS ORDERED this case is dismissed _____

_____

_____

_____　　　_____　Bar no.
Date　　　　　　　　　　　Judge

MC 09　(6/97)　**DISMISSAL**　　　　　　　　　　　　　　MCR 2.504

Appendix F: Additional Judgment Provisions

The first page of the Judgment of Divorce (GRP 4a) contains standard judgment provisions that should take care of most divorce cases without minor children. But in special cases, these standard provisions might not be enough.

Luckily, the judgment form is open-ended and expandable allowing you to add extra judgment provisions. If have you just a few additions, insert these in the blank space on the Judgment of Divorce (GRP 4c).* When you need more room, make photcopies of the GRP 4c and add these as extra pages. As you expand the judgment this way, remember to number the judgment pages consecutively in the captions of the forms.

If you're granting alimony to a party, you must use a Uniform Spousal Support Order (FOC 10b) as the alimony order. As explained in "Providing for Alimony" on page 174, the FOC 10b is a separate order which accompanies and is incorporated into the Judgment of Divorce (GRP 4) in divorces with alimony.

The sections below deal with special situations in which you might need additional judgment provisions. Sample judgment provisions are also included which you can use or adapt to your case.

Property Division Provisions

Before you can provide for a property division in your judgment, you must do a complete inventory and valuation of your property (see "Can I Get a

---

* The omitted middle page, GRP 4b, has child custody and parenting time provisions for divorce cases with minor children and therefore isn't included in this book.

Fair Property Division?" on page 31 for more about inventorying and valuing property). You and the defendant should also agree to an overall division of your property. If you have a prenuptial agreement dealing with divorce, this document will normally control the division. Otherwise, you must decide the shares each of you is to receive. Are you going to divide your property equally, 55-45, 60-40, etc.? After you do all those things, you're ready to begin the actual division of property.

Dividing Real Property

More Information

The court rules specify a judgment style which you must follow in adding provisions to your judgment:

- There must be only one subject or topic per judgment provision.

- All provisions must be numbered consecutively.

- All provisions must have a descriptive introductory heading, which is normally in bold on printed forms. However, you can underline introductory headings as a substitute for bold-face type.

All real property must be divided specifically in your divorce judgment. This rule applies both to real property owned by spouses jointly (joint real property) and real property that a spouse owns alone (solely-owned real property). The provisions below divide joint and solely-owned real property in three ways: 1) trade-off 2) buy-out (by one spouse from the other) 3) sale (to third parties). There are several other ways to divide real property, but these are far too complicated to do by yourself.

If you and your spouse don't own any real property, check the first box in paragraph #5A of the Judgment of Divorce (GRP 4a). If you are property-owners, check the second box and then divide the property in the Judgment of Divorce (GRP 4c).

As you divide real property, include the street address and legal description. Adding the legal description is important because this permits you to use the judgment as a substitute deed if one spouse refuses to sign a deed for the property (see "Transferring Property" on page 101 for more about using a judgment to transfer property this way). You can find the legal description in a deed, land contract, mortgage, abstract of title or title insurance policy for the property.

Joint Real Property

If you do nothing with joint real property in your divorce judgment, the property automatically converts to tenancy in common ownership. This might be acceptable for a while. As tenants in common, you and the defendant would each get an equal share of the property. If either of you were to die, your share would pass to your heirs/will beneficiaries, not your ex-spouse, because tenancy in common property doesn't have rights of survivorship.

But in the long run, tenancy in common ownership isn't practical for divorced persons. A tenancy in common is really like a partnership. Both tenants in common have an equal right to possess and use the property, and each has a duty to maintain it. This kind of close-knit arrangement is seldom suitable for ex-spouses.

Consequently, you should divide your joint real property in another way. The provisions below suggest several division options, some of which you may be able to handle yourself.

If enough property is available, one spouse can trade his/her share of the joint property for an equivalent amount of other property. For example, let's say that spouses jointly own a house worth $50,000 and have $50,000 of miscellaneous property. If the spouses agree to an equal property division, the defendant could trade his/her one-half share of the house for the plaintiff's half-interest in the miscellaneous property. After giving all the miscellaneous property to the defendant elsewhere in the property division, the spouses might use a provision like the one below to give the jointly-owned house to the plaintiff:

13. <u>Real Property</u>. Plaintiff is awarded the property located at 121 S. Main, Lake City, Michigan, and described below, free of any claims of defendant:

   Lot 2 of Assessor's Plat, Lake City, Ojibway County, Michigan

   Plaintiff shall be responsible for any indebtedness against the property and hold defendant harmless from liability for this debt.

Instead of a trade-off, one spouse could purchase the other's share of the joint real property. The provision below provides for a buy-out of the defendant's share by the plaintiff for cash:

13. <u>Real Property</u>. Plaintiff shall be awarded the property located at 121 S. Main, Lake City, Michigan, and described below, free of any claims of defendant, upon the payment of $25,000 to defendant:

   Lot 2 of Assessor's Plat, Lake City, Ojibway County, Michigan

   Plaintiff shall be responsible for any indebtedness against the property and hold defendant harmless from liability for this debt.

This provision lets the plaintiff buy out the defendant with a single cash payment. If the buyer-spouse can't afford to pay cash, s/he could make installment payments. But to provide for that type of buy-out, one must know about installment sales, how to secure them and their tax consequences. All these things are quite complicated, so seek legal help if you want to provide for a buy-out on an installment basis.

The sale of joint property to third parties is another way to handle joint property. You can arrange for an immediate sale at the time of your divorce or delay the sale until later. Either way, the sale provision will usually convert the joint property into a tenancy in common until the sale. Then, the provision will typically require: 1) pay-off of any mortgage or land contract against the property 2) payment of all selling costs (broker's commission, closing costs, etc.) 3) division of any remaining proceeds. A good sale provision should also say who shall possess and maintain the property before the sale. All these things are included in the immediate sale provision below:

13. <u>Real Property</u>. The property located at 121 S. Main, Lake City, Michigan, and described below, shall be owned by plaintiff and defendant as tenants in common:

   Lot 2 of Assessor's Plat, Lake City, Ojibway County, Michigan

   This property shall be sold as soon as possible at a price and terms the parties shall agree upon. After the property is sold, the proceeds of the sale shall be applied first to satisfy any indebtedness against the property, then against all the costs of sale (including any broker's commission and closing costs). Any remainder shall be divided [equally] between the parties.

   Until the closing of the sale, plaintiff shall have sole possession of the property. Plaintiff shall be responsible for any mortgage or land contract payments, taxes, insurance and other expenses of maintaining the property during this time until the day of closing.

An immediate sale is simple and provides for a clean break between the spouses. There may also be sound tax reasons for selling real property around the time of a divorce, especially when the property is the former marital home. However, an immediate sale may displace a parent and children living at the home.

A delayed sale can solve that problem. It can permit the in-home parent to live in the former marital home for a while, yet will eventually allow the other parent to receive his/her share of the property when the delayed sale occurs. The trouble is, a delayed sale is difficult to provide for in a judgment. The events triggering the delayed sale (remarriage of the in-home parent, maturity of children, etc.) must be anticipated and carefully described in the provision. The other parent may want interest on his/her share of the property, and have it protected by a mortgage or other security. Finally, the income tax consequences from a delayed sale can be unfavorable. For all these reasons, if you want a delayed sale, go to a lawyer for help.

Solely-Owned Real Property

If you fail to deal with solely-owned real property in your judgment, the owner-spouse retains ownership of the property free of any claim or interest of the other spouse (in part, that's what paragraph #6 of the Judgment of Divorce (GRP 4a) is about). But you shouldn't leave it at that. Even if you want the owner-spouse to keep his/her solely-owned property (presumably because of a trade-off or buy-out), you should say so in your judgment. When you want another disposition of the property, such as a sale to a third party, you must provide for that as well.

In this case, the nonowner is trading off his/her hypothetical share in the owner-spouse's solely-owned real property for equivalent property elsewhere in the property division. The owner-spouse keeps ownership of the property:

13. <u>Real Property</u>. Plaintiff is awarded the property located at 121 S. Main, Lake City, Michigan, and described below, free of any claims of defendant:

    Lot 2 of Assessor's Plat, Lake City, Ojibway County, Michigan

    Plaintiff shall be responsible for any indebtedness against the property and hold defendant harmless from liability for this debt.

The owner-spouse buys out the nonowner's "share" in his/her solely-owned real property for cash:*

13. <u>Real Property</u>. Plaintiff shall be awarded the property located at 121 S. Main, Lake City, Michigan, and described below, free of any claims of defendant, upon the payment of $25,000 to defendant:

    Lot 2 of Assessor's Plat, Lake City, Ojibway County, Michigan

    Plaintiff shall be responsible for any indebtedness against the property and hold defendant harmless from liability for this debt.

In this scenario, the solely-owned property must be sold as soon as possible to a third party followed by a division of the proceeds:**

13. <u>Real Property</u>. The property located at 121 S. Main, Lake City, Michigan, and described below, shall be owned by plaintiff and defendant as tenants in common:

    Lot 2 of Assessor's Plat, Lake City, Ojibway County, Michigan

    This property shall be sold as soon as possible at a price and terms the parties shall agree upon. After the property is sold, the proceeds of the sale shall be applied first to satisfy any indebtedness against

---

* As an alternative, you can provide for an installment sale. But as explained above, that's probably too difficult for you to arrange yourself.

** Instead of an immediate sale, you could choose a delayed sale. Yet, as mentioned above, you will probably need legal help to provide for that arrangement.

the property, then against all the costs of sale (including any broker's commission and closing costs). Any remainder shall be divided [equally] between the parties.

Until the closing of the sale, plaintiff shall have sole possession of the property. Plaintiff shall be responsible for any mortgage or land contract payments, taxes, insurance and other expenses of maintaining the property during that time until the day of closing.

Dividing Personal Property

You may have already divided the bulk of your personal property, such as clothing, household goods, bank accounts and motor vehicles, during or even before your divorce. Courts usually permit informal divisions of personal property because they know that you cannot wait until the end of your divorce to divide essential items. If you have already divided some or all of your personal property that way, confirm the division by checking the first box in paragraph #5B of the Judgment of Divorce (GRP 4a).

On the other hand, you should specifically mention personal property that hasn't yet been transferred to the intended recipient at the time of your final hearing. This avoids confusion about ownership later. For example, if you and the defendant have agreed that the defendant must give you an automobile, a dinette set and a $1,000 bank account, you should say so in your judgment. Check the second box in paragraph #5B of the Judgment of Divorce (GRP 4a), and include this provision in the Judgment of Divorce (GRP 4c):

13. <u>Personal Property</u>. Plaintiff is awarded the following personal property free of any claims of defendant:

1984 Dodge Aries automobile VIN VL29C4B266259

Five-piece (table and four chairs) Contemporary dinette set

Ojibway State Bank savings account #XXXXXXXXX-021, with a current balance of $1,000

Plaintiff shall be responsible for any indebtedness against this property and hold defendant harmless from liability for this debt.

You can adapt this provision to divide almost any type of personal property. But use it only for the distribution of important items of personal property. Don't clutter up your judgment by mentioning every piece of furniture or article of clothing.

Whenever you use such a provision, include a complete description of the property since this aids transfer of the item later (see "After Your Divorce" on page 101 for more information about transferring property). Describe the property fully and mention any identification numbers (account numbers for financial accounts, vehicle identification numbers (VINs) for automobiles, hull numbers for boats, etc.). You may want to disguise the full account numbers of financial accounts or credit cards because divorce judgments are public documents and this information could fall into the wrong hands. In the example above, the account number is partially disguised (as is often done on credit card receipts), with just a few digits showing.

Dividing Retirement Benefits, Businesses and Other New Property

A divorce property division isn't complete without considering so-called new property (retirement benefits, businesses, etc.). The problem is, new property is often difficult to divide. Unlike a house or an automobile, you can't put retirement benefits on the market, sell them and divide the proceeds (most retirement plans prohibit this kind of sale or transfer even if you could find a buyer).

A business can also be hard to liquidate. Some one-person businesses depend on the skill of their owner-operators and may be impossible to sell as going concerns. And even when a small business can be sold, it must often be sold as a piece because few people will buy a share of a small business.

Despite these problems, the law has devised ways to divide new property, often without actually distributing it.

Dividing Retirement Benefits

Michigan courts have approved two methods for dividing retirement benefits: 1) trade-off 2) division of payments.

In a trade-off, the nonemployee-spouse trades his/her interest in the retirement benefits for a like share of other property. As an example, let's assume that a couple owns an automobile worth $10,000 and the husband has retirement benefits with a present value of $10,000. If the spouses agree to an equal property division, the wife might trade her one-half interest in the retirement benefits for the husband's half-interest in the automobile. Thus, the retirement benefits stay with the husband, but the wife gets the automobile. By this means, the retirement benefits have been divided, but without actually distributing them.

The other method of division—division of payments—results in the actual distribution of the retirement benefits to both spouses. With this method, the retirement benefits are divided fractionally between the spouses as payments are made. For ex-

ample, if the husband is receiving monthly payments, and the parties want an equal division of property, they could assign one-half of the payments to each spouse monthly.

Each of these methods has pluses and minuses. Trade-off is nice because it gives the nonemployee-spouse value immediately, without waiting for the retirement plan to mature (pay benefits). But it requires an estimation of the present value of the benefits, which is complicated (see "Can I Get a Fair Property Division?" on page 31 for more about the valuation of retirement plans). Trade-off also places the risk that the employee-spouse will never collect the benefits (because of premature death, early retirement, discharge, bankruptcy of the employer, etc.) on the employee-spouse alone. If the employee-spouse never gets benefits, s/he has traded off other property for nothing. Finally, a trade-off may be impossible if the value of the retirement benefits is great and there is no other property that can be traded for them.

It's simpler to just divide the retirement benefits. Unlike a trade-off, you normally won't have to estimate the total value of the benefits, since your dividing the payments, not the total benefits package. This avoids making a difficult present value calculation. Dividing payments also spreads the risks associated with the retirement benefits to both spouses. If the retirement plan fails, both spouses share the loss; if benefits increase in the future, each spouse shares in the gain.

But unless the retirement plan is mature (paying benefits), dividing payments often won't give the nonemployee-spouse any property immediately after the divorce. What's more, a division-of-payments order is difficult to provide for in a divorce judgment. You must use precise language or it won't be legally effective. For this reason, if you want to divide retirement benefits during divorce yourself, you will have to use the trade-off method. To do that, simply check the first box in paragraph #8 of your Judgment of Divorce (GRP 4a), and then give or get equivalent property elsewhere in the property division. If you want to use the division-of-payments method, see a lawyer.

Individual retirement arrangements (IRAs), which are individual retirement plans, can be divided in several ways, including: 1) transfer from the owner-spouse to the other spouse 2) trade-off 3) withdrawal and division of the proceeds.

To transfer an IRA, describe the account and provide for transfer in a judgment provision, like the bank account example on page 168. This kind of divorce-related transfer isn't considered a withdrawal, so no tax or early withdrawal penalty is imposed. But tax and an early withdrawal penalty may be due if the new owner of the account withdraws money from it prematurely. If you want to trade off an IRA for other property, make sure that you have checked the first box in paragraph #8 of your Judgment of Divorce (GRP 4a), and give the nonowner-spouse equivalent property elsewhere in the judgment. You can also withdraw the money in an IRA and divide it. But if the IRA-owner is younger than 59½, that's a premature withdrawal and a penalty will be imposed.

Keogh (HR-10) plans are another type of individual retirement plan. Like IRAs, these plans can be transferred, traded or withdrawn and divided.

But transferring or withdrawing Keoghs can have bad tax consequences, leaving trade-off as the best method of division in most cases.

Dividing Businesses and Other New Property

Business interests can be transferred between spouses or liquidated and divided. In many cases, trade-off is the best method of division. To trade off a business, create a judgment provision like the one below, assigning the business to the business-owner, and then give the nonbusiness-owner equivalent property elsewhere in the property division.

13. <u>Personal Property</u>. Defendant is awarded all the assets, including inventory, supplies, fixtures, equipment, accounts and goodwill, in the House of Waterbeds, Lake City, Michigan, free of any claims of plaintiff. Defendant shall hold plaintiff harmless from any liability in connection with this business.

Division of Debts

As you end your marriage, who is responsible for debts you leave behind? If you do nothing, the following general rules govern liability for individual debts (debts incurred by a spouse alone) and joint debts (debts taken on by spouses together):

Individual debt. The spouse who incurred the debt (debtor-spouse) remains liable for it after the divorce. The nondebtor-spouse generally won't be liable for the debt unless s/he gave the debtor-spouse authority, as agent, to incur debts on the nondebtor-spouse's behalf. The agent's authority can be express, implied or even given after the fact, by ratification of what the debtor-spouse did.

Joint debt. Because both spouses incurred joint debts, each remains liable for these after divorce.

By dividing debts in your divorce judgment, you can modify this liability to an extent. A debt provision can shift the liability for an individual debt from the debtor-spouse to the other spouse. Or the provision could have one spouse assume total liability for a joint debt.

Not all debts may be reassigned that way. Educational and personal loans are better left with those incurring them, since they have a bigger incentive to pay them. Likewise, debts secured by property (mortgages, land contracts and other liens) are customarily transferred to the recipients of the secured property. (For this reason, all the sample property division provisions in this appendix transfer secured debts together with the property securing them.) On the other hand, general unsecured debts, such as credit card or charge account debts, are good choices for division.

Whatever you decide, any debt provision you insert in your judgment must describe the debt and say who is responsible for paying it, as in the following provision:

13. <u>Debts</u>. Defendant is responsible for, and must hold plaintiff harm-less from, the following debts:

Lake City Department Store charge account #XXXXXX45 with a current balance of $540

Mastercredit account #XXXX XXXX XXXX 6529 with a current balance of $1,233.33

Debt Division and Creditors' Rights

Although you and the defendant can rearrange debts in your judgment, your arrangements won't affect the rights of the creditors holding the debts. Your creditors will have the same rights after your divorce as they had before.*

Glossary

Indemnity–legal claim making someone else answerable for your obligation to a third person.

Example: A couple got a joint car loan from a bank (creditor). In their divorce, the wife received ownership of the car and the car loan was assigned to her by a debt provision in the divorce judgment. She falls behind on the car payments. The bank could sue the husband because the debt division didn't affect his liability to the bank.

If a debt division doesn't change creditors' rights, why go to the trouble of dividing debts in your divorce judgment? The advantage to debt division is that it provides a legal claim, known as indemnity, against the spouse assuming the debt. The indemnity can then be used as a defense or as a direct claim.

Example: A couple gets a joint car loan from a bank (creditor). In their divorce, the wife gets the car and agrees to pay the loan off in a debt division provision. After she falls behind in car payments, the bank sues both spouses. The husband could cite the indemnity from the debt division and shift liability to the wife. Had the bank sued the husband alone, he could add the wife to the case and raise the indemnity against her this way.

Alimony Provisions

Every divorce judgment must deal with alimony** and settle the issue for both spouses by: 1) waiver (giving up alimony totally and irrevocably) 2)

---

*   A creditor can agree to release a spouse from liability for a joint debt. In that case, the released spouse would no longer be liable to the creditor for the debt. Nevertheless, most creditors won't consent to such releases because they prefer to have two debtors rather than one.

**   In the judgment, alimony is called by its real name: spousal support.

reservation (leaving the issue open so you can ask for alimony later, with no guarantee that it will be granted then) 3) grant of alimony (resulting in an order for alimony).

When you're dealing with alimony in your judgment, make sure that you settle it for *both* parties in one of the three ways described above. If you fail to settle alimony for a party, the failure automatically reserves alimony for the neglected party.

Waiver of Alimony

When you want to waive alimony for you and/or the defendant, indicate in paragraph #4 of your Judgment of Divorce (GRP 4a) that alimony is "not granted for" that particular party. Frequently, both parties mutually waive alimony. With no alimony being ordered in the case, check the box at the end of paragraph #4 that a Uniform Spousal Support Order isn't required.

Reservation of Alimony

If you want to leave the issue of alimony open for a party, check the box in paragraph #4 of the GRP 4a indicating that alimony is "reserved for" that party. Reservation of alimony means no alimony is being ordered now, so check the box at the end of paragraph #4 saying that a Uniform Spousal Support Order isn't required.

You cannot reserve alimony merely because you find the issue of alimony bothersome and don't want to deal with it now. To reserve alimony, you must have a good reason for the reservation, such as: 1) there is only limited jurisdiction in the case (see "Can I Get a Divorce in Michigan?" on page 24 about why limited jurisdiction isn't enough for alimony) 2) the payer is elusive or has disappeared and you cannot determine his/her ability to pay alimony 3) the would-be recipient of the alimony is making a personal or career change and isn't sure of his/her financial needs now. When alimony is reserved for a party, s/he can come back to court after the divorce and ask for alimony. At that time, the court will decide whether it should be paid.

Grant of Alimony

If you and the defendant have agreed on some type of alimony, check the box in paragraph #4 of the GRP 4a that says alimony is "granted later in the judgment for" the recipient (payee). At the end of paragraph #4, check the box saying that a Uniform Spousal Support Order shall accompany and be incorporated into the judgment. You must then provide for the alimony in a uniform support order for alimony.

Providing for Alimony

Alimony used to be dealt with inside divorce judgments. As of 2006, alimony (and child support, in divorces with minor children) must now be provided for separately in state-issued uniform support orders. The state wants alimony to be handled this way to achieve greater uniformity among support orders.

There are two kinds of uniform support orders for alimony: 1) Uniform Spousal Support Order (FOC 10b) 2) Uniform Spousal Support Order, No Friend of Court Services (FOC 10c). The FOC 10b is for payment of alimony the normal way (by immediate income withholding through the SDU) and the FOC 10c is for alimony payment after a total or partial opt-out of the friend of the court system (see "Choosing an Alimony Payment Method" below for more about these payment options).

The Domestic Relations Judgment Information form (FOC 100) is now also required in divorce-with-alimony cases. The FOC 100 gives the friend of the court personal and financial information about the parties. This information was also once included in divorce judgments, but is now kept separate because of privacy concerns. Like the Verified Statement and Application for IV-D Services (FOC 23) filed at the beginning of with-alimony divorces, the FOC 100 goes to the friend of the court and parties, but isn't filed with the clerk (where sensitive information in the form would be public record).

Ordering Alimony

The Uniform Spousal Support Order (FOC 10b) allows for payment of either short- or long-term alimony. The provisions excerpted below from the FOC 10b show both kinds. The provisions make the alimony subject to several conditions. You can omit any of these or add others. But keep in mind that the death-of-the-recipient condition is necessary to qualify the payments as alimony for federal tax purposes. Without that condition, the payments won't be deductible by the payer.

Short-Term Alimony

After stating the payer and payee, amount and effective date of the alimony in paragraph #1 of the FOC 10b, you can add conditions to end the alimony in paragraph #3. The addition of an end-date makes this short-term alimony (two-year in this example).

3. This order continues until the death of the payee or until the earliest of the following events:
   ☒ Date: _5-7-91_   ☐ $_____ _____ is paid.
   ☒ Remarriage of the payee.   ☒ Death of the payer.
   ☒ Other (specify all other events): _COHABITATION BY THE PAYEE WITH A MEMBER OF THE_

   OPPOSITE SEX OR MODIFICATION BY THE COURT.

After describing the alimony in paragraph #1 of the FOC 10b, you can add conditions to end the alimony in paragraph #3. By leaving out an end-date and having the alimony open-ended, you make the alimony long-term.

3. This order continues until the death of the payee or until the earliest of the following events:
☐ Date: _____   ☐ $_____ is paid.
☒ Remarriage of the payee.   ☒ Death of the payer.
☒ Other (specify all other events): _COHABITATION BY THE PAYEE WITH A MEMBER OF THE_

    OPPOSITE SEX OR MODIFICATION BY THE COURT.

Choosing an Alimony Payment Method

When you provide for alimony, you must also arrange for a method of payment. As with the other kind of support, child support, the normal way of paying alimony is by immediate income withholding through the friend of the court system to the state disbursement unit (SDU). With this method of payment, the alimony payer's source of income (usually an employer) deducts the alimony from the payer's wages or salary and sends the money to the SDU, which forwards it to the alimony recipient (payee). The friend of the court monitors payment so it can enforce the obligation.

If you want payment of alimony by immediate income withholding to the SDU, you don't have to do anything extra because the Uniform Spousal Support Order (FOC 10b) is set up for this payment. You must also use an Order Regarding Income Withholding (FOC 5), which authorizes immediate income withholding (in some counties, the friend of the court will prepare the FOC 5 for you). And in Wayne County only, you must add an extra support form: Order Data Form-Support (FD/FOC 4002) (this form comes with instructions).

Other Methods of Payment

Immediate income withholding is popular with alimony recipients and the courts because it makes alimony easy to collect. On the other hand, some alimony payers dislike it because it creates more paperwork for their employers. They may want to avoid immediate income withholding and set up a different method of payment.

If alimony isn't immediately withheld, the payer can pay it to the SDU or directly to the alimony recipient. Alimony payers may like payment to the recipient because it's informal with less paperwork. But recipients usually prefer payment to the SDU, since this offers better collection, record-keeping and enforcement of the alimony.

You can choose these other options by opting out of the friend of the court system. You can do a limited opt-out from immediate income with-holding and choose another payment method, or elect another payment method as part of a broader (total or partial) opt-out from the friend of the court system. Appendix C has complete information about these other payment options obtained by opting out.

Obtaining Alimony at the Final Hearing

Besides the extra forms described above, you must take several special steps before and during the final hearing to obtain alimony in your divorce judgment.

Friend of the Court Recommendation about Alimony

When alimony is at stake, some friends of the court may investigate the issue during the divorce and submit a nonbinding recommendation to the judge about alimony. You will also receive a copy of any recommendation about alimony, which you should take into account as your prepare the Uniform Spousal Support Order (FOC 10b).

See if the friend of the court's recommendation coincides with your and the defendant's agreement on alimony. If it does, there shouldn't be any problem. But if the friend of the court's recommendation diverges from your view about alimony, you must be prepared to justify your position to the judge at the final hearing.

Review and Approval of the Final Divorce Papers

In divorce-with-alimony cases, some counties want the friend of the court to review the final divorce papers to make sure everything is in order (check with the friend of the court to find out the local policy). If that's necesssary in your county, submit the Judgment of Divorce (GRP 4), Uniform Spousal Support Order (FOC 10b) and Order Regarding Income Withholding (FOC 5) to the friend of the court a week or so before your final hearing. If the papers are satisfactory, the friend of the court will approve them orally or by adding a notation to the papers. If they're unsatisfactory, the friend of the court should suggest corrections.

In Wayne County, you don't need the friend of the court's approval if you can truthfully say in the Certificate of Conformity for Domestic Relations Order or Judgment (1225) that your judgment (incorporating the spousal support order) complies with the friend of the court's recommendation about alimony. If it doesn't, you must get the Wayne County Friend of the Court's approval of the judgment papers.

Serving the Judgment Information Form on the Friend of the Court

The original Domestic Relations Judgment Information form (FOC 100) should be served on the friend of the court before the final hearing. If you're submitting your other final divorce papers to the friend of the court for approval of the alimony, include the FOC 100 also. If not, deliver or send the FOC 100 to the friend of the court separately.

Either way, after service prepare a Proof of Service of Domestic Relations Judgment Information Form (GRP 7) proving service of the FOC 100 on the friend of the court, so the court will know this at the final hearing (as a result, try to have the GRP 7 in your case file before the hearing). The defendant should also get a copy of the Domestic Relations Judgment Information form (FOC 100), and you can prove service on him/her in the same GRP 7. (The GRP 7 replaces the Proof of Mailing (MC 302) cited in the FOC 100 as the suggested proof of service form.)

Bring the extra alimony-related papers (FOC 10b and FOC 5) to the final hearing, along with extra copies for the friend of the court, you and the defendant. Add these alimony papers to your final divorce papers for submission to the judge, signing by him/her and filing after the hearing, as described in "Attending the Final Hearing" on page 93.

During the final hearing itself, make sure you mention the alimony in your testimony. Describe the amount of alimony, duration (short- or long-term) and agreement with the defendant that produced the alimony. In this regard, having the defendant at the final hearing, to confirm the agreement, is helpful.

After the final hearing, file the alimony papers (FOC 10b and FOC 5) along with the other final divorce papers as described in "Filing the Final Divorce Papers" on page 93. In Wayne County only, you'll want to include the Order Data Form-Support (FD/FOC 4002) among these papers, so the Wayne County Clerk can forward this form to the friend of the court.

A little later, include the alimony papers among the other final divorce papers you send to the defendant, as described on page 94. And then list these papers in the Proof of Mailing (MC 302) as having been served on the defendant along with the Judgment of Divorce (GRP 4) and any local papers.

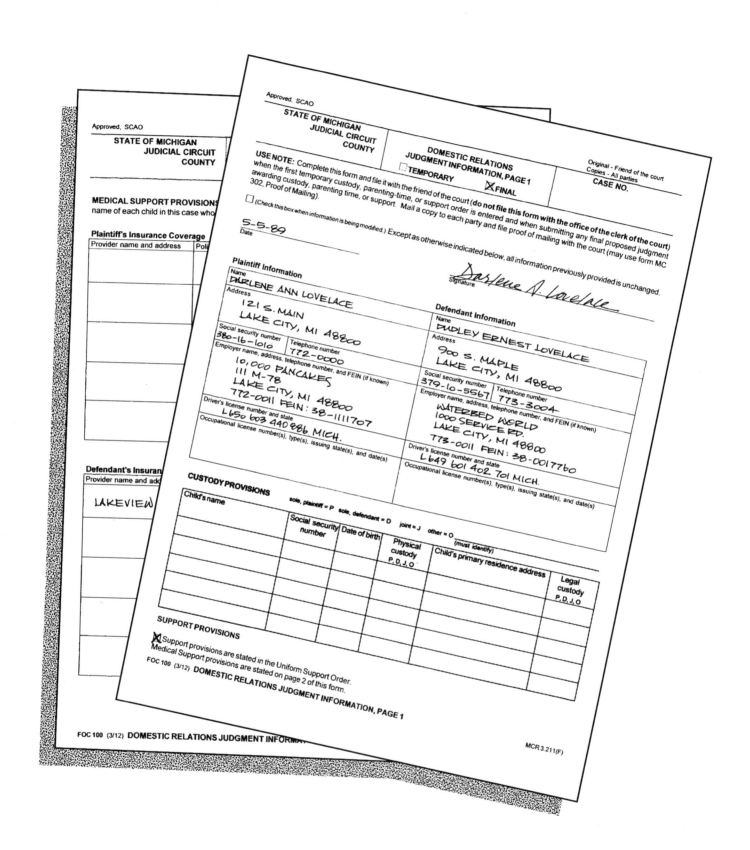

Approved, SCAO

STATE OF MICHIGAN
JUDICIAL CIRCUIT
COUNTY

MEDICAL SUPPORT PROVISION
name of each child in this case who

Plaintiff's Insurance Coverage

Provider name and address	Poli

Defendant's Insuran

Provider name and ad
LAKEVIEW

FOC 100 (3/12) DOMESTIC RELATIONS JUDGMENT INFORMA

Approved, SCAO

STATE OF MICHIGAN
JUDICIAL CIRCUIT
COUNTY

DOMESTIC RELATIONS
JUDGMENT INFORMATION, PAGE 1
☐ TEMPORARY   ☒ FINAL

Original - Friend of the court
Copies - All parties

CASE NO.

USE NOTE: Complete this form and file it with the friend of the court **(do not file this form with the office of the clerk of the court)** when the first temporary custody, parenting-time, or support order is entered and when submitting any final proposed judgment awarding custody, parenting time, or support. Mail a copy to each party and file proof of mailing with the court (may use form MC 302, Proof of Mailing).

☐ (Check this box when information is being modified.) Except as otherwise indicated below, all information previously provided is unchanged.

Date: 5-5-89

Signature: *Darlene A. Lovelace*

Plaintiff Information

Name: DARLENE ANN LOVELACE
Address: 121 S. MAIN
LAKE CITY, MI 48800

Social security number	Telephone number
380-16-1010	772-0000

Employer name, address, telephone number, and FEIN (if known)
10,000 PANCAKES
111 M-78
LAKE CITY, MI 48800
772-0011 FEIN: 38-1111707

Driver's license number and state
L650 603 440 886 MICH.

Occupational license number(s), type(s), issuing state(s), and date(s)

Defendant Information

Name: DUDLEY ERNEST LOVELACE
Address: 900 S. MAPLE
LAKE CITY, MI 48800

Social security number	Telephone number
379-10-5567	773-3004

Employer name, address, telephone number, and FEIN (if known)
WATERBED WORLD
1000 SERVICE RD.
LAKE CITY, MI 48800
773-0011 FEIN: 38-0017760

Driver's license number and state
L649 601 402 701 MICH.

Occupational license number(s), type(s), issuing state(s), and date(s)

CUSTODY PROVISIONS

sole, plaintiff = P   sole, defendant = D   joint = J   other = O
(must identify)

Child's name	Social security number	Date of birth	Physical custody P,D,J,O	Child's primary residence address	Legal custody P,D,J,O

SUPPORT PROVISIONS

☒ Support provisions are stated in the Uniform Support Order.
☐ Medical Support provisions are stated on page 2 of this form.

FOC 100 (3/12) **DOMESTIC RELATIONS JUDGMENT INFORMATION, PAGE 1**

MCR 3.211(F)

STATE OF MICHIGAN Circuit Court - Family Division ___ COUNTY	PROOF OF SERVICE OF DOMESTIC RELATIONS JUDGMENT INFORMATION FORM	CASE NO.

Plaintiff (appearing *in propria persona*):

v

Defendant:

I served the following papers in this case as described below:

1. On **5-5-89**, I ☒ delivered ☐ sent by first-class mail the original Domestic Relations Judgment Information form for the Judgment of Divorce to the friend of the court at its official address.

2. On **5-5-89**, I sent a copy of the Domestic Relations Judgment Information form for the Judgment of Divorce to defendant by first-class mail at his/her address in the caption above, which is defendant's last known mailing address.

I declare that the statements above are true to the best of my information, knowledge and belief.

Date **5-5-89**

Plaintiff *Darlene A. Lovelace*

GRP 7 (3/07) PROOF OF SERVICE/DOMESTIC RELATIONS JUDGMENT INFORMATION FORM

Original - Court
1st copy - Plaintiff

2nd copy - Defendant
3rd copy - Friend of the court

Approved, SCAO

STATE OF MICHIGAN
JUDICIAL CIRCUIT
COUNTY

UNIFORM SPOUSAL SUPPORT ORDER
(PAGE 1)
☐ EX PARTE ☐ TEMPORARY ☐ MODIFICATION ☒ FINAL

CASE NO.

Court telephone no.

Court address

Plaintiff's name, address, and telephone no.

v

Defendant's name, address, and telephone no.

Plaintiff's attorney name, bar no., address, and telephone no.

Defendant's attorney name, bar no., address, and telephone no.

Plaintiff's source of income name, address, and telephone no.

Defendant's source of income name, address

ADD SOURCES OF INCOME (EMPLOYERS) TO CAPTION

This order is entered ☒ after hearing. ☐ on stipulation/consent of the parties.

IT IS ORDERED, UNLESS OTHERWISE ORDERED IN ITEM 10: ☐ Standard provisions have been modified (see item 10).

1. **Spousal Support.** Spousal support shall be paid monthly through the Michigan State Disbursement Unit as follows:

| Payer: DUDLEY E. LOVELACE | Payee: DARLENE A. LOVELACE | Amount: $200 | Effective date: 5-7-89 |

2. Income withholding takes immediate effect for those items payable through the Michigan State Disbursement Unit.

3. This order continues until the death of the payee or until the earliest of the following events:
☒ Date: 5-7-91   ☐ $_____ is paid.
☒ Remarriage of the payee.   ☒ Death of the payer.
☒ Other (specify all other events): COHABITATION BY THE PAYEE WITH A MEMBER OF THE OPPOSITE SEX OR MODIFICATION BY THE COURT.

☒4. For tax purposes, the payments will be deductible to the payer and included in the income of the payee.

☐5. Payments that must be paid directly to the third party (not to the payee) are listed below. (Payments to be made directly to a third party are not payable through the Michigan State Disbursement Unit or friend of the court.)

Type	Amount Per Month	Start Date	Pay to	End Date
	$			
	$			
	$			
	$			

(See page 2 for the remainder of the order.)

FOC 10b (3/12) UNIFORM SPOUSAL SUPPORT ORDER, PAGE 1

MCL 552.13, MCR 3.211

Approved, SCAO

STATE OF MICHIGAN
JUDICIAL CIRCUIT
COUNTY

Original - Court
1st copy - Plaintiff

2nd copy - Defendant
3rd copy - Friend of the court

UNIFORM SPOUSAL SUPPORT ORDER
(PAGE 2)

☐ EX PARTE ☐ TEMPORARY ☐ MODIFICATION ☒ FINAL

CASE NO.

Court address

Court telephone no.

Plaintiff's name

v

Defendant's name

6. Retroactive Modification, Surcharge for Past-Due Support, and Liens for Unpaid Support. Support is a judgment the date it is due and is not retroactively modifiable. A surcharge may be added to past-due support. Unpaid support is a lien by operation of law and the payer's property can be encumbered or seized if an arrearage accrues for more than the periodic support payments payable for two months under the payer's support order.

7. Address, Employment Status, Health Insurance. Both parties shall notify the friend of the court in writing of: a) their mailing and residential addresses and telephone numbers; b) the names, addresses, and telephone numbers of their sources of income; c) their health-maintenance or insurance companies, insurance coverage, persons insured, or contract numbers; d) their occupational or drivers' licenses; and e) their social security numbers unless exempt by law pursuant to MCL 552.603. Both parties shall notify the friend of the court in writing within 21 days of any change in this information. Failure to do so may result in a fee being imposed.

8. Fees. The payer of support shall pay statutory and service fees as required by law.

9. Prior Orders. This order supersedes all prior spousal support orders. Past-due amounts owed under any prior support order are preserved.

10. Other: (Attach separate sheets as needed.)

Plaintiff (if consent/stipulation)

Date

Defendant (if consent/stipulation)

Date

Plaintiff's attorney

Date

Defendant's attorney

Date

5-7-89

Date

Lester Jubbs

Judge

Bar no.

CERTIFICATE OF MAILING

I certify that on this date I served a copy of this order on the parties or their attorneys by first-class mail addressed to their last-known addresses as defined in MCR 3.203.

Date

Signature

COURT USE ONLY

FOC 10b   (3/12)   **UNIFORM SPOUSAL SUPPORT ORDER, PAGE 2**

MCL 552.13, MCR 3.211

Approved, SCAO

STATE OF MICHIGAN JUDICIAL CIRCUIT COUNTY	Original - Court 1st copy - Friend of the court	2nd copy - Plaintiff 3rd copy - Defendant Additional copies to all sources of income
Court address	**ORDER REGARDING INCOME WITHHOLDING**	**CASE NO.**

Court telephone no.

Plaintiff's name, address, and telephone no

v

Defendant's name, address, and telephone no.

THE COURT FINDS:

1. The requirements for implementation or adjustment of income withholding
   - ☒ have
   - ☐ have not
   been met

☐ 2. The proposed administrative adjustment of income withholding
   - ☐ will
   - ☐ will not
   produce an unjust or inappropriate result

IT IS ORDERED:

3. Income withholding is
   - ☐ discontinued.
   - ☐ effective.
   - ☐ effective in an amount pursuant to the Michigan Child Support Formula to pay current support and arrears.
   - ☐ effective as follows:

5-7-89
Date

Lester Jubbs
Judge   Bar no.

CERTIFICATE OF MAILING

I certify that on this date I served a copy of this order on the parties and sources of income by first-class mail addressed to their last-known addresses as defined in MCR 3.203

Date

Signature

FOC 5 (3/08) **ORDER REGARDING INCOME WITHHOLDING**

MCL 552.601 et seq

PAGE 1 OF 2

ORDER DETAILS

ORDER DATA FORM-SUPPORT
Re: SUBMISSION FOR LOADING
ATTACHED SUPPORT ORDER INTO
MiCSES ON FOC COMPUTER SYSTEM

STATE OF MICHIGAN
COUNTY OF WAYNE
THIRD JUDICIAL CIRCUIT COURT
FAMILY DIVISION

THE ORDER WAS ENTERED ON:
5-7-89
(DATE ON ORDER STAMPED BY JUDGE'S CLERK)

JUDGE

> USE THIS FORM IN
> WAYNE COUNTY ONLY.
> SEE THE BLANK FORM
> WHICH HAS A TWO-PAGE
> PREFACE WITH MORE
> INSTRUCTIONS

(PLACE LABEL HERE)

CASE #:

JUDGE

*INDICATES REQUIRED INFORMATION
CHECK ONLY THE BOXES WHICH APPLY TO PROVISIONS IN THE SUBMITTED ORDER

* PLAINTIFF NAME:
DARLENE ANN LOVELACE

* DEFENDANT NAME:
DUDLEY ERNEST LOVELACE

*THIS ORDER IS: ☐ TEMPORARY ☒ JUDGMENT ☐ MODIFICATION
☐ EX PARTE (PROOF OF SERVICE REQUIRED) ☐ YES ☐ NO

*WERE CHILD SUPPORT GUIDELINES FOLLOWED?

*THE CHILD SUPPORT PAYER IS ☐ PLAINTIFF ☐ DEFENDANT ☐ NOT APPLICABLE.
☐ PAY DIRECT, NOT THROUGH FOC.

☐ CHILD SUPPORT. COMMENCEMENT DATE IS _____
* 3 CHILDREN PER WEEK CHILD SUPPORT AMOUNT $ _____
* 2 CHILDREN PER WEEK CHILD SUPPORT AMOUNT $ _____
* 1 CHILD PER WEEK CHILD SUPPORT AMOUNT $ _____
* 5 CHILDREN PER WEEK CHILD SUPPORT AMOUNT $ _____
* 4 CHILDREN PER WEEK CHILD SUPPORT AMOUNT $ _____

☐ INCOME WITHHOLDING: ☐ PROCESS AT GUIDELINE AMOUNT ☐ PROCESS AT $ _____ PER WEEK

☐ CHILD SUPPORT ARREARAGE: ☐ SET AT $ _____ AS OF DATE: _____
☐ PRESERVED ☐ CANCELED AS OF DATE: _____ PER WEEK, COMMENCEMENT DATE IS _____;

☐ CHILD CARE EXPENSES: $ _____
END DATE IS ☐ GUIDELINE DATE **OR** ☐ DATE: _____ ☐ SET AT $ _____ AS OF DATE: _____

☐ CHILD CARE ARREARAGE:
☐ PRESERVED ☐ CANCELED AS OF DATE: _____

☐ ARREARAGE ADJUSTMENT: ☐ ADD ADDITIONAL OBLIGATION IN AMOUNT OF $ _____
☐ DIRECT CREDIT IN AMOUNT OF $ _____

☐ MEDICAL INSURANCE IN ORDER.
☐ CHILD SUPPORT PAYER RESPONSIBLE FOR _____ % OF UNINSURED MEDICAL EXPENSES.

☐ PARENTING TIME ABATEMENT: _____ % PARENTING TIME CREDIT AFTER _____ CONSECUTIVE OVERNIGHTS.
☐ PARENTING TIME ORDERED: (CHECK ONE): ☐ RESERVED ☐ REFER TO FAMILY COUNSELING/OTHER
☐ REASONABLE ☐ SPECIFIC ☐ SUPERVISED

*THE SPOUSAL SUPPORT PAYER IS ☐ PLAINTIFF ☒ DEFENDANT ☐ NOT APPLICABLE.
☒ SPOUSAL SUPPORT: ☒ $ **200** PER WEEK, COMMENCEMENT DATE: **5-7-89** ☐ PAY DIRECT, NOT THROUGH FOC
☐ PERMANENT ☒ END DATE **5-7-91** ☐ SET AT $ _____ AS OF DATE: _____
☐ SPOUSAL SUPPORT ARREARAGE:
☐ PRESERVED ☐ CANCELED AS OF DATE: _____

☐ ORDER REFERS MATTERS TO DIVORCE INVESTIGATION/MODIFICATION FOR FURTHER INVESTIGATION.

I CERTIFY THAT THE ABOVE INFORMATION IS TRUE TO THE BEST OF MY KNOWLEDGE,
INFORMATION AND BELIEF, AND IS IN FULL CONFORMITY WITH THE REQUIREMENTS SET FORTH
BY STATUTE AND COURT RULE AND THE DECISION OF THE COURT. (NOTE: FOC WILL NOT READ
THE ORDER WHEN ENTERING IT ON MiCSES.)   *Darlene Lovelace*   BAR NO. _____
5-5-89   SIGNATURE OF ATTORNEY PLAINTIFF
DATE:
PLEASE PRINT:
ATTORNEY NAME
121 S. MAIN
ADDRESS
LAKE CITY, MI 48800
CITY/STATE/ZIP   **772-0000**
                                                 TELEPHONE NO.

FD/FOC 4002 (11/06/02) ORDER DATA FORM-SUPPORT

☐ PLAINTIFF ☐ DEFENDANT
HOME TELEPHONE NO:
FIA/TANF NO.:
NOW ACTIVE. ☐ YES ☐ NO
EMPLOYER FED I D. NO.:

☐ PLAINTIFF ☐ DEFENDANT
HOME TELEPHONE NO:
FIA/TANF NO.:
NOW ACTIVE. ☐ YES ☐ NO
EMPLOYER FED I D. NO.:

* SOCIAL SECURITY NUMBER(S)

Regular Forms

Note: To remove the forms cleanly from the book, follow these steps: 1) keep the back of the book as flat as possible on a table or other hard surface 2) open the book at the form you want to remove and pull gently on the form at its perforated edge, keeping the back of the book flat 3) if the form won't pull away easily, take a knife and cut the perforated edge of the form around 1" at the top and bottom, and resume steps 1 and 2.

STATE OF MICHIGAN JUDICIAL DISTRICT JUDICIAL CIRCUIT COUNTY PROBATE	SUMMONS AND COMPLAINT	CASE NO.

Court address | **Court telephone no.**

Plaintiff's name(s), address(es), and telephone no(s).	v	Defendant's name(s), address(es), and telephone no(s).
Plaintiff's attorney, bar no., address, and telephone no.		

SUMMONS **NOTICE TO THE DEFENDANT**: In the name of the people of the State of Michigan you are notified:

1. You are being sued.
2. **YOU HAVE 21 DAYS** after receiving this summons to **file a written answer with the court** and serve a copy on the other party **or take other lawful action with the court** (28 days if you were served by mail or you were served outside this state). (MCR 2.111[C])
3. If you do not answer or take other action within the time allowed, judgment may be entered against you for the relief demanded in the complaint.

Issued	This summons expires	Court clerk

*This summons is invalid unless served on or before its expiration date.
This document must be sealed by the seal of the court.

COMPLAINT *Instruction: The following is information that is required to be in the caption of every complaint and is to be completed by the plaintiff. Actual allegations and the claim for relief must be stated on additional complaint pages and attached to this form.*

Family Division Cases

☐ There is no other pending or resolved action within the jurisdiction of the family division of circuit court involving the family or family members of the parties.

☐ An action within the jurisdiction of the family division of the circuit court involving the family or family members of the parties has been previously filed in _____ Court.
The action ☐ remains ☐ is no longer pending. The docket number and the judge assigned to the action are:

Docket no.	Judge	Bar no.

General Civil Cases

☐ There is no other pending or resolved civil action arising out of the same transaction or occurrence as alleged in the complaint.

☐ A civil action between these parties or other parties arising out of the transaction or occurrence alleged in the complaint has been previously filed in _____ Court.
The action ☐ remains ☐ is no longer pending. The docket number and the judge assigned to the action are:

Docket no.	Judge	Bar no.

VENUE

Plaintiff(s) residence (include city, township, or village)	Defendant(s) residence (include city, township, or village)
Place where action arose or business conducted	

Date _____ Signature of attorney/plaintiff _____

If you require special accommodations to use the court because of a disability or if you require a foreign language interpreter to help you fully participate in court proceedings, please contact the court immediately to make arrangements.

MC 01 (3/08) **SUMMONS AND COMPLAINT** MCR 2.102(B)(11), MCR 2.104, MCR 2.105, MCR 2.107, MCR 2.113(C)(2)(a), (b), MCR 3.206(A)

TO PROCESS SERVER: You are to serve the summons and complaint not later than 91 days from the date of filing or the date of expiration on the order for second summons. You must make and file your return with the court clerk. If you are unable to complete service you must return this original and all copies to the court clerk.

CERTIFICATE / AFFIDAVIT OF SERVICE / NONSERVICE

☐ **OFFICER CERTIFICATE**
I certify that I am a sheriff, deputy sheriff, bailiff, appointed court officer, or attorney for a party (MCR 2.104[A][2]), and that: (notarization not required)

OR

☐ **AFFIDAVIT OF PROCESS SERVER**
Being first duly sworn, I state that I am a legally competent adult who is not a party or an officer of a corporate party, and that: (notarization required)

☐ I served personally a copy of the summons and complaint,
☐ I served by registered or certified mail (copy of return receipt attached) a copy of the summons and complaint, together with _____
List all documents served with the Summons and Complaint

_____

_____ on the defendant(s):

Defendant's name	Complete address(es) of service	Day, date, time

☐ I have personally attempted to serve the summons and complaint, together with any attachments, on the following defendant(s) and have been unable to complete service.

Defendant's name	Complete address(es) of service	Day, date, time

I declare that the statements above are true to the best of my information, knowledge, and belief.

Service fee $	Miles traveled	Mileage fee $	Total fee $

Signature _____

Name (type or print) _____

Title _____

Subscribed and sworn to before me on _____ , _____ County, Michigan.
Date

My commission expires: _____ Signature: _____
Date   Deputy court clerk/Notary public

Notary public, State of Michigan, County of _____

ACKNOWLEDGMENT OF SERVICE

I acknowledge that I have received service of the summons and complaint, together with _____
Attachments

_____ on _____
                                        Day, date, time

_____ on behalf of _____.

Signature

STATE OF MICHIGAN Circuit Court - Family Division COUNTY	COMPLAINT FOR DIVORCE	CASE NO.

Plaintiff: ☐ Husband ☐ Wife

Defendant:

	v	

Plaintiff's name before this marriage:

Defendant's name before this marriage:

1. Plaintiff's residence: at least ☐ 180 days in Michigan ☐ 10 days in this county immediately before filing of this complaint.

and/or

Defendant's residence: at least ☐ 180 days in Michigan ☐ 10 days in this county immediately before filing of this complaint.

2. Date of marriage _____ Place of marriage _____

3. The parties stopped living together as husband and wife on or about _____

4. There has been a breakdown of the marriage relationship to the extent that the objects of matrimony have been destroyed and there remains no reasonable likelihood that the marriage can be preserved.

5. There are no children of the parties or born during the marriage who are: a) minors (under 18) b) adults age 18-19½ entitled to support.

6. The wife ☐ is not pregnant. ☐ is pregnant, and the estimated date of birth is _____

7. There ☐ is ☐ is no property to be divided; ☐ division of property is controlled by the parties' prenuptial agreement attached as exhibit 1.

8. I request a judgment of divorce, and:

   a. property ☐ award to each party the property in his/her possession
             ☐ divide

☐ b. change wife's last name to _____

☐ c. spousal support for: ☐ plaintiff ☐ defendant

   plaintiff/defendant earns _____ monthly at _____ and needs support

   plaintiff/defendant earns _____ monthly at _____ and can pay support

☐ d. other:

Date _____ Plaintiff _____

GRP 1 (1/04) **COMPLAINT FOR DIVORCE, extension page to MC 01**

STATE OF MICHIGAN **Circuit Court - Family Division** COUNTY	**DEFAULT** Request, Affidavit, Entry and Notice of Entry	**CASE NO.**

Plaintiff (appearing *in propria persona*):

Defendant:

v

REQUEST

1. As shown by the proof of service on file, defendant was served with a summons and complaint on _____ , but did not respond to the complaint within 21 days (28 days if served by mail or out of state).

I request the clerk to enter the default of defendant for failure to plead or defend as provided by law.

Date _____   Plaintiff _____

AFFIDAVIT

Plaintiff, being sworn, says:

2. Defendant is not a minor or an incompetent person.

3. Defendant's (non)military status:

☐ a. Based on ☐ my personal knowledge, ☐ attached military status report, defendant
    ☐ is not in active-duty military service.
    ☐ is in active-duty military service, and ☐ has appeared and waived all lawsuit relief rights
        under the Servicemembers Civil Relief Act and/or MCL 32.517 (or similar military relief law
        from another state) in the attached appearance and waiver form.
        ☐ other: _____

☐ b. I am unable to determine whether or not defendant is in active-duty military service.

Date _____   Plaintiff _____

Subscribed and sworn to before me on _____ , _____ County, Michigan

My commission expires _____ Signature _____

Notary public, State of Michigan, County of _____

ENTRY AND NOTICE OF ENTRY

The default of defendant is entered for failure to plead or defend as provided by law.

Date _____   Court clerk _____

TO DEFENDANT: Please take notice of this entry of default against you.

PROOF OF MAILING

On the date below, I sent a copy of this Default to defendant by ordinary first-class mail at his/her address in the caption above, which is defendant's last known address.

I declare that the statement above is true to the best of my information, knowledge and belief.

Date _____   Plaintiff _____

GRP 2 (3/07)   **DEFAULT, Request, Affidavit, Entry and Notice of Entry**

STATE OF MICHIGAN **Circuit Court - Family Division** **COUNTY**	**MOTION TO ENTER DEFAULT JUDGMENT OF DIVORCE**	**CASE NO.**

Plaintiff (appearing *in propria persona*):

Defendant:

v

1. After entry of defendant's default on _____, I request the court to enter a default Judgment of Divorce granting the relief I requested in my Complaint for Divorce; ☐ and grant the following new/different relief_____

I declare that the statement above is true to the best of my information, knowledge and belief.

Date _____   Plaintiff _____

NOTICE OF HEARING

A hearing on this motion will be held in the courtroom of the judge assigned to this case, located at

(place)_____ on (date) _____ at (time) _____

PROOF OF MAILING

On the date below, I sent a copy of this motion to defendant by ordinary first-class mail at his/her address in the caption above, which is defendant's last known address.

I declare that the statement above is true to the best of my information, knowledge and belief.

Date _____   Plaintiff _____

GRP 3 (3/07)   **MOTION TO ENTER DEFAULT JUDGMENT OF DIVORCE**

STATE OF MICHIGAN Circuit Court - Family Division COUNTY	JUDGMENT OF DIVORCE Page 1 of pages	CASE NO.

Plaintiff (appearing *in propria persona*):

Defendant:

v

Date of hearing _____   Judge _____

After the defendant's default, **IT IS ORDERED:**

1. **DIVORCE:** The parties are divorced.

2. **CHILDREN:** There are no children of the parties or born during their marriage who are under 18 or adult and entitled to support.

☐ 3. **NAME CHANGE:** Wife's last name is changed to _____

4. **SPOUSAL SUPPORT:** Spousal support is
☐ not granted for   ☐ wife. ☐ husband.
☐ reserved for   ☐ wife. ☐ husband.
☐ granted later in the judgment for ☐ wife. ☐ husband.

A Uniform Spousal Support Order ☐ is not required because spousal support is not being ordered.
☐ shall accompany and be incorporated into this judgment because spousal support is granted.

5. **PROPERTY DIVISION:**

A. **Real property:**   ☐ The parties do not own any real property.
   (Land and buildings)   ☐ Real property is divided elsewhere in this judgment.

All real property owned by the parties in joint tenancy or tenancy by the entirety is converted to tenancy in common, unless this judgment provides otherwise.

B. **Personal property:**   ☐ Each party is awarded the personal property in his or her possession.
   (All other property)   ☐ Personal property is divided elsewhere in this judgment.

6. **STATUTORY RIGHTS:** All interests of the parties in the property of the other, now owned or later acquired, under MCL 700.2201-700.2405, are extinguished, including those known as dower under MCL 558.1-558.29.

7. **BENEFICIARY RIGHTS:** The rights each party has to the proceeds or policies or contracts of life insurance, endowments or annuities upon the life of the other as a named beneficiary or by assignment during or in anticipation of marriage, are ☐ extinguished. ☐ awarded later in the judgment.

8. **RETIREMENT BENEFITS:** Any rights of either party in any pension, annuity or retirement plan benefit of the other, whether these rights are vested or unvested, accumulated or contingent, are ☐ extinguished. ☐ awarded later in the judgment.

9. **DOCUMENTATION:** Each party shall promptly and properly execute and deliver to the other documents to carry out the terms of this judgment.

10. **PRIOR ORDERS:** Except as otherwise provided in this judgment, any nonfinal orders or injunctions entered in this action are terminated.

☐ 11. **SUSPENDED FEES AND COSTS:** The previously suspended fees and costs in this case of _____ shall be ☐ paid by ☐ plaintiff ☐ defendant   to the clerk. ☐ waived finally.

12. **EFFECTIVE DATE OF JUDGMENT:** This judgment shall become effective immediately after it is signed by the judge and filed with the clerk.

GRP 4a (3/07)   **JUDGMENT OF DIVORCE, page 1**

<table>
<tr>
<td>

STATE OF MICHIGAN
Circuit Court - Family Division
COUNTY

</td>
<td>

JUDGMENT OF DIVORCE
Final of   pages

</td>
<td>

CASE NO.

</td>
</tr>
</table>

Plaintiff:

Defendant:

v

IT IS ALSO ORDERED:

This judgment ☐ resolves ☐ does not resolve   the last pending claim in this case, and   ☐ closes ☐ does not close   the case, except to the extent jurisdiction is retained by law.

Date _____   Judge _____

GRP 4c (1/06)   JUDGMENT OF DIVORCE, final page

Testimony

1) My name is [full name] , my address is [address], and I am the plaintiff in this case.

2) I was married to the defendant on _____ at _____ by a person authorized to
perform marriages.
Date and place of marriage

3) Before the marriage, my/[my wife's] name was _____ .
Wife's former name

4) I filed my complaint for divorce on _____ . Before I filed the complaint, I had resided in Michigan since
Filing date
_____ and in this county since _____ .
State residence   County residence

5) As I said in my complaint, there has been a breakdown in our marriage relationship to the extent the objects of matrimony
have been destroyed because _____and there remains no
Brief facts to support grounds
reasonable likelihood that our marriage can be preserved because _____ .
Brief facts to support grounds

6) The defendant and I have no minor children, and I/[my wife] am not now pregnant.

7) I am working at_____ and am able to support myself. As a
result, no alimony is being ordered.
Source of support

8) We own some _____ that we have split between us. We have also agreed that
General description of personal property
the defendant is to give me_____ and I will pay off the debt on it.
Specific items of personal property transferred in judgment

9) We also own_____ worth around_____ .
Description of any real property   Value
We have agreed to _____ .
Manner of division

10) I would like my former name of _____ back.
Wife's name change

11) My court fees were suspended when I filed this divorce. Since then, _____ .
Current financial condition

12) Does the court have any questions?

STATE OF MICHIGAN **JUDICIAL DISTRICT** **JUDICIAL CIRCUIT**	**PROOF OF MAILING**	CASE NO.

Court address   Court telephone no.

Plaintiff(s)

v

Defendant(s)

On the date below I sent by first class mail a copy of _____

to:

Names and addresses

I declare that the statements above are true to the best of my information, knowledge and belief.

Date _____

Name (typed) _____

Signature _____

MC 302 (5/88) **PROOF OF MAILING**

Optional Forms

Approved, SCAO

REQUEST FOR ACCOMMODATIONS

Court name and location

Today's date

Instructions for completing form. *Provide your name, address, and telephone number. Check the boxes which apply to you and provide any necessary details. When you have completed this request, please return it to the court at the above address.*

1. Name

   Address

City	State	Zip	Telephone no.

2. Court activity you need accommodations for:

   ☐ Hearing _____
   Date

   ☐ Jury duty _____
   Date(s)

   ☐ Mediation meeting _____
   Date

   ☐ Other (specify): _____
   include dates if relevant

3. What is the nature of your disability?

   ☐ Physical mobility impairment (wheelchair, walker, crutches, etc.)

   ☐ Speech impairment (specify):_____

   ☐ Visual impairment

   ☐ Hearing impairment (specify):   ☐ deaf   ☐ hard of hearing   ☐ deaf-blind

   ☐ Other (specify): _____

4. What type of accommodation are you requesting?

   ☐ Interpreter for deaf (specify whether ASL, tactile, oral, etc.):_____

   ☐ Assistive listening device (specify):   ☐ headphones   ☐ neckloop   ☐ computer-assisted real-time captioning (CART)
   ☐ other: _____

   NOTE: To determine if other accommodations are available, contact the Division on Deaf and Hard of Hearing, 201 N. Washington Square, Suite 150, Lansing, MI 48913, telephone 517-335-6004, T/V toll free 877-499-6232, T/V fax 517-335-7773.

   ☐ Physical location accessible for persons with a physical mobility concern.

   ☐ Other (specify):_____

5. If the request for accommodation is denied or if the accommodation does not successfully establish effective communication, the applicant may file a grievance in accordance with the court's established grievance procedure. Upon request, the court shall provide the applicant a copy of the court's established grievance procedure.

For court use only

Original - Court file
1st copy - Assignment clerk/Extra
2nd copy - Friend of the court/Extra

3rd copy - Opposing party
4th copy - Moving party

Approved, SCAO

STATE OF MICHIGAN JUDICIAL DISTRICT JUDICIAL CIRCUIT COUNTY	MOTION AND ORDER FOR APPOINTMENT OF FOREIGN LANGUAGE INTERPRETER	CASE NO.

Court address   Court telephone no.

Plaintiff's name(s) ☐ moving party		Defendant's name(s) ☐ moving party
Plaintiff's attorney, bar no., address, and telephone no.	v	Defendant's attorney, bar no., address, and telephone no.

MOTION

1. I state that I am unable to speak English sufficiently to understand and participate in the proceedings in this case.

2. ☐ I am represented by an attorney.   ☐ I am not represented by an attorney.

3. I request the court to appoint a foreign language interpreter to interpret for me.

4. I request an interpreter who speaks the _____ language.

5. If required, place my request on the motion calendar.

_____
Date

_____
Signature

To be completed only if the court
requires a hearing on the motion.

NOTICE OF HEARING

You are notified that a hearing has been scheduled on this matter for:

Judge	Bar no.	Date	Time
Hearing location			
☐ Court address above ☐			

If you require special accommodations to use the court because of a disability or if you require a foreign language interpreter to help you fully participate in court proceedings, please contact the court immediately to make arrangements.

_____
Date

_____
Signature

CERTIFICATE OF MAILING

I certify that on this date I served a copy of this motion on the parties or their attorneys by first-class mail addressed to their last-known addresses as defined in MCR 2.107(C)(3).

_____
Date

_____
Signature

ORDER

IT IS ORDERED the above motion is   ☐ granted.   ☐ denied.

_____
Date

_____
Judge

MC 81 (3/08) **MOTION AND ORDER FOR APPOINTMENT OF FOREIGN LANGUAGE INTERPRETER**

Original - Friend of the court
Copy - Filing party

STATE OF MICHIGAN JUDICIAL CIRCUIT COUNTY	CHANGE IN PERSONAL INFORMATION	CASE NO.

Friend of the court address   **Telephone no.**

Please type or print information. Complete only those sections that apply. You can only file changes for yourself or those minor children of whom you have physical custody. Use another form when making changes for more than one person. **You must sign this form and send it to the friend of the court.**

☐ for party and minor child(ren)　　☐ for party only

1. New Address and/or Telephone Number ☐ for minor child _____ no longer living with custodial parent
Name

Street address			
City	State	Zip	Area code and telephone number

I understand that by filing this change of address, it will be used to automatically update address information on any other child-support cases I have in Michigan. This change is effective for (check all that apply)

☐ all addresses you have listed for me.
☐ residence address only (where I live).
☐ an address that is confidential by court order and which remains confidential with this change.
☐ the single mailing address to which all notices and papers will be served.

2. Alternate Address

The court has entered an order making my address confidential under Michigan Court Rule 3.203(F). The following is an alternate address for the court, the friend of the court office, and the other party to use in serving me with notice and other court papers. I will retrieve all my mail regarding this case from this alternate address.

Street address	City	State	Zip

3. Name Change (Attach order changing name or certificate of marriage.)

New name

4. New Employer　☐ Employer information is confidential by court order.

Employer name	Street address		
City	State	Zip	Area code and telephone number

5. New Driver's License

Issuing state	License number	Expiration date

6. New Occupational License

Issuing state	Type of occupation	License number	Expiration date

7. New Social Security Number　☐ for you　☐ for minor child _____
Name

Social security number

8. Health Care Insurance Provider

Provider name	Provider address and telephone number	Group number	Policy number

9. Other Information: (To be provided as ordered by the court.) (Attach separate sheet.)

Name of party filing the change (type or print)	Social security number	Date of filing
Signature of party filing the change	Name of other party (type or print)	

FOC 108 (5/10) **CHANGE IN PERSONAL INFORMATION**

Approved, SCAO

Original - Court
1st copy - Applicant

2nd copy - Friend of the court
(when applicable)
PROBATE JIS CODE: OSF

STATE OF MICHIGAN JUDICIAL DISTRICT JUDICIAL CIRCUIT COUNTY PROBATE	WAIVER/SUSPENSION OF FEES AND COSTS (AFFIDAVIT AND ORDER)	CASE NO.

Court address _____ Court telephone no.

Plaintiff/Petitioner name		Defendant/Respondent name
Plaintiff's/Petitioner's attorney and bar no.	v	Defendant's/Respondent's attorney and bar no.

☐ Probate   In the matter of _____

NOTE: Requests for waiver/suspension of transcript costs or mediation fees must be made separately by motion.

AFFIDAVIT

1. I ask the court to waive/suspend fees and costs for the following reason: (check either a or b)
   ☐ a. I am currently receiving public assistance: My DHS case number is _____ .
   (MCR 2.002[C] requires the court to suspend payment of fees and costs.)
   OR
   ☐ b. I am unable to pay fees and costs because of indigency, based on the following facts:
   My average gross income is about $ _____ every ☐ week. ☐ two weeks. ☐ month.
   ☐ I am receiving unemployment benefits.
   ☐ I am not employed.
   ☐ I have a vehicle: Year: _____ Make: _____ Model: _____ Amount Owed: $_____
   The total amount in all my bank accounts is: $ _____
   Write down any other assets and how much they are worth. If you need more space, attach a separate sheet.

   I pay $ _____ in rent/mortgage every month. I pay $ _____ in utilities (water, electricity, gas) every month. I pay $ _____ for court-ordered child support. I pay $_____ for court-ordered_____ .
   specify
   Write down any other obligations and how much you pay. If you need more space, attach a separate sheet.

2. The number of people living in my household is_____ .
☐ 3. I am signing this affidavit for a person who ☐ is a minor. ☐ has the following disability_____

_____
Applicant signature

_____
Name (type or print)

Subscribed and sworn to before me on _____ , _____ County, Michigan.
                                           Date

My commission expires:_____ Signature:_____
                            Date   Deputy clerk/Register/Notary public

Notary public, State of Michigan, County of _____

ORDER

IT IS ORDERED:

☐ 1. The applicant has shown by ex parte affidavit that he/she is
   ☐ a. receiving public assistance, and payment of fees and costs are waived/suspended pursuant to MCR 2.002(C).
   ☐ b. indigent and payment of fees and costs are waived/suspended pursuant to MCR 2.002(D).
   The applicant is required to notify the court if the reason for waiving/suspending the fees and costs no longer exists.
☐ 2. The application is denied.

_____   _____
Date   Judge

MC 20 (8/12) WAIVER/SUSPENSION OF FEES AND COSTS (AFFIDAVIT AND ORDER)   MCR 2.002

INSTRUCTIONS FOR USING FORM MC 20, WAIVER/SUSPENSION OF FEES AND COSTS (AFFIDAVIT AND ORDER)

»» CAN I FILE MY LEGAL PAPERS WITH THE COURT FREE OF CHARGE?

When you file a legal paper with the court or are ordered to case evaluation, you are often required to pay certain fees. If you cannot afford these fees, you can ask the court to "waive" or "suspend" them using this form (MC 20).

»» FILING AN AFFIDAVIT

1. **Prove That You Cannot Afford to Pay a Filing Fee**

   You must show the court that you cannot afford to pay the fees. If you receive public assistance, you must give the court your DHS case number. If you do not receive public assistance, you must give the court information about your assets and obligations. An asset is something you own, such as money, a car, a house, or other property. An obligation is something you owe, such as rent, a loan payment, utilities, court-ordered child support, etc.

2. **Complete Form MC 20**

   After you prepare the legal papers you want to file with the court, complete form MC 20.

   If you are receiving public assistance, check the box in front of item 1a. Write in your DHS case number. Public assistance means you are receiving help from the Michigan Department of Human Services and/or are receiving federal social security income (SSI), which includes Medicaid (a DHS program). It does not include benefits such as veterans assistance (VA benefits) or unemployment. Do not check the box in front of item 1b. Gross income means before any deductions.

   If you are not receiving public assistance, check the box in front of item 1b. Check all the boxes that apply to you. If you are not employed, check that box. Write in all the requested information about your assets and obligations.

   Do not sign the form until you are in front of a notary public or the clerk of the court.

3. **Sign the Affidavit Under Oath**

   After form MC 20 is completed, sign it under oath in front of a notary public or a clerk of the court. You must bring your photo identification with you when you sign the affidavit. There may be a fee to have your affidavit signed in front of a notary public.

4. **Make Copies**

   After you have signed the affidavit under oath, make a copy of the completed form for your records. If your court case is a domestic relations case, such as divorce, paternity, separate maintenance, etc., make another copy of the completed form for the friend of the court office. If you are at the court when you sign the affidavit, you can ask the clerk of the court to make copies for you. There may be a cost to make the copies.

5. **File Form MC 20**

   Take or mail the original and all copies of this form (MC 20) to the clerk of the court along with any other legal papers you want to file. If your court case is a domestic relations case, such as divorce, paternity, separate maintenance, etc., include the friend of the court copy you made in step 4. If you mail the form, include a postage-paid envelope with your return address.

»» GETTING A SIGNED ORDER

When you file your affidavit with the court, the clerk of the court will give it to the judge. The judge will make a decision and will sign the order. The clerk of the court will keep the original and return a signed copy to you. The clerk of the court will send a copy to the friend of the court if you filed that copy.

Approved, SCAO

STATE OF MICHIGAN JUDICIAL DISTRICT JUDICIAL CIRCUIT COUNTY PROBATE	MOTION AND VERIFICATION FOR ALTERNATE SERVICE	CASE NO.

Court address | **Court telephone no.**

Plaintiff name(s), address(es), and telephone no(s).		Defendant name(s), address(es), and telephone no(s).
	v	

In the matter of _____

1. Service of process upon _____ cannot reasonably be made as otherwise provided in MCR 2.105, as shown in the following verification of process server.

2. Defendant's last known home and business addresses are:

_____
Home address   City   State   Zip

_____
Business address   City   State   Zip

   a. I believe the ☐ home / ☐ business address shown above is current.

   b. I do not know the defendant's current ☐ home / ☐ business address. I have made the following efforts to ascertain the current

      address: _____

      _____

      _____

3. I request the court order service by alternate means.

I declare that the statements above are true to the best of my information, knowledge, and belief.

_____
Date

_____
Plaintiff/Plaintiff's attorney signature

_____
Address

_____
Name (type or print)   Bar no.

_____
City, state, zip   Telephone no.

VERIFICATION OF PROCESS SERVER

1. I have tried to serve process on this defendant as described: State date, place, and what occurred on each occasion.

I declare that the statements above are true to the best of my information, knowledge, and belief.

_____
Date

_____
Signature

_____
Process server (type or print)

MC 303 (3/11) **MOTION AND VERIFICATION FOR ALTERNATE SERVICE**   MCR 2.105

Approved, SCAO

STATE OF MICHIGAN JUDICIAL DISTRICT JUDICIAL CIRCUIT COUNTY PROBATE	ORDER REGARDING ALTERNATE SERVICE	CASE NO.

Court address _____ Court telephone no.

Plaintiff name(s), address(es), and telephone no(s).		Defendant name(s), address(es), and telephone no(s).
	v	
Plaintiff's attorney, bar no., address, and telephone no.		

THE COURT FINDS:

☐ 1. Service of process upon the defendant, _____ ,

cannot reasonably be made as provided in　　☐ MCR 2.105　　☐ MCR 2.107(B)(1)(b)　　and service of process

may be made in a manner that is reasonably calculated to give the defendant actual notice of the proceedings and an opportunity

to be heard.

IT IS ORDERED:

☐ 2. Service of the　　☐ summons and complaint　　☐ other: _____

and a copy of this order shall be made by the following method(s).

☐ a. First-class mail to _____ .

☐ b. Tacking or firmly affixing to the door at _____ .

☐ c. Delivering at _____

to a member of the defendant's household who is of suitable age and discretion to receive process, with instructions to

deliver it promptly to the defendant.

☐ d. Other: _____

_____

For each method used, proof of service must be filed promptly with the court.

☐ 3. The motion for alternate service is denied.

_____　　　　　　　　　　　_____　　　　　_____
Date　　　　　　　　　　　　　　　　　　　　　　　Judge　　　　　　　　　　　　　　　　Bar no.

MC 304 (9/09) **ORDER REGARDING ALTERNATE SERVICE**　　　　　　　　　　MCR 2.103, MCR 2.105

PROOF OF SERVICE	ORDER REGARDING ALTERNATE SERVICE Case No.

TO PROCESS SERVER: You must serve the copies of the order regarding alternate service and file proof of service with the court clerk. If you are unable to complete service, you must return this original and all copies to the court clerk.

CERTIFICATE / AFFIDAVIT OF SERVICE / NONSERVICE

☐ **OFFICER CERTIFICATE**	**OR**	☐ **AFFIDAVIT OF PROCESS SERVER**
I certify that I am a sheriff, deputy sheriff, bailiff, appointed court officer, or attorney for a party (MCR 2.104[A][2]), and that: (notarization not required)		Being first duly sworn, I state that I am a legally competent adult who is not a party or an officer of a corporate party, and that: (notarization required)

I served a copy of the ☐ summons and complaint ☐ other: _____

and a copy of the order for alternate service upon _____ by

☐ 1. First-class mail to _____, on _____ .
                                                                    Date

☐ 2. Tacking or firmly affixing to the door at _____, on _____ .
                                                                        Date

☐ 3. Delivering at _____, on _____ .
                                                        Date

   to a member of the defendant's household who is of suitable age and discretion to receive process, with instructions to deliver

   it promptly to the defendant.

☐ 4. Other: _____, on _____ .
          specify   Date

I declare that the statements above are true to the best of my information, knowledge, and belief.

Service fee $	Miles traveled Fee $	
Incorrect address fee $	Miles traveled Fee $	TOTAL FEE $

Signature _____

Name (type or print) _____

Title _____

Subscribed and sworn to before me on _____ , _____ County, Michigan.
                                              Date

My commission expires: _____ Signature: _____
                              Date   Deputy court clerk/Notary public

Notary public, State of Michigan, County of _____

, Approved, SCAO

STATE OF MICHIGAN JUDICIAL DISTRICT JUDICIAL CIRCUIT COUNTY PROBATE	ORDER FOR SERVICE BY PUBLICATION/POSTING AND NOTICE OF ACTION	CASE NO,

Court address   **Court telephone no.**

Plaintiff name(s), address(es), and telephone no(s).

v

Defendant name(s), address(es), and telephone no(s).

Plaintiff's attorney, bar no., address, and telephone no.

TO: _____

IT IS ORDERED:

1. You are being sued in this court by the plaintiff to _____

_____ . You must file your answer or take other action

permitted by law in this court at the court address above on or before _____ . If you fail to do
    Date

so, a default judgment may be entered against you for the relief demanded in the complaint filed in this case.

2. A copy of this order shall be published once each week in _____
    ☐ three consecutive weeks,   Name of publication

for ☐ _____ , and proof of publication shall be filed in this court.

3. _____ shall post a copy of this order in the courthouse, and
  Name

at _____   _____ and
  Location

at _____
  Location

    ☐ three continuous weeks,

for ☐ _____ , and shall file proof of posting in this court.

4. A copy of this order shall be sent to _____ at the last-known address
    Name   ☐ date of the last publication,

by registered mail, return receipt requested, before the ☐ last week of posting,   and the affidavit of mailing shall be

filed with this court.

_____   _____
Date   Judge   Bar no.

MC 307 (9/09) **ORDER FOR SERVICE BY PUBLICATION/POSTING AND NOTICE OF ACTION**   MCR 2.106, MCR 5.101(C)

AFFIDAVIT OF PUBLISHING

Name of ☐ publisher ☐ agent of publisher	Attach copy of publication here.

Name of newspaper	County where published

This newspaper is a qualified newspaper. The order for service was published in this newpaper at least once each week for three consecutive weeks on the following dates.

_____

Date _____   Affiant signature _____

Subscribed and sworn to before me on _____ , _____ County, Michigan.
Date

My commission expires: _____   Signature: _____
Date   Court clerk/Notary public

Notary public, State of Michigan, County of _____

AFFIDAVIT OF POSTING

I have posted this order in a conspicuous place in the _____ courthouse and the

following places as ordered by this court: _____

_____

_____

It has been posted for   ☐ three continuous weeks ☐ _____ continuous weeks   as ordered by this court.

Date _____   Affiant signature _____

Subscribed and sworn to before me on _____ , _____ County, Michigan.
Date

My commission expires: _____   Signature: _____
Date   Court clerk/Notary public

Notary public, State of Michigan, County of _____

AFFIDAVIT OF MAILING

As ordered, on _____ I mailed a copy of the summons and complaint
Date

and this order to _____
Name

at _____
Address

The mailing receipt and return receipt are attached at right.

Attach mailing receipt and return receipt here.

Date _____   Affiant signature _____

Subscribed and sworn to before me on _____ , _____ County, Michigan.
Date

My commission expires: _____   Signature: _____
Date   Court clerk/Notary public

Notary public, State of Michigan, County of _____

STATE OF MICHIGAN JUDICIAL CIRCUIT COUNTY	VERIFIED STATEMENT AND APPLICATION FOR IV-D SERVICES	CASE NO.

1. Mother's last name First name Middle name	2. Any other names by which mother is or has been known

3. Date of birth	4. Social security number	5. Driver's license number and state

6. Mailing address and residence address (if different)

7. Eye color	8. Hair color	9. Height	10. Weight	11. Race	12. Scars, tattoos, etc.

13. Home telephone no.	14. Work telephone no.	15. Maiden name	16. Occupation

17. Business/Employer's name and address	18. Gross weekly income

19. Has mother applied for or does she receive public assistance? If yes, please specify kind. ☐ Yes ☐ No	20. DHS case number

21. Father's last name First name Middle name	22. Any other names by which father is or has been known

23. Date of birth	24. Social security number	25. Driver's license number and state

26. Mailing address and residence address (if different)

27. Eye color	28. Hair color	29. Height	30. Weight	31. Race	32. Scars, tattoos, etc.

33. Home telephone no.	34. Work telephone no.	35. Occupation

36. Business/Employer's name and address	37. Gross weekly income

38. Has father applied for or does he receive public assistance? If yes, please specify kind. ☐ Yes ☐ No	39. DHS case number

40. a. Name of Minor Child Involved in Case	b. Birth Date	c. Age	d. Soc. Sec. No.	e. Residential Address

41. a. Name of Other Minor Child of Either Party	b. Birth Date	c. Age	d. Residential Address

42. Health care coverage available for each minor child

a. Name of Minor Child	b. Name of Policy Holder	c. Name of Insurance Co./HMO	d. Policy/Certificate/Contract/Group No.

43. Names and addresses of person(s) other than parties, if any, who may have custody of child(ren) during pendency of this case

If any of the public assistance information above changes before your judgment is entered, you are required to give the friend of the court written notice of the change.

☐ I request support services under Title IV-D of the Social Security Act.

I declare that the statements above are true to the best of my information, knowledge, and belief.

Date _____   Signature _____

FOC 23 (3/12) **VERIFIED STATEMENT AND APPLICATION FOR IV-D SERVICES**   MCR 3.206(B)

STATE OF MICHIGAN JUDICIAL CIRCUIT COUNTY	ADVICE OF RIGHTS REGARDING USE OF FRIEND OF THE COURT SERVICES (PAGE 1)	CASE NO.

Friend of the court address   **Telephone no.**

1. Right to Refuse Friend of the Court Services

a. You have the right to refuse friend of the court services for custody, parenting time, and support. To decline friend of the court services, you must file with the court a motion requesting that friend of the court services not be required. You must attach a signed copy of this advice of rights to the motion. The court will grant the motion provided both parties agree and have signed this advice of rights and it determines that all the following are true.
   1) Under MCL 552.505a, neither of you receives or has received public assistance or requests friend of the court services.
   2) There is no evidence of domestic violence or of an uneven bargaining position between you.
   3) The court finds that declining to receive friend of the court services is not against the best interests of a child.

b. If you already have a friend of the court case, you can file a motion to discontinue friend of the court services provided both parties agree and have signed this advice of rights and the court finds that all the following are true.
   1) Neither of you receives public assistance or requests friend of the court services.
   2) There is no evidence of domestic violence or an uneven bargaining position between you.
   3) The court finds that declining to receive friend of the court services is not against the best interests of a child.
   4) No money is due the governmental entity because of past public assistance.
   5) No arrearage or violation of a custody or parenting-time order has occurred in the last 12 months.
   6) Neither of you has reopened a friend of the court case in the last 12 months.

2. Friend of the Court Services (you will not receive these services if you choose not to use the friend of the court)

a. Accounting Services
Friends of the court must collect support and disburse it within 48 hours. Friend of the court accounting services include: 1) friend of the court accounting for payments received and sent, 2) adjustments of support for parenting time or other credits, and 3) annual statements of accounts, if requested.

b. Support Enforcement Services
The friend of the court must begin to enforce support when one month of support is overdue. For friend of the court cases, child-support enforcement services include:
- paying support out of tax refunds.
- asking the court to order the nonpaying party to come to court to explain the failure to pay.
- having unpaid support paid out of property the payer owns.
- reporting support arrearage to a consumer reporting agency or requesting that the payer's license(s) be suspended.
- collecting support by an income withholding order.

If you choose not to receive friend of the court services, any existing income withholding source will be notified that the friend of the court is no longer responsible for income withholding. **The parties will be solely responsible for stopping or changing income withholding as the law allows.** The friend of the court will stop any unfinished collection actions.

c. Medical Support Enforcement Services
The friend of the court is required to recommend how the parents divide health-care expenses and to take action to collect the amounts that a parent fails or refuses to pay. When a parent is required to insure the children, the friend of the court is authorized to instruct an employer to enroll the children in an insurance plan when the parent fails or refuses to do so.

d. Support Review and Modification Services
Once every three years, persons with friend of the court cases may request the friend of the court to review the support amount. After completing the review, the friend of the court must file a motion to raise or lower support, or inform the parties that it recommends no change. It must also review support when changed circumstances lead it to believe that support should be modified.

e. Custody and Parenting-Time Investigation Services
For disputes about custody or parenting time in friend of the court cases, the friend of the court sometimes must investigate and provide reports to the parties and the court.

f. Mediation Services
Friend of the court offices must provide mediation services to help parties with friend of the court cases settle custody and parenting-time disputes.

g. Custody and Parenting-Time Enforcement Services
For friend of the court cases, the friend of the court must enforce custody and parenting time when a party complains that it is violated. Child-custody and parenting-time enforcement services include:

(See page 2)

STATE OF MICHIGAN JUDICIAL CIRCUIT COUNTY	ADVICE OF RIGHTS REGARDING USE OF FRIEND OF THE COURT SERVICES (PAGE 2)	CASE NO.

Friend of the court address   Telephone no.

2. Friend of the Court Services (you will not receive these services if you choose not to use the friend of the court)
(continued from page 1)

   g. **Custody and Parenting-Time Enforcement Services** (continued from page 1)
   - asking the court to order the noncooperating party to come to court to explain the failure to obey the parenting-time order.
   - suspending the licenses of individuals who deny parenting time.
   - awarding makeup parenting time.
   - joint meetings to resolve complaints.

3. Michigan State Disbursement Unit and IV-D Services

   a. **Michigan State Disbursement Unit (MiSDU)**
   If you choose not to receive friend of the court services, you may continue to make payments to, and receive payments through, MiSDU. MiSDU will keep track of the amount paid and sent out. However, MiSDU cannot provide you with all the accounting functions the friend of the court provides. All payments made through MiSDU must be distributed according to the amounts due as required by federal law. When a payer has more than one case, federal law determines how a payment is divided among the cases. **Even if you choose not to receive friend of the court services, payments through MiSDU must be divided among all a payer's cases and distributed in the same manner as payments on friend of the court cases. You cannot discontinue friend of the court services if you want to use MiSDU unless you first provide to MiSDU all the information that MiSDU needs to set up an account.**

   b. **Your Rights Under Title IV-D of the Social Security Act**
   Title IV-D of the Social Security Act provides federal government resources to collect child support and it allows certain funding to be used for parenting-time and custody services. In Michigan, critical Title IV-D services are delivered by the friend of the court. **If you choose not to receive friend of the court services, you cannot receive most Title IV-D services.**

4. Public Assistance

   Receipt of public assistance means receipt of any of the following benefits: cash assistance, medical assistance, food assistance, foster care, and/or child care.

$$\boxed{\text{ACKNOWLEDGMENT REGARDING SERVICES}}$$

Check below only if you do not want to receive friend of the court services. Then date, print name, and sign.

I have read this advice of rights and I understand the friend of the court services I am entitled to receive.

☐ I acknowledge that by signing below **I am choosing not to receive** any friend of the court services. I understand that before this choice can take effect, a motion requesting this choice and the other party's agreement must be filed with the court for approval. I also understand that the court may deny this choice if certain conditions are not met as stated in this advice of rights.

Name (type or print)	Name (type or print)

Signature	Date	Signature	Date

If you did not check the above box, you are choosing to receive friend of the court services. **For the most effective friend of the court services**, you can request Title IV-D services by dating and signing below.

I request Title IV-D services through the friend of the court office.

Date	Signature

	Original - Court 1st copy - Plaintiff	2nd copy - Defendant 3rd copy - Friend of the court
STATE OF MICHIGAN **JUDICIAL CIRCUIT** **COUNTY**	**ORDER EXEMPTING CASE FROM** **FRIEND OF THE COURT SERVICES** **(PAGE 1)**	**CASE NO.**

Court address   Telephone no.

Plaintiff's name, address, and telephone no.		Defendant's name, address, and telephone no.
	v	

Attorney: Attorney:

Date of hearing: _____   Judge: _____

                                                                                   Bar no.

THE COURT FINDS:

1. There is no evidence of domestic violence or of an unequal bargaining position between the parties to the case.

2. Granting the parties the relief they have requested would not be against the best interests of any child in the case.

3. The parties have filed executed copies of a form advising them of services they will not receive if their motion is granted.

4. Neither party receives public assistance.

5. No money is due the governmental entity because of past public assistance in the case.

6. No arrearage or custody or parenting-time order violation has occurred in the last 12 months in this case.

7. Neither party has reopened a friend of the court case in the last 12 months.

☐ 8. The parties do not want Title IV-D services and have requested that any existing Title IV-D case be closed. (Note: This box should be checked unless exceptional circumstances exist that entitle the Title IV-D case to remain open.)

IT IS ORDERED:

9. Subject to the provisions of item 14 below, this case is not a friend of the court case.

☐ 10. This case is not a Title IV-D case. (Note: This box should be checked if item 8 has been checked.)

11. The friend of the court shall not be involved in the enforcement, investigation, or accounting functions for custody, parenting time, or support in this case.

12. The parties are responsible for all enforcement and accounting functions for custody, parenting time, or support in this case.

13. Except as indicated below, there is no income withholding in this case, support will be paid directly by the payer to the payee, and the friend of the court shall terminate any existing income withholding. Should this case become a friend of the court case, the payer must keep the friend of the court advised of the name and address of the payer's source of income and any health-care coverage that is available to the payer as a benefit of employment or that the payer maintains, including the name of the insurance company, health-care organization, or health maintenance organization; the policy, certificate, or contract number; and the names and birth dates of the persons for whose benefit the payer maintains the coverage.

    ☐ a. Support shall be paid through the Michigan State Disbursement Unit (MiSDU). Support shall be paid by income withholding to the extent allowed by statutes and court rules; however, the friend of the court is not responsible for income withholding. The friend of the court shall notify the employer that it is no longer involved in the case and that any further information concerning income withholding will be provided by the parties.

(See page 2 for the remainder of the order.)

STATE OF MICHIGAN JUDICIAL CIRCUIT COUNTY	ORDER EXEMPTING CASE FROM FRIEND OF THE COURT SERVICES (PAGE 2)	CASE NO.

Court address _____ Telephone no. _____

Plaintiff's name	v	Defendant's name

13. (continued)

   ☐ b. Support shall be paid through MiSDU.

   If support payments are to be made through MiSDU by income withholding or otherwise, the friend of the court shall not close the friend of the court case until MiSDU notifies the friend of the court that it has been provided with the information necessary to process the child-support payments. There will be no accounting for support that is not paid through MiSDU.

14. The friend of the court shall open a friend of the court case if a party applies for public assistance, a child is placed in foster care, or either party submits to the friend of the court a written request to reopen the friend of the court case. If this case becomes a friend of the court case for any reason, the following provisions shall apply.

   a. The parties must cooperate fully with the friend of the court in establishing the case as a friend of the court case.

   b. The parties must provide copies of all orders in their case to the friend of the court.

   c. The parties must supply any documents that a party to a friend of the court case is required to supply if they have not already done so.

   d. The friend of the court is not responsible for determining any support arrearage that is not indicated by payment made through MiSDU.

   e. Support is payable through MiSDU effective the date the case becomes a friend of the court case.

   f. The friend of the court may prepare and submit, ex parte, a uniform support order that contains all the statutory requirements of a Michigan support order as long as the order does not contradict the existing support order.

   g. At the request of the friend of the court, the parties shall complete a Verified Statement and Application for Title IV-D Services.

_____
Date

_____
Judge

CERTIFICATE OF MAILING

I certify that on this date I served a copy of this order on the parties or their attorneys by first-class mail addressed to their last-known addresses as defined in MCR 3.203.

_____
Date

_____
Signature

STATE OF MICHIGAN	REQUEST TO REOPEN	CASE NO.
JUDICIAL CIRCUIT	FRIEND OF THE COURT CASE	
COUNTY		

Court address   **Telephone no.**

| Plaintiff's name, address, and telephone no. | | Defendant's name, address, and telephone no. |
| | v | |

Attorney: Attorney:

1. On _____ an order was entered exempting this case from friend of the court services.
   Date

I REQUEST that the friend of the court case be reopened upon filing of this request with the friend of the court office. Attached is a completed Verified Statement (form FOC 23).

☐ I request support services under Title IV-D of the Social Security Act.

_____   _____
Date   Signature

CERTIFICATE OF MAILING

I certify that on this date I served a copy of this request on the friend of the court and on the parties or their attorneys by first-class mail addressed to their last-known addresses as defined in MCR 3.203.

_____   _____
Date   Signature

FOC 104 (3/09) **REQUEST TO REOPEN FRIEND OF THE COURT CASE**   MCL 552.505, MCL 552.505a

Approved, SCAO

STATE OF MICHIGAN JUDICIAL CIRCUIT COUNTY	AGREEMENT SUSPENDING IMMEDIATE INCOME WITHHOLDING	CASE NO.

Court address

Court telephone no.

Plaintiff's name, address, and telephone no.

v

Defendant's name, address, and telephone no.

NOTE: MCL 552.604(3) requires that all new and modified support orders after December 31, 1990. include a provision for immediate income withholding and that income withholding take effect immediately unless the parties enter into a written agreement that the income withholding order shall not take effect immediately.

We understand that by law an order of income withholding in a support order shall take effect immediately. However, we agree to the following.

1. The order of income withholding shall not take effect immediately.

2. An alternative payment arrangement shall be made as follows:

3. Both the payer and the recipient of support will notify the friend of the court, in writing, within 21 days of any change in
   a. the names, addresses, and telephone numbers of their current sources of income;
   b. any health-care coverage that is available to them as a benefit of employment or that is maintained by them; the names of the insurance companies, health-care organizations, or health-maintenance organizations; the policy, certificate, or contract numbers; and the names and birth dates of the persons for whose benefit they maintain health-care coverage under the policies, certificates, or contracts; and
   c. their current residences, mailing addresses, and telephone numbers.

4. We further understand that proceedings to implement income withholding shall commence if the payer of support falls one month behind in his/her support payments.

5. We recognize that the court may order withholding of income to take effect immediately for cause or at the request of the payer.

Date _____

Date _____

Plaintiff's signature _____

Defendant's signature _____

FOC 63 (3/08) **AGREEMENT SUSPENDING IMMEDIATE INCOME WITHHOLDING**

MCL 552.604

STATE OF MICHIGAN JUDICIAL CIRCUIT COUNTY	ORDER SUSPENDING IMMEDIATE INCOME WITHHOLDING	CASE NO.

Court address | Court telephone no.

```
┌─────────────────────────────────────────────┐
│ Plaintiff's name, address, and telephone no.  │
│                                               │
│                                               │
│                                               │
└─────────────────────────────────────────────┘

                    v

┌─────────────────────────────────────────────┐
│ Defendant's name, address, and telephone no.  │
│                                               │
│                                               │
│                                               │
└─────────────────────────────────────────────┘
```

1. Date of hearing: _____ Judge: _____

Bar no.

2. **THE COURT FINDS:**

☐ a. There is good cause for the order of income withholding not to take effect immediately as follows.
  1) It is in the best interest of the child for immediate income withholding not to take effect for the following reasons:

  2) Proof of timely payment of previously-ordered support has been provided.

☐ b. The parties have entered into a written agreement that has been reviewed and entered in the record as follows.
  1) The order of income withholding shall not take effect immediately.
  2) An alternative payment arrangement has been agreed upon and is attached.

3. Both the payer and the recipient of support will notify the friend of the court, in writing, within 21 days of any change in
  a. the names, addresses, and telephone numbers of their current sources of income;
  b. any health-care coverage that is available to them as a benefit of employment or that is maintained by them, the names of the insurance companies, health-care organizations, or health-maintenance organizations; the policy, certificate, or contract numbers; and the names and birth dates of the persons for whose benefit they maintain health-care coverage under the policies, certificates, or contracts; and
  c. their current residencea, mailing addresses, and telephone numbers.

IT IS ORDERED:

4. Income withholding shall not take effect immediately.
5. Income withholding shall take effect if the fixed amount of arrearage is reached, as specified in law.

_____   _____
Date   Judge

STATE OF MICHIGAN JUDICIAL CIRCUIT COUNTY	UNIFORM SPOUSAL SUPPORT ORDER, NO FRIEND OF COURT SERVICES (PAGE 1) ☐ EX PARTE ☐ TEMPORARY ☐ MODIFICATION ☐ FINAL	CASE NO.

Court address

Court telephone no.

Plaintiff's name, address, and telephone no.	v	Defendant's name, address, and telephone no.
Plaintiff's attorney name, bar no., address, and telephone no.		Defendant's attorney name, bar no., address, and telephone no.
Plaintiff's source of income name, address, and telephone no.		Defendant's source of income name, address, and telephone no.

This order is entered ☐ after hearing. ☐ on stipulation/consent of the parties.

IT IS ORDERED, UNLESS OTHERWISE ORDERED IN ITEM 8: ☐ Standard provisions have been modified (see item 8).

1. **Spousal Support.** Spousal support shall be paid monthly as follows:

Payer:	Payee:	Amount: $	Effective date:

2. This order continues until the death of the payee or until the earliest of the following events:
   ☐ Date: _____ ☐ $ _____ is paid.
   ☐ Remarriage of the payee. ☐ Death of the payer.
   ☐ Other (specify all other events): _____
   _____

☐ 3. For tax purposes, the payments will be deductible to the payer and included in the income of the payee.

☐ 4. Payments that must be paid directly to the third party (not to the payee) are listed below.

Type	Amount Per Month	Start Date	Pay to	End Date
	$			
	$			
	$			
	$			

(See page 2 for the remainder of the order.)

FOC 10c (3/12) **UNIFORM SPOUSAL SUPPORT ORDER, NO FRIEND OF COURT SERVICES, PAGE 1** MCL 552.13, MCR 3.211

	Original - Court 1st copy - Plaintiff	2nd copy - Defendant 3rd copy - Friend of the court

STATE OF MICHIGAN JUDICIAL CIRCUIT COUNTY	UNIFORM SPOUSAL SUPPORT ORDER NO FRIEND OF COURT SERVICES (PAGE 2) ☐ EX PARTE ☐ TEMPORARY ☐ MODIFICATION ☐ FINAL	CASE NO.

Court address   **Court telephone no.**

Plaintiff's name	v	Defendant's name

5. **Retroactive Modification and Liens for Unpaid Support.** Support is a judgment the date it is due and is not retroactively modifiable. Unpaid support is a lien by operation of law and the payer's property can be encumbered or seized if an arrearage accrues for more than the periodic support payments payable for two months under the payer's support order.

6. **Change of Address, Employment Status, Health Insurance.** Both parties shall notify each other in writing within 21 days of any change in: a) their mailing and residential addresses and telephone numbers; b) the names, addresses, and telephone numbers of their sources of income; c) their health-maintenance or insurance companies, insurance coverage, persons insured, or contract numbers; d) their occupational or drivers' licenses; and e) their social security numbers unless exempt by law pursuant to MCL 552.603.

7. **Prior Orders. This order supersedes all prior spousal support orders and all continuing provisions are restated in this order.** Past-due amounts owed under any prior support order are preserved.

8. **Other: (Attach separate sheets as needed.)**

Plaintiff (if consent/stipulation)	Date	Defendant (if consent/stipulation)	Date

Plaintiff's attorney	Date	Defendant's attorney	Date

Date		Judge	Bar no.

CERTIFICATE OF MAILING

I certify that on this date I served a copy of this order on the parties or their attorneys by first-class mail addressed to their last-known addresses as defined in MCR 3.203.

Date	Signature

COURT USE ONLY

STATE OF MICHIGAN **Circuit Court - Family Division** **COUNTY**	**APPEARANCE AND WAIVER OF MILITARY RELIEF LAW RIGHTS**	CASE NO.

Plaintiff (appearing *in propria persona*):

v

Defendant:

Defendant says:

1. I am in the active duty of the following unit of the U.S. military:

2. I am currently stationed at:

3. I previously received copies of the summons and complaint for divorce and any other initial divorce papers in this case.

4. I make a general appearance and waive all lawsuit relief rights, including the right to request a stay or adjournment of proceedings, provided to me in this case by the Servicemembers Civil Relief Act (50 USC App. 501 et seq.) and/or Michigan's military relief law (MCL 32.517) (or similar military relief law from another state).

Date _____   Defendant _____

GRP 6   (3/07)   **APPEARANCE AND WAIVER OF MILITARY RELIEF LAW RIGHTS**

Request for Military Status Report

TO:

Defense Manpower Data Center
Attn: Military Verification
1600 Wilson Blvd.
Suite 400
Arlington, VA 22209-2593

RE:

Case name _____

Case number _____

Full name of defendant _____

Defendant's date of birth_____

Defendant's social security number _____

    I am the plaintiff in the divorce case above seeking a default judgment of divorce against the defendant. I must know whether or not the defendant is currently in the active duty of the U.S. military service, to comply with the Servicemembers Civil Relief Act and/or Michigan Compiled Law 32.517 or a similar military relief law from another state.

    Please respond by providing a military status report on defendant as soon as possible. A self-addressed stamped envelope is enclosed for your response.

Date _____

Signature _____

Name _____

Address _____

_____

Telephone:_____

Military Locator Request

TO:

Army
Army World Wide Locator Service
Enlisted Records and Evaluation Center
8899 East 56th Street
Indianapolis, IN 46249-5301

Air Force
Air Force Manpower and Personnel Center
ATTN: Air Force Locator/MSIMDL
550 C Street West, Suite 50
Randolph Air Force Base, TX 78150-4752

Navy
Bureau of Naval Personnel
PERS-312E
5720 Integrity Drive
Millington, TN 38055-3120

Coast Guard
Commander
Coast Guard Personnel Command
4200 Wilson Blvd., Suite 1100 (CGPC-adm-3)
Arlington, VA 20598-7200

Marine Corps
Commandant of The Marine Corps
Headquarters, U.S. Marine Corps (MMSB10)
2008 Elliott Road, Suite 201
Quantico, VA 22134-5030

RE:

Case name _____

Case number _____

Full name of defendant _____

Defendant's date of birth_____

Defendant's social security number _____

Defendant's rank and service number (if known)_____

Defendant's last duty assignment (if known) _____

Defendant's last military address (if known)_____

I am the plaintiff in the case above seeking a divorce against the defendant. I request information about the defendant's *current* rank, service number, unit of assignment and military address. I need this information for service of the divorce papers, to satisfy the military relief laws and other reasons related to this divorce case. A self-addressed stamped envelope is enclosed for your response.

As the defendant's spouse, I ask for waiver of the locator request fee.

Date _____   Signature _____

Name _____

Address _____

_____

Telephone:_____

STATE OF MICHIGAN	DISMISSAL	CASE NO.
JUDICIAL DISTRICT JUDICIAL CIRCUIT COUNTY PROBATE		

Court address		Court telephone no.

Plaintiff name(s) and address(es)	v	Defendant name(s) and address(es)
Plaintiff's attorney, bar no., address, and telephone no.		Defendant's attorney, bar no., address, and telephone no.

☐ **NOTICE OF DISMISSAL BY PLAINTIFF**

☐ with
☐ without   prejudice as to:

1. Plaintiff/Attorney for plaintiff files this notice of dismissal of this case
   ☐ all defendants.
   ☐ the following defendant(s): _____

2. I certify, under penalty of contempt, that:
   a. This notice is the first dismissal filed by the plaintiff based upon or including the same claim against the defendant.
   b. All costs of filing and service have been paid.
   c. **No answer or motion has been served upon the plaintiff by the defendant** as of the date of this notice.
   d. A copy of this notice has been provided to the appearing defendant/attorney by ☐ mail ☐ personal service.

_____   _____
Date   Plaintiff/Attorney signature

☐ **STIPULATION TO DISMISS**

☐ with
☐ without   prejudice as to:

I stipulate to the dismissal of this case
☐ all parties.
☐ the following parties: _____

_____   _____
Date   Plaintiff/Attorney signature

_____   _____
Date   Defendant/Attorney signature

☐ **ORDER TO DISMISS**

☐ with
☐ without   prejudice. Conditions, if any: _____

IT IS ORDERED this case is dismissed

_____

_____

_____   _____   _____
Date   Judge   Bar no.

MC 09 (6/97) **DISMISSAL**   MCR 2.504

STATE OF MICHIGAN JUDICIAL CIRCUIT COUNTY	DOMESTIC RELATIONS JUDGMENT INFORMATION, PAGE 1 ☐ TEMPORARY ☐ FINAL	CASE NO.

USE NOTE: Complete this form and file it with the friend of the court (**do not file this form with the office of the clerk of the court**) when the first temporary custody, parenting-time, or support order is entered and when submitting any final proposed judgment awarding custody, parenting time, or support. Mail a copy to each party and file proof of mailing with the court (may use form MC 302, Proof of Mailing).

☐ (Check this box when information is being modified.) Except as otherwise indicated below, all information previously provided is unchanged.

Date _____

Signature _____

Plaintiff Information

Name

Address

Social security number	Telephone number

Employer name, address, telephone number, and FEIN (if known)

Driver's license number and state

Occupational license number(s), type(s), issuing state(s), and date(s)

Defendant Information

Name

Address

Social security number	Telephone number

Employer name, address, telephone number, and FEIN (if known)

Driver's license number and state

Occupational license number(s), type(s), issuing state(s), and date(s)

CUSTODY PROVISIONS

sole, plaintiff = P   sole, defendant = D   joint = J   other = O _____ (must identify)

Child's name	Social security number	Date of birth	Physical custody P, D, J, O	Child's primary residence address	Legal custody P, D, J, O

SUPPORT PROVISIONS

☐ Support provisions are stated in the Uniform Support Order.
Medical Support provisions are stated on page 2 of this form.

FOC 100 (3/12) **DOMESTIC RELATIONS JUDGMENT INFORMATION, PAGE 1**   MCR 3.211(F)

STATE OF MICHIGAN JUDICIAL CIRCUIT COUNTY	DOMESTIC RELATIONS JUDGMENT INFORMATION, PAGE 2 ☐ TEMPORARY ☐ FINAL	CASE NO.

MEDICAL SUPPORT PROVISIONS: List the name of each insurance provider for the plaintiff and the defendant. Then enter the name of each child in this case who is covered by that provider and the type of coverage provided.

Plaintiff's Insurance Coverage

Provider name and address	Policy/Group no.	Cert. no.	Child(ren)'s name(s)	Medical	Dental	Optical	Other

Defendant's Insurance Coverage

Provider name and address	Policy/Group no.	Cert. no.	Child(ren)'s name(s)	Medical	Dental	Optical	Other

STATE OF MICHIGAN **Circuit Court - Family Division** COUNTY	PROOF OF SERVICE OF DOMESTIC RELATIONS JUDG- MENT INFORMATION FORM	CASE NO.

Plaintiff (appearing *in propria persona*):

Defendant:

v

I served the following papers in this case as described below:

1. On_____, I ☐ delivered ☐ sent by first-class mail   the original Domestic Relations Judgment Information form for the Judgment of Divorce to the friend of the court at its official address.

2. On_____, I sent a copy of the Domestic Relations Judgment Information form for the Judgment of Divorce to defendant by first-class mail at his/her address in the caption above, which is defendant's last known mailing address.

I declare that the statements above are true to the best of my information, knowledge and belief.

Date _____   Plaintiff _____

STATE OF MICHIGAN JUDICIAL CIRCUIT COUNTY	UNIFORM SPOUSAL SUPPORT ORDER (PAGE 1) ☐ EX PARTE ☐ TEMPORARY ☐ MODIFICATION ☐ FINAL	CASE NO.

Court address   Court telephone no.

Plaintiff's name, address, and telephone no.	v	Defendant's name, address, and telephone no.
Plaintiff's attorney name, bar no., address, and telephone no.		Defendant's attorney name, bar no., address, and telephone no.
Plaintiff's source of income name, address, and telephone no.		Defendant's source of income name, address, and telephone no.

This order is entered   ☐ after hearing.   ☐ on stipulation/consent of the parties.

IT IS ORDERED, UNLESS OTHERWISE ORDERED IN ITEM 10: ☐ Standard provisions have been modified (see item 10).

1. **Spousal Support.** Spousal support shall be paid monthly through the Michigan State Disbursement Unit as follows:

Payer:	Payee:	Amount: $	Effective date:

2. Income withholding takes immediate effect for those items payable through the Michigan State Disbursement Unit.

3. This order continues until the death of the payee or until the earliest of the following events:
   ☐ Date: _____   ☐ $_____ is paid.
   ☐ Remarriage of the payee.   ☐ Death of the payer.
   ☐ Other (specify all other events): _____

   _____

☐ 4. For tax purposes, the payments will be deductible to the payer and included in the income of the payee.

☐ 5. Payments that must be paid directly to the third party (not to the payee) are listed below. (Payments to be made directly to a third party are not payable through the Michigan State Disbursement Unit or friend of the court.)

Type	Amount Per Month	Start Date	Pay to	End Date
	$			
	$			
	$			
	$			

(See page 2 for the remainder of the order.)

FOC 10b (3/12) **UNIFORM SPOUSAL SUPPORT ORDER, PAGE 1**   MCL 552.13, MCR 3.211

Original - Court
1st copy - Plaintiff

2nd copy - Defendant
3rd copy - Friend of the court

STATE OF MICHIGAN JUDICIAL CIRCUIT COUNTY	UNIFORM SPOUSAL SUPPORT ORDER (PAGE 2) ☐ EX PARTE ☐ TEMPORARY ☐ MODIFICATION ☐ FINAL	CASE NO.

Court address

Court telephone no.

Plaintiff's name	v	Defendant's name

6. **Retroactive Modification, Surcharge for Past-Due Support, and Liens for Unpaid Support.** Support is a judgment the date it is due and is not retroactively modifiable. A surcharge may be added to past-due support. Unpaid support is a lien by operation of law and the payer's property can be encumbered or seized if an arrearage accrues for more than the periodic support payments payable for two months under the payer's support order.

7. **Address, Employment Status, Health Insurance.** Both parties shall notify the friend of the court in writing of: a) their mailing and residential addresses and telephone numbers; b) the names, addresses, and telephone numbers of their sources of income; c) their health-maintenance or insurance companies, insurance coverage, persons insured, or contract numbers; d) their occupational or drivers' licenses; and e) their social security numbers unless exempt by law pursuant to MCL 552.603. Both parties shall notify the friend of the court in writing within 21 days of any change in this information. Failure to do so may result in a fee being imposed.

8. **Fees.** The payer of support shall pay statutory and service fees as required by law.

9. **Prior Orders. This order supersedes all prior spousal support orders.** Past-due amounts owed under any prior support order are preserved.

10. **Other: (Attach separate sheets as needed.)**

Plaintiff (if consent/stipulation)	Date	Defendant (if consent/stipulation)	Date

Plaintiff's attorney	Date	Defendant's attorney	Date

Date		Judge	Bar no.

CERTIFICATE OF MAILING

I certify that on this date I served a copy of this order on the parties or their attorneys by first-class mail addressed to their last-known addresses as defined in MCR 3.203.

Date		Signature	

COURT USE ONLY

STATE OF MICHIGAN JUDICIAL CIRCUIT COUNTY	ORDER REGARDING INCOME WITHHOLDING	CASE NO.

Court address

Court telephone no.

Plaintiff's name, address, and telephone no.

v

Defendant's name, address, and telephone no.

THE COURT FINDS:

1. The requirements for implementation or adjustment of income withholding
   ☐ have
   ☐ have not
   been met.

☐ 2. The proposed administrative adjustment of income withholding
   ☐ will
   ☐ will not
   produce an unjust or inappropriate result.

IT IS ORDERED:

3. Income withholding is
   ☐ discontinued.
   ☐ effective.
   ☐ effective in an amount pursuant to the Michigan Child Support Formula to pay current support and arrears.
   ☐ effective as follows:

Date

Judge

Bar no.

CERTIFICATE OF MAILING

I certify that on this date I served a copy of this order on the parties and sources of income by first-class mail addressed to their last-known addresses as defined in MCR 3.203.

Date

Signature

FOC 5 (3/08) **ORDER REGARDING INCOME WITHHOLDING**

MCL 552.601 *et seq.*

Local Forms
(for Wayne County only)

<table>
<tr><td>Certificate of Conformity for Domestic Relations Order or Judgment</td><td>1225</td></tr>
<tr><td>Order Data Form-Support</td><td>FD/FOC 4002</td></tr>
</table>

STATE OF MICHIGAN THIRD JUDICIAL COURT WAYNE COUNTY	CERTIFICATE OF CONFORMITY FOR DOMESTIC RELATIONS ORDER OR JUDGMENT	CASE NO.
Penobscot Bldg. 645 Griswold Ave. Detroit, MI 48226		*313-224-5372*

PLAINTIFF'S NAME		DEFENDANT'S NAME
	V	

I certify the attached Order of Judgment as presented for entry to be in full conformity

with the requirements set forth by statute, **INCLUDING A PROVISION FOR IMMEDIATE**

INCOME WITHHOLDING (WHICH SHALL BE IMPLEMENTED BY THE FRIEND OF THE COURT).

THE PAYER'S SOCIAL SECURITY NUMBER AND THE NAME AND ADDRESS OF HIS/HER

SOURCE OF INCOME, IF KNOWN, UNLESS OTHERWISE ORDERED BY THE COURT, and with

Michigan Court Rules 3.201 and following and if applicable, includes all provisions of the

Friend of the Court recommendation or is in conformity with the decision of

_____ rendered on the _____ day of

_____, 20_____.

_____   _____

Date

Instructions: Please sign and present this certificate to the Court Clerk when the Order or Judgment is presented for entry. If an ex parte interim order is being presented to the Judge, please complete the "Certificate on behalf of Plaintiff regarding Ex Parte Interim Support Order: and follow Local Court Rule 3.206.

#1225(11/04) CERTIFICATE OF CONFORMITY FOR DOMESTIC RELATIONS ORDER OR JUDGMENT

THE CIRCUIT COURT
FOR THE THIRD JUDICIAL CIRCUIT OF MICHIGAN
FAMILY DIVISION – FRIEND OF THE COURT

ORDER DATA FORM-SUPPORT
FOR SUBMISSION OF DOMESTIC RELATIONS ORDER FOR ENTRY INTO
Michigan Child Support Enforcement System (MiCSES) BY FOC

NON-EX PARTE ORDERS:

1.   Complete legibly and attach this form to the Friend of the Court (FOC) True Copy of the Order.

2.   Please note that the FOC worker will not review the order. If required fields are not completed (noted by asterisk *), the Order Data Form and the Order will be returned to you.

3.   Do not submit Orders with non-specific dates, such as orders that start support as of the date of sale of the marital home.

4.   If an order provides for different support amounts for different periods of time, complete an Order Data Form for each period. Label each with "1 of 'n', ..., 'n' of 'n', in the upper right corner.

5.   The Judge's Circuit Court Clerk will forward the FOC copy of the Order, with attached Order Data Form, to FOC for entry into the MiCSES System.

EX PARTE ORDERS:

1.   Attach the Proof of Service if the Order is an Ex Parte Order. (The Order will not be entered into the MiCSES System unless the Proof of Service is attached.)

2.   Ex Parte Orders, with completed Order Data Form and Proof of Service, should be faxed or mailed to:

Order Entry Department
3rd Floor, Penobscot Building
645 Griswold   **or delivered to:**
Detroit, Michigan 48226
FAX: (313) 237-9290

Attorney Window
2nd Floor, Penobscot Building
645 Griswold
Detroit, Michigan 48226
FAX: (313) 237-9290

**THE ORDER DATA FORM IS AVAILABLE FOR DOWNLOAD TO YOUR COMPUTER
OR FOR PRINTING
ON THE COURT WEBSITE AT http://3rdcc.org OR FAX LIBRARY: (313) 967-3662**

Rev. 11/06/02

ABOUT THE NEW AND REQUIRED "ORDER DATA FORM-SUPPORT"

Friend of the Court, with the support of the Family Law Bench, has developed a data form, now called ORDER DATA FORM-SUPPORT (ODF-S), (formerly known as Fast Track Form) to assist the FOC in the task of loading the provisions of a support order into the Michigan Child Support Enforcement System. (MiCSES) It is now two pages.

A completed ODF-S must be attached to the FOC copy of any domestic relations order.

The old Fast Track form you have used was developed before and during the transition to the Michigan Child Support Enforcement System and is now obsolete.

Here are some features of the new form, as well as some practical considerations that should be noted when an order is being prepared for entry.

First, please note that it is the responsibility of the party submitting the order to the court for signature to enter all the relevant details of the new order into the ODF-S [ORDER DETAILS). The FOC worker will rely upon that information when loading the order and will not consult the attached order, nor any other previously entered order(s).

Second, the information required on page one, "ORDER DETAILS", of the ODF-S should be garnered only from the order attached. If the order results in a change in a certain element of the account, you check the relevant boxes and complete the relevant text areas. If the order does not impact a certain element of the account, then you do not check those boxes and no change would be noted on MiCSES for that aspect of the account.

For example: the order modifies child support but not childcare. You would check the relevant boxes and enter the ordered amounts and dates into the text fields in the child support section. You would not check any of the childcare boxes. The worker will load the new child support, with its commencement date, and leave the childcare portion of the account as is.

For example: an order might provide for a certain cycle for one period of time, then a different amount for a subsequent period of time [for example, $10/wk from 04-01-02 to 05-31-02, then $40/wk from 06-01-02 until further order of the court]. You will prepare a "1 of 2" ODF-S (ORDER DETAILS) sheet for the '04-01-02 to 05-31-02 period' and a "2 of 2" ODF-S (ORDER DETAILS) sheet for the '06-01-02 until further order of the court' period of time. Only one copy of page 2, ODF-S (DEMOGRAPHICS) would need to be attached.

The only time an arrearage amount would be entered would be when the order, by its specific terms, sets a specific amount of arrearage for a date certain.

Again, the first page of the form (ORDER DETAILS) should contain the specifics of only the attached order.

The second page, DEMOGRAPHICS is also attached to the new order being submitted for entry. FOC will check and correct/update the account for any changes or errors. The information required is standard information you obtain from your clients. Your client's and the other parties' information should be on the verified statement initially and updated in your client file as you interact with your client and opposing counsel. Family Independence Agency account #'s, children's dates of birth and social security numbers, etc. are known to your clients and should be in your client files.

MiCSES has an automated Income Withholding Notice feature. The worker, as a part of the order loading activity that day, reviews the Demographics page and updates the employer, if necessary. Upon entry into MiCSES of a new support order, the system generates an Income Withholding Notice (IWN) that night, in batch, to the active employer. If the order specifies a certain $ amount to be wage deducted, that amount is loaded into MiCSES and the IWN is generated in that amount. If the order does not specify a certain amount to be withheld, the system calculates the guideline amount and the IWN is generated in that amount.

I believe that, especially if you download the template version of this form from the Website, you will find that it is very straightforward and quick to complete. The boxes and text areas, which are impacted by the order, are checked and filled and the balance of the choices are left blank.

ORDER DETAILS

| STATE OF MICHIGAN
COUNTY OF WAYNE
THIRD JUDICIAL CIRCUIT COURT
FAMILY DIVISION | **ORDER DATA FORM-SUPPORT**
Re: SUBMISSION FOR LOADING
ATTACHED SUPPORT ORDER INTO
MiCSES ON FOC COMPUTER SYSTEM

THE ORDER WAS ENTERED ON:
_____
(DATE ON ORDER STAMPED BY JUDGE'S CLERK) | (PLACE LABEL HERE)

CASE #:
_____
_____
JUDGE |

*INDICATES REQUIRED INFORMATION

CHECK ONLY THE BOXES WHICH APPLY TO PROVISIONS IN THE SUBMITTED ORDER

* PLAINTIFF NAME:	* DEFENDANT NAME:

*THIS ORDER IS:
☐ EX PARTE (PROOF OF SERVICE REQUIRED)   ☐ TEMPORARY ☐ JUDGMENT ☐ MODIFICATION

*WERE CHILD SUPPORT GUIDELINES FOLLOWED?   ☐ YES   ☐ NO

*THE CHILD SUPPORT PAYER IS   ☐ PLAINTIFF ☐ DEFENDANT   ☐ NOT APPLICABLE.

☐ **CHILD SUPPORT.**   COMMENCEMENT DATE IS _____   ☐ **PAY DIRECT, NOT THROUGH FOC.**

* 5 CHILDREN PER WEEK	* 4 CHILDREN PER WEEK	* 3 CHILDREN PER WEEK	* 2 CHILDREN PER WEEK	* 1 CHILD PER WEEK
CHILD SUPPORT AMOUNT	CHILD SUPPORT AMOUNT	CHILD SUPPORT AMOUNT	CHILD SUPPORT AMOUNT	CHILD SUPPORT AMOUNT
$	$	$	$	$

☐ **INCOME WITHHOLDING:**   ☐ PROCESS AT GUIDELINE AMOUNT   ☐ PROCESS AT $ _____ PER WEEK

☐ **CHILD SUPPORT ARREARAGE:**
☐ PRESERVED ☐ CANCELED AS OF DATE: _____   ☐ SET AT $ _____ AS OF DATE: _____

☐ **CHILD CARE EXPENSES:** $ _____ PER WEEK, COMMENCEMENT DATE IS _____ ;
END DATE IS ☐ GUIDELINE DATE **OR** ☐ DATE: _____
☐ **CHILD CARE ARREARAGE:**
☐ PRESERVED ☐ CANCELED AS OF DATE: _____   ☐ SET AT $ _____ AS OF DATE: _____

☐ **ARREARAGE ADJUSTMENT:**
☐ DIRECT CREDIT IN AMOUNT OF $ _____   ☐ ADD ADDITIONAL OBLIGATION IN AMOUNT OF $ _____

☐ **MEDICAL INSURANCE IN ORDER.**
☐ **CHILD SUPPORT PAYER RESPONSIBLE FOR** _____ **% OF UNINSURED MEDICAL EXPENSES.**

☐ **PARENTING TIME ABATEMENT:** ____ % PARENTING TIME CREDIT AFTER ___ CONSECUTIVE OVERNIGHTS.
☐ **PARENTING TIME ORDERED: (CHECK ONE):**
☐ REASONABLE   ☐ SPECIFIC   ☐ SUPERVISED   ☐ RESERVED   ☐ REFER TO FAMILY COUNSELING/OTHER

*THE SPOUSAL SUPPORT PAYER IS   ☐ PLAINTIFF ☐ DEFENDANT   ☐ NOT APPLICABLE.
☐ **SPOUSAL SUPPORT:** ☐ $ _____ PER WEEK, COMMENCEMENT DATE: _____ .
☐ PERMANENT   ☐ END DATE _____   ☐ **PAY DIRECT, NOT THROUGH FOC**
☐ **SPOUSAL SUPPORT ARREARAGE:**
☐ PRESERVED ☐ CANCELED AS OF DATE: _____   ☐ SET AT $ _____ AS OF DATE: _____

☐ **ORDER REFERS MATTERS TO DIVORCE INVESTIGATION/MODIFICATION FOR FURTHER INVESTIGATION.**

I CERTIFY THAT THE ABOVE INFORMATION IS TRUE TO THE BEST OF MY KNOWLEDGE, INFORMATION AND BELIEF, AND IS IN FULL CONFORMITY WITH THE REQUIREMENTS SET FORTH BY STATUTE AND COURT RULE AND THE DECISION OF THE COURT. (NOTE: FOC WILL NOT READ THE ORDER WHEN ENTERING IT ON MiCSES.)

DATE: _____   SIGNATURE OF ATTORNEY _____   BAR NO. _____

PLEASE PRINT:

_____
ATTORNEY NAME

_____
ADDRESS

_____   _____
CITY/STATE/ZIP   TELEPHONE NO.

FD/FOC 4002 (11/06/02) **ORDER DATA FORM-SUPPORT**

DEMOGRAPHICS

| STATE OF MICHIGAN
COUNTY OF WAYNE
THIRD JUDICIAL CIRCUIT
COURT
FAMILY DIVISION | **ORDER DATA FORM-SUPPORT**
Re: SUBMISSION FOR LOADING
ATTACHED SUPPORT ORDER INTO
MiCSES ON FOC COMPUTER SYSTEM

THE ORDER WAS ENTERED ON:

_____
(DATE ON ORDER STAMPED BY JUDGE'S CLERK) | (PLACE LABEL HERE)

CASE #:
_____

_____
JUDGE |

*INDICATES REQUIRED INFORMATION

CHECK ONLY THE BOXES WHICH APPLY TO PROVISIONS IN THE SUBMITTED ORDER

* PLAINTIFF NAME:	* DEFENDANT NAME:

* NAME(S) OF CHILDREN (OLDEST TO YOUNGEST)	* DATE(S) OF BIRTH	* SOCIAL SECURITY NUMBER(S)

(ADD ADDITIONAL CHILDREN ON SEPARATE SHEET)

NON-CUSTODIAL PARENT (OR FATHER IF JOINT CUSTODY) ☐ PLAINTIFF ☐ DEFENDANT

* NAME:	* DATE OF BIRTH:	* SOC. SEC. NO.	HOME TELEPHONE NO:
* RESIDENTIAL ADDRESS:	* CITY, STATE, ZIP	OTHER TELEPHONE NUMBERS: ☐ WORK ☐ MOBILE	FIA/TANF N0.: NOW ACTIVE: ☐ YES ☐ NO
* EMPLOYER:	* EMPLOYER ADDRESS:	EMPLOYER TELEPHONE NO.:	EMPLOYER FED I.D. NO.:

CUSTODIAL PERSON (OR MOTHER IF JOINT CUSTODY) ☐ PLAINTIFF ☐ DEFENDANT

* NAME:	* DATE OF BIRTH:	* SOC. SEC. NO.	HOME TELEPHONE NO:
* RESIDENTIAL ADDRESS:	* CITY, STATE, ZIP	OTHER TELEPHONE NUMBERS: ☐ WORK ☐ MOBILE	FIA/TANF N0.: NOW ACTIVE: ☐ YES ☐ NO
* EMPLOYER:	* EMPLOYER ADDRESS:	EMPLOYER TELEPHONE NO.:	EMPLOYER FED I.D. NO.:

I CERTIFY THAT THE ABOVE INFORMATION IS TRUE TO THE BEST OF MY KNOWLEDGE, INFORMATION AND BELIEF, AND IS IN FULL CONFORMITY WITH THE REQUIREMENTS SET FORTH BY STATUTE AND COURT RULE AND THE DECISION OF THE COURT. (NOTE: FOC WILL NOT READ THE ORDER WHEN ENTERING IT ON MiCSES.)

DATE: _____ SIGNATURE OF ATTORNEY _____ BAR NO. _____

PLEASE PRINT: _____
ATTORNEY NAME

FD/FOC 4002 (11/06/02) **ORDER DATA FORM-SUPPORT**